THE RAGS OF TIME

THE *R*AGS OF *T*IME

A Fragment of Autobiography

William Buchan

ASHFORD, BUCHAN & ENRIGHT
Southampton

First published in 1990 by
Ashford, Buchan & Enright,
an imprint of Martins Publishers Ltd,
1 Church Road, Shedfield,
Southampton SO3 2HW

British Library Cataloguing in Publication Data

Buchan, William, *1916–*
The rags of time: a fragment of autobiography.
I. Title
823. 912

ISBN 0 907675 91 3

Typeset in 11/12 Bembo by Print Origination
(Southern) Ltd, Aldershot, Hants.
Printed and bound in Great Britain by Hartnolls
Ltd, Bodmin, Cornwall

CONTENTS

ILLUSTRATIONS

between pages 118 and 119

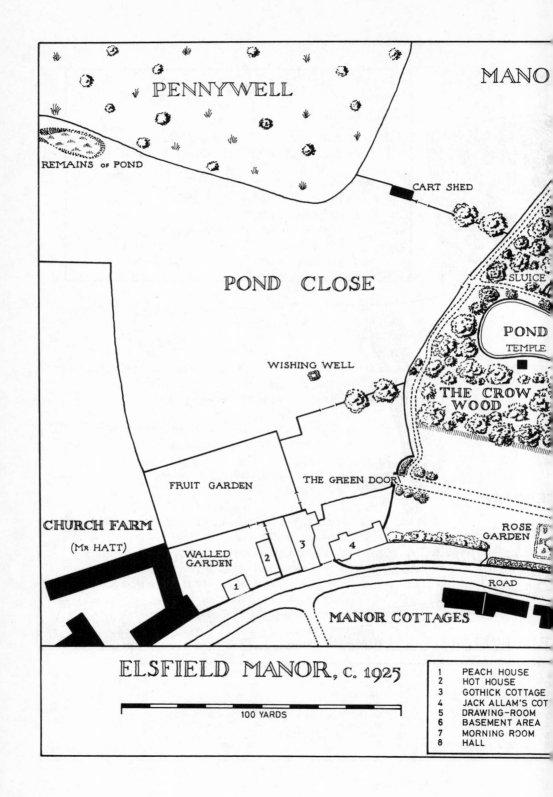

PENNYWELL

MANO

REMAINS of POND

CART SHED

POND CLOSE

SLUICE

POND

TEMPLE

THE CROW WOOD

WISHING WELL

FRUIT GARDEN

THE GREEN DOOR

ROSE GARDEN

CHURCH FARM

(Mr HATT)

WALLED GARDEN

3

4

2

1

ROAD

MANOR COTTAGES

ELSFIELD MANOR, c. 1925

100 YARDS

1	PEACH HOUSE
2	HOT HOUSE
3	GOTHICK COTTAGE
4	JACK ALLAM'S COT
5	DRAWING-ROOM
6	BASEMENT AREA
7	MORNING ROOM
8	HALL

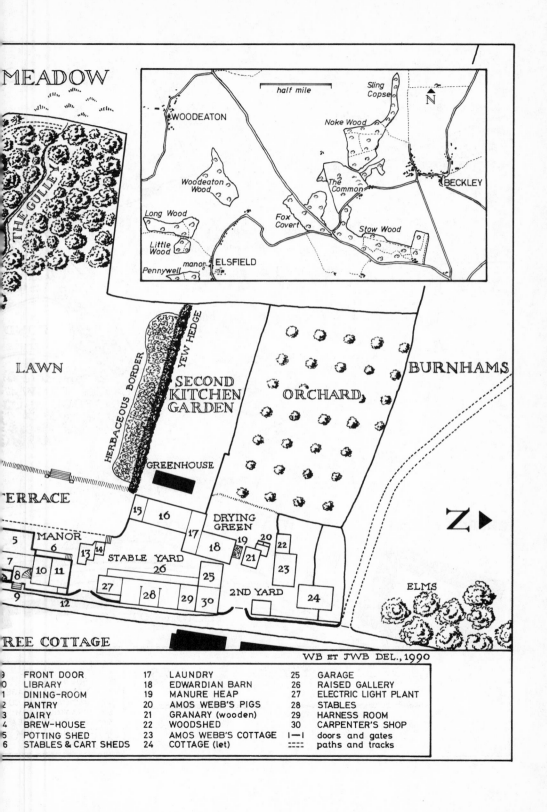

MEADOW

half mile

WOODEATON

Sling Copse

Noke Wood

N

Woodeaton Wood

The Common

BECKLEY

Long Wood

Fox Covert

Stow Wood

Little Wood

Pennywell

manor ELSFIELD

THE GULLIE

LAWN

HERBACEOUS BORDER

YEW HEDGE

SECOND KITCHEN GARDEN

ORCHARD

BURNHAMS

GREENHOUSE

TERRACE

15

16

DRYING GREEN

17

19

20

22

MANOR

5

6

18

21

23

13 14

7

STABLE YARD

8

10 11

26

25

24

9

27

28

29 30

2ND YARD

12

ELMS

Z ▶

REE COTTAGE

WB ET JWB DEL., 1990

9	FRONT DOOR	17	LAUNDRY	25	GARAGE
0	LIBRARY	18	EDWARDIAN BARN	26	RAISED GALLERY
1	DINING-ROOM	19	MANURE HEAP	27	ELECTRIC LIGHT PLANT
2	PANTRY	20	AMOS WEBB'S PIGS	28	STABLES
3	DAIRY	21	GRANARY (wooden)	29	HARNESS ROOM
4	BREW-HOUSE	22	WOODSHED	30	CARPENTER'S SHOP
5	POTTING SHED	23	AMOS WEBB'S COTTAGE	I—I	doors and gates
6	STABLES & CART SHEDS	24	COTTAGE (let)	::::	paths and tracks

SAURÉ, FOR SO MUCH . . .

Love, all alike, no season knows, nor clime,
Nor hours, days, months, which are the rags of time.

John Donne, 'The Sun Rising'

Ce que j'ai appris je ne le sais plus —
le peu que je sais je l'ai deviné.

Sébastien Roch Nicolas Chamfort

INTRODUCTION

Ogden Nash, the most typical New Yorker of my time, once said that, were he to produce an autobiography, he would call it *I am a Stranger Here Myself*. This wry use of a phrase familiar to anyone who has ever had to ask his way in a strange place, expresses perfectly the rather desperate irony of much American humour in the thirties. It occurred to me when I first heard it, and comes back to me still, that the same title would do very well for me, should I ever have the temerity to attempt such a work.

Newborn babies were sometimes referred to as 'little strangers' and, for the most part, very sincere efforts were made to make them feel at home. Sometimes that result was achieved quite easily, the little stranger laying hold on life with energy and swiftly taking command of his or her surroundings; but, as I shall suggest later, not all children greet their universe with unalloyed enthusiasm. Those are the ones who refuse to participate in cheerful party games, hanging about instead on the fringe of the merry, competitive crowd, looking at once yearning and disdainful, to the great irritation and even shame of those who would like to see them popular, successful, a social asset of which to be proud. Those, also, are the ones for whom childhood is truly a cosmos, limitless, worthy in itself of a lifetime's exploration. Physical growth, therefore, and the steadily accumulating years can themselves be a source of anxiety, even perhaps of anguish. The child comes to feel that he has been pushed too hard and too quickly into a state thought to be adult, and thus denied the chance to explore fully and satisfactorily that other state which seemed to hold so much meaning. 'Late developers' are of this breed and often show an infuriating childishness, a sporadic irrationality by adult standards, well into later life.

If one has the audacity, being neither famous nor even notorious, to invite attention to a life passed during some especially troubled moments of history, that history must provide justification. It may be just permissible to offer personal recollec-

1

tions of people, places, ways of doing things, states of affairs, which are already the meat of a thousand serious researchers, if only because historical conjecture, even where historical fact is still within recollection, can so often be grotesquely wide of the mark; which fact leads one to wonder about the same conjecture where neither contemporary record nor reminiscence is available. It may be that history is too important a study to be left to historians.

Having embarked on this rash exercise I have been struck by two things. Firstly, it is well known that recollection in old age tends to produce its clearest pictures from the distant past, from childhood itself and from early youth. This may be simply the first declaration of approaching senility, but it remains, nevertheless, a fact. Of the often turbulent years of middle life, and of five years of war service in my twenties, certain recollections possess a sharp and sometimes horrid clarity; but they are unconnected scenes, clear-lit, sharp-edged, surrounded by shifting clouds of strife and muddle, as though battle-smoke were rolling about them, and only intermittently blown aside. Secondly — and this is saddening — it is also, for me, a fact that errors, inanities, follies, gaffes, unwise actions, failures of one kind and another, return to memory far more often than anything likely to give a feeling of satisfaction. Such recollections, occurring in the small hours, can still make me go cold all over, when I should naturally prefer a warmer glow, remembering tasks well performed, wise counsel given, good ideas brought to fruition, the presentation of a *bella figura* to an admiring world. It is possible that there may have been times when I gave sound advice, behaved with moderate courage, fulfilled the expectations and justified the love of others: there may have been, but they do not recur in memory with anything like the force and frequency of the others I have mentioned.

If a tendency to precipitate and ill-considered action is not restrained in childhood, restraint will have to be learned in many hard ways later in life. Mr Ernest Marples, once Minister of Transport, has never, to my knowledge, been described as either a profound philosopher or a great aphorist; yet that Marcus Aurelius among Transport Ministers coined a most telling phrase, still to be read in large letters wherever, at the conjunction of four traffic-lights, yellow lines forming a square are painted on the road. 'Do not enter box until you see your exit is clear.' How I wish that this admirable injunction had penetrated to me in my early years. How many boxes have I entered without seeing how undesirable their issue was likely to be.

2

Much of what I have written in this book concerns childhood, a childhood which, in spite of friction caused by my own self-will and general intransigence, must be accounted happy. This record, therefore, may have some small use as an illustration of a kind of upbringing, normal enough in its time, which, even if it were thought other than embarrassingly old-fashioned, would now be impossible to reproduce. For the rest, it happened that I, through no virtue of my own, but simply as beneficiary of the condition into which I was born, had many chances of meeting, seeing at close quarters, pehaps even loving, men and women whose lives possess, nowadays, great interest for many people. From my earliest days I stood at the edge of an arena where great affairs were considered, great careers made, great ambitions proclaimed. If upon so much 'greatness' I sometimes cast a sceptical eye, having a child's clear insight to vanity and hollow pretension in the adult world, I could sympathize with my parents' idealistic view of that world and of certain people, even though I could never wholly share it. It was the world's fault, not theirs, that I should live to see their hopes frustrated, their conclusions falsified. They honestly believed what they professed; and it is to that honesty that I must pay tribute.

It has been a depressing habit amongst critics in recent years to apply the ominous expression 'self-indulgent' to any writer who lets himself go, either in exuberant fine writing, or in extended examination of a private emotion inspired by art, architecture or mortal love. It is as though that writer were thought to have strayed from the strict conditions of a disciplined communal exercise, for example a Boy Scouts' field day, to slope off and stuff himself with blackberries whilst his more admirable colleagues were busy laying trails, marking trees and tying knots. As far as I am concerned, in what I have written here, I must risk the harsh impeachment. Far better than any indulgence from myself I would hope for the indulgence of my reader.

I

LONDON 1916

It is a January day in Mayfair, a typical one I imagine, overcast and still, with a cold never far above freezing. I must imagine this because no one could ever describe the weather for me. Perhaps I may ask the Meteorological Office if its records have anything significant to say about 10 January 1916, during some part of which day, early or middle or late — no one could ever say for certain which — I am being born. All that my mother could tell me was that, at the moment of my birth, bugles were blowing in Hyde Park.

My grandmother's house in Upper Grosvenor Street stood on the south side and was, I think, the last but one before Park Lane. No doubt Hyde Park at that time was given over to tented army camps, and certainly, then, the piercing, sad cry of the bugles could be easily heard over the hoofbeat and jingle of horse traffic and the grinding gears of army lorries: otherwise this definite recollection of my mother's is not of much help in pinpointing the moment of my arrival in a world deeply preoccupied by war. Could those bugles have been blowing Reveille, perhaps, or 'Come To The Cookhouse Door', or even Lights Out? Borne through the pains of childbirth on a tide of 'twilight sleep' — or so I hope sincerely — my mother, deeply disliking the whole process, must have heard the bugles sounding, perhaps, a note of triumph, a celebration of the end of her ordeal. But of the exact time of day she had no recollection, and so I have never been able to commission a horoscope, correctly cast.

There exists a photograph of the room in which I was born. That house, Number 30, was built in the mid eighteenth century, to an ample and stately plan, by Sir Thomas Grosvenor when he was busy 'developing' his Mayfair estate. The second-floor bedroom had sober, heavy cornices, a plain but elegant chimney-piece in grey marble, and was furnished, at the time of the photograph, in the pleasant, unpretentious country-house style of the days before interior decoration became an industry and a

5

matter for acute self-consciousness. Besides a large brass bedstead, there were a comfortable sofa, chintz-covered, next to the fireplace where, in the picture, a good coal fire is ready for lighting and, comfortably placed, a round table with a lamp on it which strikes an up-to-date note, being covered with a cloth of the same chintz as the sofa's, reaching to the floor. At the foot of the bed is a writing-table, with all that might be needed for composing those letters which guests, arriving at tea-time, were expected to want to polish off between tea and the dressing-gong. On the table is a row of what look like enticing new books.

On the day of my arrival, no doubt, all that clutter would have been cleared away, not so much for reasons of hygiene as to give free passage to an impressive, frock-coated doctor, and a nurse in a high, frilled cap secured with a bow under her chin. I can imagine that the house, on that day, would have been hushed, that the servants would have spoken in low voices and gone about the place on tiptoe, while my grandmother sat in her green drawing-room looking out on to the gardens of old Grosvenor House, and the tall, classical bay of its famous picture-gallery, with her beautiful, short-sighted eyes, composed as ever, but betraying anxiety by an extra alertness, a readiness to rise to any emergency which might present itself upstairs. Meanwhile, from the second floor where the bedroom was — the first being fully occupied by staircase and landing and the big, L-shaped drawing-room — there must have come down to her noises of muted but purposeful activity, the tread of feet over the floors, and the sounds of steps ascending as more and more hot water was brought up from the kitchen far below; and then perhaps, very faintly, and in opposition to the bugle-calls blowing from the park, that sound of all sounds least likely to be misinterpreted, the cry of a human infant just born.

It was not an ideal moment for me to put in an appearance. The war with Germany was not going well: indeed, in that January of 1916 — the year of the Battle of the Somme — it would have been possible to believe that it might be lost. For seventeen months, day by day, people had had to brace themselves to read the casualty lists where, amongst the dead and missing, would almost every time be found the names of friends, relations, young men known since childhood, or, most dreadfully, of husbands and lovers, fathers and sons. I think that my mother at that time may have been spared one continual anxiety, since my father was back in London from France. He had been severely ill in August 1914, with what was to become his perpetual duodenal trouble. He was then thirty-nine years old, well beyond the age of enlistment, and very evidently medically unfit. Doctors and friends, together with all those to whom he applied for serious war-work, had sternly told him to rest, relax, wait for an opportunity to be useful at a later date. None of that would he accept, arranging instead to be sent to the front as correspondent for *The Times* and so, added to the misery of the casualty lists, there was usually constant anxiety for my mother, as much for her husband's health as for the dangers into which, she knew, he would frequently put himself.

It may be, then, after my newborn person had been washed and swaddled and put to rest in its beribboned bassinet, that my mother may have known a moment of pure peace and freedom from her most pressing anxieties; may even have heard in the sour notes of the bugles, melancholy yet somehow triumphant, something positive and hopeful for the future of her world and of her latest child.

My elders, Alice, eight, and Johnnie, four, would have been sent away to the country while their mother was engaged in mysteries about which they would not have been directly informed until the abrupt announcement that they had acquired a baby brother. For Alice, this was the second time round, and she may well have heard the news with mixed feelings. For a first-born, such new arrivals must often suggest a watering-down or diversion of much-desired parental attention: may be, in short, more of a nuisance than an unqualified delight.

My recollections of Number 30 are sketchy because, not long after my birth, my family moved to 76 Portland Place, a fine house of the 1770s, designed by the Adam brothers, and, as in many of their houses of that time, given a drawing-room ceiling painted by Angelica Kauffmann. Those details I know, without claiming to remember them. What I can remember (as is most usual with children) are the kitchen quarters and the stone stairs down to them, and the stone-deaf man in a green apron who carried coals; and the stone floor of the hall, a sense of a gracefully curving staircase, leading to the white paint and hot coal fire, with brass railed fireguard, of the nursery. I am sure, also, that I remember the deep cupboard under the stairs into which we children were hurried when, as happened quite frequently, the Germans had a go at bombing London. Something which I do not recollect, but about which I was told often enough, is that one nearby explosion coming unheralded, had dislodged me from an upstairs sofa on which I was lying and landed me on the floor. That must have been very shortly after the move to Portland Place, when I was still only a few months old, and (if true) may account for an almost hysterical aversion to loud noises, especially when I am not prepared for them.

At two years and eight months I, too, was presented with a younger brother, born in September 1918, just eight weeks before the Armistice, and I do not suppose that I was any more pleased with the gift than my elder siblings had been with me. Until that moment I had had the nursery to myself for much of the time, and the almost undivided, if not always welcome, attention of Miss Frances Earl, our nurse, later to be known as Old Nanny. She was a commanding, somewhat domineering person, swift to irritability, and inclined to be heavy-handed, even though, like so many of her kind, she preferred boys to girls, and babies to anyone. My sister, I know, suffered a good deal of unkindness at her hands. I was too young to be able to take reasoned likes or dislikes but, after Alastair's birth, I know for certain that I set my affections firmly on Nanny's adjutant, a young nurserymaid called Millie, who was as consistently kind and gentle as Nanny was sporadically harsh.

Alastair's arrival caused a lot of disturbance in my life, including being sent away to Kent while he was being born. Returning to Portland Place I found the little stranger not merely the focal point of nursery life, but causing infinite upheaval in various daily routines. What was worse, from my self-centred point of view, was that he appeared, every day, the object of so much cooing attention and so many complimentary exclamations, as if he were to be sincerely congratulated on his cleverness in being born.

Those two houses of my earliest years are now gone, Number 30 to the 'developers', when the Duke of Westminster sold his London residence, Grosvenor House, and some acres adjoining it in 1929, for the erection of an hotel; and Number 76 to a German bomb in the Second World War. I have worked out that my birthplace was somewhere in the upper air of the ballroom of that vast hotel which is now called Grosvenor House. From later visits to Number 30 I remember the hall, which had a black stone diamond at each corner of its large square flags, and a little breakfast-room, wonderfully cosy in winter, its fire blazing behind a club-fender with a padded red leather top, where I remember being deposited after an early train journey and a taxi-ride from Paddington through cold fog and tall, bewildering traffic, to an immense feeling of security, of a life as timeless, ordered and traditional in its own way as that which I had left behind in Oxfordshire. Otherwise I tend to remember best the high-up sewing-room where I would have tea with Alice Butterfield, the lady's-maid, and quite often with Amy Sutch, who came for days at a time to sew for the household. Neither was used to children, in any sense which might have prompted to cynicism, and so, on my visits, I was comfortably spoiled, and treated as an individual of great interest.

Alice Butterfield took me one late-winter evening for a treat much talked about beforehand, and much looked forward to — a view of the illuminations at Piccadilly Circus, then a wonder comparatively new, and a source of pride to all good Londoners. We went on the upper deck of a bus. Motorbuses in those days were topless, as buses had been when horses pulled them, and, on wet days, showed an undulating upper surface of umbrellas, like the back of some sea-monster. That evening, though, was fine, and the display, when we reached the Circus, almost as exciting as the fireworks which I looked forward to so much every 5th of November. I was fascinated by electric light in all its forms, and there it was, running and rippling and changing colour, in whorls and wheels and geometrical patterns, spelling out and erasing and spelling again, the names of products or, better still, showing a brilliant shower of drops falling from a bottle into a waiting glass. It would be asking too much of memory to state accurately what all those products were, but Bovril I certainly remember, together with Sandeman's Port. Meanwhile the coloured lights, red, yellow and green, set off by streams of a dazzling, diamond-white, coloured all the air of Piccadilly Circus and the sky above. Coloured lights and water, or lights simulating water, could always hold my attention, leave me dreaming. Later in life there would be the Lalique glass fountains at the Rond Point of the Champs-Elysées, later still, the illuminations in Times Square which, by comparison with London and Paris, seemed a trifle overdone. Piccadilly Circus was frankly vulgar, but comforting, popular, a joyous expression of pleasure in a clever new technology, and Londoners, who had not then lost the capacity to marvel, found it an endless delight. As to Paris, those fountains with their milky glass doves and flowers, they too expressed a faith and pleasure in new things, and a poetic fantasy not always to be found in French public works.

9

2

THE MANOR OF ELSFIELD

Past times and their inhabitants and outmoded objects, which continue to be the present day and the dear familiars of recollection, crop up again and again, in after days, almost unrecognizable, dressed up or distorted by succeeding generations' half-taught guesses, assumptions, wishful thoughts. Looking at photographs of children and grown-ups belonging to my earliest years, I can see little consonance between these odd clothes, stiff attitudes, unfamiliar expressions and what memory tells me of the living originals. Skirt-lengths, for example, which date more tellingly even than hair-styles, have no place whatever in my recollections. When we left London in the winter of 1919, adult women wore their skirts to the ground, or nearly; young girls still in the school room to below the knee. For the latter there were stockings, black, brown or grey, lisle thread or wool; of their elders' legs little was to be seen. Yet I have no reminiscent feeling of stiffness or stuffiness where my female acquaintance was concerned. No photograph can show the flux of materials, or convey softness or warmth, or catch the grace of movement, the fugitive brilliance of a smile. In any case, young children are obliged to accept what is offered to their senses by their surroundings: warmth they remember, and scent and softness, clear colours, floating stuffs, and the sympathy or its opposite which they receive from the beings in whose subordination they find themselves.

What is apt to be disconcerting, in later life, is to discover that clothes and objects familiar in childhood have acquired, with passing time and technical restlessness, the status of antiques or, at least, of what are now known as 'bygones'.

Almost immediately after our move to Elsfield Manor, near Oxford, I had my fourth birthday. My sister and elder brother, emancipated from the nursery, were more familiar than I with the splendours of library and drawing-room, the latter being places which Alastair and I rarely entered except to say goodnight to our parents or, dressed in shorts and silk jerseys, our hair slicked down with Yardley's solidified brilliantine and smelling strongly of lavender, to be propelled by our nurse into the company of visitors. The kitchen was another matter. We were lucky to have, in Mrs Charlett, the kindest and least upsettable of cooks, who seemed even to welcome our incursions and to be remarkably intuitive about the hunger which comes to children in the course of a long morning's strenuous exploration. She was always good for a snack of raisins or brown sugar and might even, at round about eleven o'clock, give us each a scaled-down version of the manly hunks of bread and thick slices of yellow cheese which were available to men coming in from garden or stable-yard.

Now the remembered furnishings of Mrs Charlett's kitchen, and of its adjacent offices, are increasingly often brought to my notice when I gaze, as I always do, anywhere, into the windows of junk-shops. How difficult, incidentally, it has become to find a proper junk-shop, which I take to be an almost impenetrable hugger-mugger of other people's leavings, smelling of stewed tea and dirty carpet, and always worth exploring by any devotee who has ever had the luck to find, amongst the foundered plenishings of the dead, the bankrupt, the absconded, an item or two fitting to his personal taste. In the kitchen for example, at Elsfield, there was a range of six blue and white china jugs, descending in size, and all moulded with the same pattern of recessed bands. There was the heavy iron coffee-grinder, with its brass funnel, wooden-knobbed crank-handle, and small drawer beneath to catch the grounds. There were, for a while, in the earliest days, a couple of large drum-shaped wooden knife-cleaners, also crank-handled, held upright (as a drum would be held by a marching bandsman) on cast-iron legs, and used for cleaning such steel-bladed knives as were still in use. Oakey's Wellington Knife Polish was fed into these machines, and the knife blades were inserted in slots at the top. Stainless steel soon made obsolete such unwieldy labour-savers. For a while they hung about in the space where boots and shoes were cleaned, and then disappeared. Specimens now turn up, smartly refurbished, in the windows of dealers in the forgotten and the quaint. Those dealers no longer resemble the red-eyed, unshaven, beer-smelling character in a squashed homburg hat who used to lurk in a cavern composed of broken chairs and stained mattresses at the back of his shop; more likely they are brisk matrons with blue hair, or smooth young men in tight jeans,

11

both equally up-to-the-minute in their feeling for 'trends' and usually far too knowledgeable about any *objets* of real *vertu* among their wares. They would know exactly how to present, and price, that row of china jugs, that coffee-grinder, those knife-cleaners, but might regretfully decline to handle the big ice-chest, wood-grained without, zinc-lined within, where a half-hundredweight block of ice from the Oxford fishmonger, wrapped in a blanket, kept milk and cream and butter in condition throughout memory's invariably torrid summer days.

By the time of my childhood professional photography had advanced enormously since my parents' youth. What Julia Cameron began in England in the 1860s, and others pursued in Europe, had brought a quality, sometimes, of high art to studio portraiture. This influence, however, had scarcely affected the general run of Kodak-wielders, who were responsible for the contents of the average family album. My Uncle Walter, for instance (my father's only surviving brother) used to make, with my grandmother and my Aunt Anna, a regular yearly visit from Scotland to Elsfield, in April, bringing with him a complicated and expensive camera. That camera, in other hands than his, might have provided a wonderful record of the period I am writing about, but whatever excellent qualities my uncle may have had, an appreciation of photography as an art was not one. His ambitions as a photographer seldom went further than groups, and of these he took a great number. In many of them my family looks ill-assorted and, as the children grow older, a reminiscent eye can detect signs of boredom and rebellion amongst junior members, who are obviously fed up with being called from more interesting ploys to repeat this tiresome ritual, in contrast with the patient benevolence of their elders, whose affection and respect for Walter, as also for tradition, made them willing victims of his de-romanticizing lens. Unfortunately, because I should so much have liked a good set of pictures of Elsfield interiors, since it seems that they have now been altered past recognition, Uncle Walter never came to terms with such things as tripods, extra lenses, or time-exposures. Consequently his interior shots are dark, foggy and infuriatingly unrevealing.

Hands play an important part in the first impressions of a young child. It is unlikely that he will consciously remember the soapy, slippery hands which gentled him through his bathing, or the competent, dry ones which arranged his limbs for sleep. Quite soon, however, he will have come to prefer certain hands above others. Old Nanny's, for example, were hard, bony and impatient; my mother's sometimes hurt me with their rings. There were kind hands that picked me up when I fell, and others that held me, sometimes painfully, when I was being dressed or got ready, say, for a winter walk in a London park, when it was a question of doing up my many-buttoned leggings with a button-hook.

There were also the floury hands of cooks, the many-textured hands of visitors, the oily hands of chauffeurs and, perhaps by me most significantly remembered, the brown hands of a gardener, thick-fingered, black-nailed, with earth engraved in every line of palm and finger, so delicately demonstrating the art of taking cuttings.

I was fascinated, as most growing children must be, by the things which hands could do. Knitting and crochet could hypnotize me, as I watched the product unfurl from the purposeful needles and marked how a mechanical action, in skilled hands, could fulfil a task while mind and tongue were busy with something quite else. Needles and tongues clicked and clacked in rhythm. The knitting steadily increased, as though with a life of its own, and so did the embroidered ribbon of gossip, comment and speculation coming from the mouths above. Much of the same effect was to be observed, although the terms of the talk might be different, when I was allowed to sit quietly on a stool, watching my beautiful Aunt Hilda Grenfell at work on her embroidery while she talked with my mother across the drawing-room fire. Half-hypnotized again by the movement of her delicate hands, dipping into and withdrawing, from a square of canvas, a needleful of coloured silk, I was lulled also by the tones of the two voices, so alike, family voices full of identical cadences and a delicious die-away, mock-despairing tone when deploring some human idiocy or recounting something absurd. Friends since childhood, those two first cousins could inspire each other to extravagant flights of fancy, and, in the end to paroxysms of helpless laughter, where letter-writing and embroidery had to be abandoned until calm could be restored.

If, however, hands could often be remembered for their kindness, their power to heal and to reassure, they could also be cruel, as I was to find out one day when I had my first real taste of the outside world at my preparatory school.

The outside world! I wonder if, nowadays, there can be many children able to feel that the immediate surroundings of home and

13

family are so sufficient (for good or ill) that any excursion beyond that circle can seem an adventure, a taste of freedom or, perhaps, a peril. The circumstances of my growing up which, to some, might appear enviable, to others might seem fraught with dangerous omens for later years. For my childhood's world was a complete one, and one which provided nourishment and to spare for the most romantically inclined child, and friction enough for the most pugnacious. For one thing, much of the structure of life as lived at Elsfield belonged to times much older than the 1920s of my earliest recollection. The house had been the home of Herbert Parsons, of Parsons and Thompson, the Oxford bankers, whose premises were the Old Bank in the High Street. He had remodelled a portion of the Jacobean house (with eighteenth-century additions) which had been the home of Dr Johnson's friend, the scholar and cleric Francis Wise. A very little of Wise's elaborate garden plan remained; the house, in its older part, had the panelled stone-paved hall, the panelled reception rooms and elegant staircase of his time. The Victorian addition — fortunately, because its design was heavy and somewhat out of scale — had been built of grey Cotswold stone and roofed with Cotswold tiles. Kitchen and offices were all in a deep basement like those of a London house. Beyond the kitchen was the stable-yard, a wide rectangle sloping down the side of the hill on which the house was built and which, elsewhere, afforded the famous view. There was stabling for a large number of horses — hunters and carriage horses, work-horses and hacks — a laundry, a dairy, a brewhouse, and a dark high-ceilinged harness-room in which the modest saddlery of our horse and ponies occupied only a corner of the pitch-pine walls from which jutted brackets for every size of saddle and harness of every known kind. In our time the former coach-house, with room for two carriages, became a garage for cars. Only one trio of loose-boxes was needed for my father's steady old horse and a succession of ponies. The rest were used to store potatoes and turnips, odds and ends of machinery, and bales of hay and straw. One of them, at a much later date, became the home of a badger, Mrs Brock; another housed my elder brother's hawks. All the buildings, except the brick garage, were built of Cotswold stone.

When we first went to Elsfield, the village, although a mere five miles from Oxford, could still be thought of as remote. Accordingly, a reduced version of Banker Parsons's self-contained economy went on working for a few years after our arrival. The dairy continued in use, to deal with the product of two cows which lived in the meadow below the lawn. The laundry, which occupied a corner of the stable-yard, came into its own once a fortnight, when the big copper was heated and a team of women scrubbed and pummelled, wrung and rinsed and mangled various linens, cottons and woollens, all in a thick atmosphere of steam and the biscuity smell of hot wet textiles. Peering in at the door, I could see moving figures, half blotted out by steam or by sheets hanging from the long wooden airers, red faces, red arms, hair coming loose as seaweed in the damp, and hear the laughter, the merry exchanges between the women of the village who had come with their own laundry; a party-like atmosphere which showed that many hands were, indeed, making light work.

Beside the garage there was a narrow passage leading out of the stable-yard into another smaller but equally steeply sloping space beyond. One wall of that passage was the side of a tall, buttressed barn, much the oldest building on the place. When, later, my sister heard a visiting architect speak respectfully of that building as, very likely, Edwardian, she was enchanted, seeing a vision of plush and gilding, hearing waltz-music and the popping of corks. The architect, of course, meant to date the barn to the reign of Edward VI, perhaps even of Edward IV — simply, none of us had heard the expression in that context before.

The smaller yard contained a brick manure-pit, a wooden granary standing on staddle-stones, a woodshed and, high on the road side, backing on to the harness-room, a capacious carpenter's shop. Downhill below the granary lay the orchard, the drying green, the sties of Amos Webb's cherished pigs, and the runs for Mrs Webb's hens. In my earliest childhood, all these aspects of domestic economy were in some sort of use, and we should have had to be dull children indeed not to find entertainment among them even on the worst of days.

Elsfield Manor stands, as many such houses do in the Cotswolds, directly on the village street, and the line of the house, past the first yard-gates, is continued by the stable-range as far as the carpenter's shop. This range had, on the yard side, a raised, railed footway and looked down on the buildings opposite. Above the stables there was a big, raftered loft, wood-floored, with a door opening on to air, which had once been used for hoisting bales of feed. At that level, on the house side, were the quarters known as the grooms' room — two rooms in fact, reached by a steep staircase. Those rooms had a great attraction for me,

15

although untenanted because the groom lived out in the village, their floors covered in fallen plaster, their windows cobwebbed, and the air full of a sweetish smell of damp and decay. I should have liked to have had them to myself to live in, particularly when at odds with my family, as I fairly often was. Beyond and below the grooms' room, and hard by the yard gates, was the shed which housed the Lister-Bruston engine which made the electric light. In those days, before the coming of the National Grid (which did not reach Elsfield until 1936), if you wanted electricity you had to make it yourself.

There it all was, a small-scale version of something to be found in every English country house of any size, a complete arrange-ment for living made to a pattern which, barring motor-cars, plumbing and electric light, had seen little radical change over many centuries. In our time, certainly, bread was bought from a baker, and meat and fish in Oxford, but milk, cream and butter were all produced on the premises; pigs were killed, and sides of bacon salted down in long wooden troughs; meat and game were hung in the tall meat-safe, with its panels of perforated zinc, which stood on wooden legs at the corner of the stable yard nearest to the house. Apart from bread, all other kinds of baking were done in the kitchen, where jam was also made. Vegetables and fruit were supplied from the kitchen gardens, the orchard and the hothouse. Provisions for the store-cupboard — chests of tea, sacks of sugar, dry groceries of many kinds, came, as they did to many families living our kind of life, from London, from the Army & Navy Stores. 'The Stores', that nearly universal provider, standby of colonial families and people living in the deep country, had had for its first chairman my mother's uncle, and so she enjoyed the privilege of a 'family discount' on anything that she ordered. I particularly remember the sweets and crystallized fruits which came in blue and white striped boxes and, of course, as really fascinating reading, the famous catalogue, which is now a collectors' item.

One summer when my father had taken for the holidays a rather leaky shooting-lodge, Ben More, on the island of Mull, we found that the library consisted of one Edgar Wallace novel, minus its back, and an Army & Navy Stores catalogue, intact and weighty between its stiff red covers. My father, who usually went on holiday with a large wooden box of books, was never short of reading, and each of us brought some of his own; yet I was happy to read the catalogue very carefully from end to end, and found continual amusement in imagining how I might furnish, say, a lawyer's office, or a sporting estate, or an operating theatre, from its pages, or equip myself beyond reason or desire as a fisherman, a motorist, or a big-game hunter.

The village of Elsfield lies along the edge of a hill strung out over a distance of nearly a mile. The road, which comes in a series of short, straight stretches and sharp turns from Beckley to the north, and which crosses the old Worcester-London road a mile and a half away, was once no more than a track giving access to fields, and it follows their contours with respectful exactitude. It crosses the plateau which looks down on to Otmoor and then descends gently but steadily on its way southwards to the flat lands at the foot of Elsfield hill, to the Marstons, Old and New, and the city of Oxford. The first dwelling to the north is Forest Farm, whose name, with that of Stow Wood, nearer to Beckley, recalls the great Stow Forest, in a clearing of which, in Saxon times, the settlement of Elsfield — known earlier as Esefelde — came to life.

The first village houses, of unguessable age, but probably early nineteenth century, a red-brick, semi-detached Victorian intruder, more stone cottages, thatched, and a smithy, were all on one side of the road, sharing the wide view over the Cherwell valley towards Gloucestershire which had been one of my parents' chief reasons for choosing the manor house as their home. Seen from that height, woods and meadows, and water-meadows beside the river, stretched away westwards to the first ridges of the Cotswolds. On a clear day we could make out the masts of the Leafield wireless station, near Burford and, in exceptional weather, Cleeve Beacon, above Cheltenham, a good fifty miles away.

After that first flush of housing the village of Elsfield seemed to come to an end. The end, on one side, was a pretty pair of attached houses in grey stone; on the other were the ruins of a much older cottage, beside a tip full of empty HP Sauce and Camp Coffee bottles, and blue-enamelled saucepans burned into holes. Then came a fine double rank of elm-trees, a high green tunnel in summer, and, at the end of that, the village began again with, on its lower side (our side) the semi-detached Victorian cottages — gabled brick, two-storeyed — in one of which lived the family of Amos Webb. Thereafter came the smaller yard, with its solid wooden gates, the higher stable range, equivalent gates to the stable-yard, and then the manor house itself, standing tall and, at that approach, rather forbidding in all its stony verticals, directly above the road. Beyond the front door with an ecclesiastical-looking porch, there ran for twenty yards or so a ten-foot wall of grey stone, ending amongst the upper branches of an old yew tree. Set back a little, beyond that, was the long, low, thatched cottage of Jack Allam, the keeper, which had 1706 on a small plaque to one side. Then came a wide farm-gate, with a wicket, which led to Pond Close and to the main kitchen garden and glasshouses. Beyond the gate a stone cottage in the 'gothick' taste, one of the few conceits of Francis Wise which had survived, housed the head gardener. His own small garden was backed by the wall of the hothouse, which held a door for his convenience. Another high wall ran on beside the road for the length of the kitchen garden and ended at the gate to the property of one of Elsfield's farmers, Mr Hatt.

Opposite the gardener's cottage, and standing well back from the road, in a cool, green garden stood the small but distinguished Queen Anne house, in grey stone with white window-sashes, where lived Miss Parsons, unmarried daughter of our banker predecessor, in an interior and with a style which might have belonged to a story by Walter de la Mare. There was no electricity in Miss Parsons's house and little plumbing; the lavatory held a beautifully kept and most intriguing earth-closet. Each year Miss Parsons gave a children's party at Christmas time, and the village children sat down by candle-light to the sort of spread of jellies and cream, cream cakes and chocolate biscuits at which present-day children, not severely rationed for sweet stuffs as we were, would probably turn up their noses.

Miss Parsons always wore a hat, usually of grey felt with a grosgrain ribbon, held on by hatpins. I cannot see her without it, even indoors. For all the time that I remember her she never varied her austere and entirely suitable style of dress. Generally she wore coats and skirts of grey material. Whatever might be happening to fashions in a wider world, those skirts were never shortened. They reached nearly to the ground, just disclosing stout black boots.

My parents had been at pains not to make Miss Parsons feel that her position in the village of her birth had been, in any way, usurped. She continued to visit, for gossip or consolation or, most often, practical charity, the families which she had known all her life. On Miss Parsons and her devotion to the village — *her* village

18

as she undoubtedly saw it — I would quote my mother: 'It is difficult to think back. The Welfare State...creates a barrier between us and the past. So I have to shut my eyes and try hard to recall life in the 1920s. Miss Parsons ran the War Savings in the village, the coal club, the shoe club; she decorated the church at all festivals with a real Victorian love of lavishness, so that portions of our tiny church almost sank under swathes of greenery and holly at Christmas, and mounds of primroses and moss at Easter. She walked into and out of Oxford sometimes three times a week until she was much advanced in years.' Few in Elsfield owned bicycles. The carrier's cart from Beckley went through to Oxford twice a week but could seldom take passengers. We alone had a car. Those who needed to go to Oxford, or to another village, simply walked or bicycled the distance, to and fro. Three visits to Oxford in one week meant thirty miles of walking for Miss Parsons, in addition to the mile or so each day on her Elsfield rounds.

The coal club...the shoe club...such expedients must sound strangely to generations brought up on child-benefit and the many official reliefs to poverty which have come into being since the Second World War, not to mention the relatively vast increase in income to farmers and those who work for them. The whole village of Elsfield, apart from our own property, and all the land around it, belonged to an Oxford college, Christ Church, and although rents were small and, I think, compassionately administered, its people were very poor. My sister remembers something which, if I noticed it at the age of four I have since forgotten — that many children, in our earliest days, went barefoot. That might, anyway, have struck me as an advantage, an enviable kind of freedom, when my own boots pinched. Oxfordshire winters are long and damp and sometimes very cold. For women who had to clothe, feed and warm a family on the agricultural wage of thirty shillings a week, their small contributions to coal club, shoe club and other things of the sort, gave at least the chance of acquiring necessities too costly ever to be bought from the weekly wage.

The 1914 war had brought a measure of ease to farmers and their employers. Frequently neglected in times of peace, and victims at all times of the savage fluctuations in prosperity to which their industry had always been subject, agriculturalists in time of war found themselves cherished, wooed, and encouraged by every means to supply food to a beleaguered country. That moderate wartime benefit to farm labourers did not last for long after 1918, and all through the twenty-one years until conflict was resumed they had a hard time indeed. The farmers, themselves struggling, were often obliged to lay off men, and so there was little security in employment. I think that my father sometimes took on a gardener or two more than were strictly needed, in an attempt to alleviate some obvious distress.

A further complication came with the expansion of Morris's motor works at Cowley, a few miles away at the northern edge of Oxford. That organization offered high wages, and even transport from the nearer villages, but no guarantee whatever of a steady job. Men were trained, and employed during moments of high production, and then, at short notice, laid off; a stupidly unimaginative system, although doubtless an economical one, which created an atmosphere of anxiety to add to the perennial precariousness of village life. Mr William Morris (later to be Lord Nuffield) had begun his commercial career with a bicycle shop in Oxford. My father, in undergraduate days, had often hired bicycles from him. When I was at New College my scout, Tom Berry, used to speak slightingly of 'little Billy Morris' who had had, he implied, the awful lack of discretion to become a millionaire. In Tom's view he was a classic example of someone who did not know his place.

The three farmers of the old village, their names all monosyllables, Mr Watts, Mr Brown and Mr Hatt, were its chief employers. Serious, responsible men they were, living in comfortable old farmhouses, with numbers of busy, attractive children and handsome, capable wives. This sounds as if kindly memory were overdoing it but, turn the proposition about as I may, I cannot see it as anything but true. Why else should I have so much enjoyed being sent on errands to the farmhouses, and have retained so strong a recollection of geniality, of purposeful industry, of good looks and robust physical health? One of the three farmers, Watts, had a high reputation beyond the county for shrewdness and skill and an ability to prosper at a time when prosperous farmers, all over Britain, were as rare as hens' teeth. In a community of unimpassioned Anglicans he and his family were the only Methodists.

There can never have been much to record of such a village as Elsfield, close kin but for its strung-out character, and the fact that it had no public house, to so many in the county at that time. The 'old village' consisted of the long row of thatched cottages opposite the Manor's garden wall, the farms, the church and vicarage; and then another couple of cottages, the schoolhouse, part thatched stone, part slate-roofed red brick, and the Watts's farm on the edge of the hill. From there the ground dropped away, pretty steeply for that neighbourhood, and Hill Farm, as it was called, had what was then an ideal view of Oxford. The city, framed by great elms, all now destroyed, and itself bowered in green, with nothing modern showing in any direction, presented a group of its finest buildings as serene and heart-catching as a celestial city in the background of an Italian primitive. So compellingly splendid was the view, and charming the farmhouse itself in its Georgian dignity, that Christ Church, which owned the property, found it necessary to have printed a standard form of refusal, applicants to buy it were so numerous.

There, then, was the place which was to contain my family's life for a small number of years, which yet provided the frame and setting for much that was formative in our lives. I write 'a small number of years': in all it was thirty-four, and I suppose, in what Hardy called our 'disordered century', that might be counted a reasonably long time. Neither we children nor our parents had any thought of merely perching, with the idea of moving on, as so many nowadays must, or feel that they must. Elsfield, for my father, was a homecoming to places — Oxford, the Cotswolds — where, as a young man, he had been intensely happy. After the misery of the Great War he wanted country life; above all he wanted to put down roots and, in rooting his own life satisfactorily he would have expected also to root his children's. For example, when he was appointed Governor-General of Canada in 1935, and needed a title for the peerage which he had to take, he chose Tweedsmuir of Elsfield, in honour, first, of the beloved land of his childhood and, second, of the solid if unostentatious material fruit of his successful career.

In the 1920s it was still just possible to sustain a belief, buttressed by a rather desperate hope, that there would not be another war, that 1914-1918 had indeed ended wars for good. Consequently it was also possible, at least for great optimists like my father, to plant trees which would not reach full stature for a hundred years, or make moderate alterations to house and garden which would play their part in the secular development of the place. It was just possible to believe that the property might yet be handed on from one generation to another. Vain hopes! Too soon war came again and, like all wars, in addition to accelerating technological progress, it vastly accelerated social and economic change. Numerous family discussions, after 1945, found no resolution. The house, built with a full staff of servants in mind, had become difficult to manage. What had always been thought of as a small country house had steadily come to seem unmanageably large. Consultations with market gardeners revealed the impossibility of converting the gardens into anything commercially worthwhile. The two highly productive kitchen gardens were separated from one another by the whole spread of the pleasure grounds. To make market gardening possible, on a truly commercial scale, lawns would have to be ploughed up, trees felled, walls pulled down to give adequate runs for the cultivators then coming into use. Moreover the house, of several different dates of construction, and containing several different levels, was not thought a good prospect for conversion into flats. Since the huge post-war expansion of the motor industry was then only just getting under way, the idea of making dwellings in the stable buildings — something which might, in the end, have saved the situation — was thought too risky. In recent years dons and others from Oxford, now thoroughly motorized, have flooded out into the adjacent villages, and made homes for themselves even farther afield; but that social trend, in the late 1940s, was not yet perceptible. Meanwhile the place attracted heavy taxes and, in the end, my elder brother decided to sell. Such properties, at that time, were little in demand. House and dependencies went for what would now seem a negligible sum, to a member of a millionaire family who offered what I suppose must have been its exact market value at the time.

The house was sold in 1953. Towards the end I lived in it myself, with my then family, already feeling that I was wearing someone else's topcoat, not a really good fit, and anyway only temporarily on my back. They were all there, the familiar things, books and pictures and furniture. Nothing material had changed since my childhood but, with the certain prospect hanging over me of having to leave the house, and although it was nearly as comfortable as ever, I found that I could no longer live in it properly. It had more echoes than our small commotion could still. The house and I were going to have to part and, whether I liked it or not, I was already booked for departure.

That last summer at Elsfield I was able to observe, with sorrow and a kind of admiration, what happens when old gardens begin to run down. Many years of meticulous cultivation had gone to

22

maintaining the health and the high productivity of the ground given to vegetables and fruit, the glasshouses, the flower borders and the large expanses of lawn. By the early 1950s domestic staff had had to be greatly reduced. My mother had left, with her companion, to inhabit an hotel in north Oxford, whilst quartering the county to find a new home. The gardens were looked after by James Adams (successor to our first head gardener, Martin Newall), with only sporadic assistance. He tended the hothouse himself and, not liking any more than I did the changes too easily foreseeable, continued to supply the household with flowers and vegetables and, in their season, with asparagus, grapes and peaches, even as weeds and grass took hold all round their places of growth. It was as though he thought, by displaying the gardens' bounty, that he could ward off the inevitable end. When that came, I had to make a round of farewells, explaining once again how necessity had forced us to sell the property, and how I was sure that the new owner would wish to keep on good and experienced staff. Adams shook my hand, his face expressionless, and then turned his back on me and looked out over Pond Close towards his fruit garden. Feeling miserable enough, I felt also a kind of guilt. That thin, stiff back seemed to say, quite plainly: 'You couldn't hold on, could you? And what's to become of me?' He said no word. A few months later, turning into the heavy traffic on the Oxford bypass, a mile away, his bicycle was struck by a car and he was killed instantly.

3

THE FRIENDLY FIELDS

It is a June morning in Oxfordshire, and I suppose that I am about seven years old. From the moment of waking the day has shown promise of being fine and hot: a sky more white than blue, a light mist over meadows drenched by the night's dew, no wind at all, no birds about except a few rooks testing the thermal currents, soaring and gliding beyond the nursery window.

This is a day much looked forward to, the day of the machine which will come to cut the hay in our meadow. It comes early, just after breakfast, and I am there to greet it as it manoeuvres through the wide gateway beside Jack Allam's cottage and goes plunging off down the steep slope of Pond Close, clashing and chattering, drawn by a sensible-looking brown horse, myself running beside. The gate at the bottom of Pond Close leads into Manor Meadow beneath the towering elm trees of the Crow Wood. Men are already waiting there, young and middle-aged, recruited from the village to help with a job which seems also, in some way, a kind of festival, a familiar stage in the cycle of the year. They are all in shirt-sleeves, their collarless shirts open on red-brown necks, and are in a jovial, somewhat holiday mood, although a hard, hot day's work lies ahead of them.

The mowing team included Jack Allam, but must otherwise have been borrowed, or rather hired, from the various village farms. For one or two of them the day may have made a kind of outing, a change from a daily routine and that, partly, was what gave a holiday air to the proceedings. The meadow was a broad rectangle of somewhat uneven surface. Wind and rain, that year, must have spared the hay which stood up thick and strong, the colour of oatmeal on top, with here and there a poppy or a moon daisy and a plentiful sprinkling of clover.

The mowing machine, with its steadily plodding horse, cut its first swathes around the edges of the field, as near as might be to the enclosing hedges and the iron-railed bank at the foot of the lawn. The driver sat on a metal seat with holes in it, and the cutting was done by reciprocating blades in a long, many-toothed projection at right angles to the machine. That machine was a little bit of a wonder still, although its design went back to the last century, because older village people could remember when the work of haymaking was done by men with scythes moving in line across a field.

As each side of the meadow was mown, the machine leaving behind it flat rows of moist grass, the driver went for the next line still standing, so that he compassed a diminishing square which would end as a small piece, a few feet across, to be demolished in a single sortie. One or two of the men had brought their dogs, mongrel terriers of different sorts, all expert rabbiters and ratters. As the square of standing hay in the meadow's centre grew smaller a horde of little creatures, desperate as the fearful thunder and clash of the machine became unbearable, bolted from their shelter out into the stubble, to be fallen upon by the dogs with squeals of glee. One sight, on that day, would stay in my mind for ever, that of a young rabbit which had stood pat a moment too long. The blades of the cutter had half severed a leg so that it hung bleeding by a strip of skin. I watched with horror its short-run three-legged race into the jaws of the nearest dog. That massacre of rabbits and field mice which had not had the sense to get out of the grass before the cutter came near them — but how could they know what the mechanical noise and the shaking of the ground really portended? — very nearly spoilt my pleasure in the day. But that pleasure was a potent one. Not even to save small animals could I have forgone the sense of importance gained from carrying jugs of beer to the men, when they settled in the shade for their dinner, and being allowed to help with the tedding of the hay into neat piles, with seeds and scraps of grass pricking my hot skin inside my shirt, and dust in my nose until, exhausted, my face burning from the fierce sun of that cloudless day, I was recalled to dusky interiors and supper, and the luxury, denied to my fellow labourers, of a long, deep bath.

That day's work was not the end of haymaking, nor of visiting machinery. Quite soon, when the hay was dry enough, a special excitement made itself felt, not only in our household but throughout the village. The hay-elevator arrived, drawn by a traction engine, and both were installed at the top of the field. Then began the process of making a rick, when the hay, carted up from the meadow, was fed to the elevator, the endless, spiked moving stairway running up and over with it, powered by a belt

25

from a driving wheel on the side of the steam engine. From the top of the elevator the dried grass fell in sheaves on to the rapidly rising rectangle which, before long, would show the familiar shape of a haystack. Meanwhile the traction engine made a fine snorting, railway-like sound and the warm air was full of the smell of hay, hot oil and coal smoke, and everybody who could came to look on as the stack, solid and wholesome-looking as a new-baked loaf, grew till it touched the top of the elevator and the work of thatching could begin.

As I have said, the world of my childhood was an enclosed one. It was also intensely active. Life at that time, and in that kind of establishment, moved to the rhythm of a repeated set of functions, where various activities, working like cogs in machinery, inter-locked to sustain momentum in all the human lives concerned.

Visiting important houses managed by the National Trust, or put on show by private owners, I am always aware of a particular lack. The places themselves are usually in splendid order: enormous care, knowledge and technical skill have been expended on details of display, arrangement and repair: useful information is everywhere supplied. But — guides and the visiting public apart — *there is nobody about.* Not so very long ago a big country house was a kind of community where many hands were engaged in maintaining or improving an august status quo. What one misses — since a crowd of visitors standing about looking bemused, or plodding docilely through gilded suites of rooms can never produce the same effect — is the continual movement to and fro of people with jobs to do, whether humble or important, fulfilling the needs of a living organism.

Once in Udaipur, in what is now Rajastan, I came early one morning to the courtyard of the Maharana's palace, and the scene which met my eyes, transposed to western terms, could have been that of a seventeenth-century study of some great European house. In one corner of the courtyard turbaned grooms were lunging a superb Arab stallion. Other grooms and palace servants were hurrying about — for it was the cool, the energetic time of day — and, waiting in knots of two or three beside the low and narrow doorway which, for good reasons of security, was the only way up to the splendours within, were Rajput noblemen in elegant kaftans and dazzling white jodhpurs, wearing small round turbans in the colours of boiled sweets, and each carrying a short, curved, silver-hilted ceremonial sword. That palace, at that time, was very much a going concern, and so, in times past, were the great houses which, with pathetic vulgarity, and in probably unacknowledged debt to Mrs Hemans, we now call 'stately homes'. That expression anyway seems a contradiction in terms, since 'home' to the average Briton means an enfolding cosiness, a wrap-around domesticity which in no way can apply to the palaces and noble mansions so described. 'Great houses' is surely a much more justly descriptive pair of words.

There was nothing stately about my home; nevertheless some sort of house had been on its site for a very long time, and the collection of buildings which I knew, having fulfilled its functions throughout several centuries, had acquired a certain dignity and character entirely its own. Except on Sundays or holidays or in the hottest hours of a July day there would always be somebody about, doing something that needed doing, in garden or stables, carpenter's shop or garage. Similarly, for most of the day, there was continual movement in the house, from an early hour in the morning when fires were attended to, and polishing and dusting got under way; and, whenever my father was there, his own especial energy and speed of movement could not have failed to animate a household many times the size. Movement was also a two-way flow, as people came into or went out of the house or outbuildings; a gardener with vegetables already scrubbed and trimmed for presentation to the kitchen, women from the village to help in dairy or laundry, men to consult with Amos Webb about needed repairs, or to bring wood for the carpenter's shop or hay for the stables; gardeners at work in the kitchen gardens or moving between them with tools, wheelbarrows, or a huge zinc water-butt on wheels. In summer a skewbald pony called Daisy, whose main duty was to pull the trap which was used for journeys not requiring the car, would be shod with leather overshoes and put to hauling a big square mowing-machine up and down the lawns. The somehow musical clash and rumble of that old machine, could I ever hear it again, would bring back clearly, not only the joy of summer weather, but the comforting sense that all was in order, that competent people had my surroundings well in hand.

The charm of any garden, its possibilities as landscape, as a variation on the theme presented by neighbouring fields, or woods, or wilds, must always be enhanced by differences of level. After spending some years working on two entirely flat gardens I

look back, as to an ideal, to the garden of my earliest home. The house, as I have said, was set on the side of a hill. Below it was a long grass terrace which stretched from the stable-yard on one side, across the west front of the house, and the whole length of the wall which fronted the village street, to the angle of another wall, part of which made the side of Jack Allam's cottage. That wall ran for a short distance across the end of the terrace, where a raised gravel walk, shaded at its end by a large yew tree and tall bushes of philadelphus, met a green-painted door. Beside that door the stone wall petered out into iron fencing of the kind which may still be seen, more or less dilapidated, bounding country properties,
and which, now, might be almost impossibly expensive to replace.

Below the terrace the ground fell away. Where it fronted the house a few steps led down to a long sloping lawn. Away to the left the terrace met, at its farther edge, the mixture of old broad-leaved trees, beech, elm and chestnut, which was known as the Crow Wood, for the colonies of rooks which nested there every year. At the wood's lower end were the temple, the pond, and, lower still, a sort of ravine which we called the Gully, also surrounded by trees, and then more iron fencing before the meadows began.

If an old print is to be taken seriously, Mr Francis Wise had created for himself, at the end of the eighteenth century, a very decent example of the Picturesque on a property of no great size. In the picture, taken from the lowest point, the Doric temple stands proudly among trees above a pond, or small lake, handsomely revetted with stone. In the nearer foreground is a stone screen, artfully designed as a ruin, from which, at a depth of about fifteen feet below the level of the pond, a cascade issues into a rectangular canal, also properly bordered in stone.

In our time it was hard to see that picture as anything but highly idealized. All that remained to be seen were the temple, still in good repair, the pond, its stone edges crumbled away or overgrown with ivy and its surface more often than not covered in green weed, and beyond and below, nothing: no ruin, no canal with neat stone borders, no cascade. The Gully, it is true, held a long depression which might once have been a canal, but time and vegetation had all but obliterated any revealing lines. There remained, however, a sluice at the pond's edge, still in working order, which could release water from the pond into a narrow channel at the bottom of the Gully. The pond was evidently fed by springs but, a century and a half after Mr Wise, those springs must have become partly choked, for there was never movement enough in the water to keep it free from pond-weed.

However, what was left of such agreeable follies was intriguing enough, and what must once have been a quite considerable work of garden design had left something, an impression, a sense of space and order, which could feed speculation and provide a satisfaction of its own. Meanwhile, since the garden contained woodland, if of a tamed and brushwood-free variety, it provided endless opportunities for games, for the making of fires, the construction of dams and fortifications in the Gully's thin, trickling stream, or the baking of the dark, greasy Oxford clay into prehistoric-looking pots and bowls.

We did not have to go very far to find the pleasures of the countryside, in a modified form, available for investigation. There were birds and their nests, and a selection of wild flowers, for calmer study, and enough large shrubs and small thickets for strenuous games of flight and pursuit, and enough space to evade sibling attention and get away on one's own.

When very young we were always turned out of doors after breakfast in almost any weather. If it rained too heavily; if slushing about in black wellingtons and mackintoshes and waterproof hats became too dreary and inhibiting, there were always the barns and lofts to explore, and a reasonable dryness was usually to be found inside the huge ilex tree which stood for ten years of our time, until uprooted by a freak gale, near the Crow Wood, at the left-hand side of the lawn as one faced the view. That was a magnificent tree, one of the finest I have seen, even in Italy, a perfectly rounded dome of shining dark green, clothed to the ground with leaves on every side. Entry, for a child, was not difficult. One had only to slip between two of the low, sweeping branches to find oneself in a considerable space, large enough for a small chapel. The tree's powerful stem branched, at about four feet from the ground, into several stout arms which, branching again in a symmetrical fashion, provided a series of comfortable sitting-places, or the means to climb almost to the height of the dome. The floor, where no herbage grew, was beaten earth carpeted with dead leaves, a brown, rustling carpet which could be swept aside to make space for building the funeral pyres which, at one time, I had a fondness for constructing. It must have been the Viking's Funeral in P.C. Wren's *Beau Geste* which had put such things into my mind; that or some half-understood random

29

reading about Mayan or Aztec customs. Usually the pyres were made for their own sake, for the pleasure of choosing dry sticks of equal length and laying them lengthways and crossways to form a neat structure which would burn easily but not too fast, and with a certain fatality which I found satisfying. Sometimes a lead soldier would be immolated, sometimes a dead mouse or shrew which I had found in the garden; but those were rare and special occasions when I improved the ceremony, rendering it more solemn by building with stones and mud a terrace and wall, even a temple-like small edifice — open to the air, since I could not manage roofs — as setting for the final rites.

Most children of that era were forbidden to play with matches, but this prohibition does not seem to have applied to us, or at least not out of doors; and even indoors I must have used them when experiments in chemistry needed something to be heated in a test-tube over a spirit lamp. From an early age I carried a box of matches on my walks in case I should want to make a fire, or to burn any scraps of paper I might find littering the countryside. My parents approved of the latter activity, which was not then much needed, for few people passed by my favourite ways, and if they did had nothing to throw down but an empty paper packet labelled Woodbine, or a bit of greasy paper which had wrapped a labourer's lunch.

Perhaps it was a useful thing to 'play with fire' at an early age. Not only did the making of it satisfy some primal instinct, not only was it beautiful in itself, but the lessons learned in keeping it under control had applications in many other spheres. Somehow, in a quite unformulated way, an understanding was achieved concerning the need, if things were to be both enjoyable and beneficial, to keep them from getting out of hand: a valuable lesson, unfortunately to be sometimes forgotten or flouted, with rather dire results, in later life.

Active children who spend much time out of doors are inevitably hungry at times not catered for by regular meals. Milk and biscuits were provided for us at eleven in the morning, and sometimes there were more enticing snacks to be had from Mrs Charlett in the kitchen. Any additional food was always welcome, and so another use for outdoor fires was the baking of potatoes, which were eaten charred black all over so that hands and face grew black as well. If one imagines mashed potato encased in hot charcoal, that is how they turned out. We found them delicious. More ambitious cookery took place once in a while, when Johnnie was at home, and he and I decided on a picnic on Beckley Common. Generously provided by Mrs Charlett with the needed materials — bread, butter, lard, sausages, bacon, eggs and a large iron frying-pan — we set off to walk the two miles to Beckley, carrying a heavy knapsack by turns.

On our way, at the place where we crossed the old Worcester-London road on its stretch between Islip and Forest Hill, we would pass an ancient elm tree which still had hanging from it a loop of rusty chain. That had been the gallows tree on which the last local highwayman had been hanged for robbing the Oxford coach and shooting its driver. We knew the highwayman's name, and knew too that his descendants, who lived not far away, were still entirely at odds with the law, so that any police investigations invariably began with them.

At the corner of Stow Wood, just beyond the crossroads, where our road resumed its way to Beckley, an oak tree still bore a notice, faintly discernible on a wooden board, which read: 'Beware! Man-traps and Spring-guns!'. That was a reminder of the 'poaching wars' of the last century. It may only have been a try-on, like the dummy burglar alarms which some people put on their houses, but I should certainly have thought twice about poaching in Stow Wood a hundred years ago.

Beckley Common, so called, is an open space, part grazing land, part thickets of gorse and bramble, which lies along the edge of the same escarpment as Elsfield, on the near side of Beckley village, with a wide view towards Otmoor. In about 1923, having received a legacy, and having the landowning instinct strong in her, my mother had bought the property which thereafter was always referred to as hers. I hasten to add that this was no wicked latter-day attempt at enclosure. In spite of its name Beckley Common had long ceased to be common land. In addition to the area so named there was another big field at the foot of the hill, enclosing the wooded promontory jutting out above which was thought to have been a British or Roman camp. The westward view encompassed Woodeaton with its woods, the rise above Islip and the hamlet of Noke, and a large part of Otmoor cut off to the north by the long, dark bulk of Noke Wood. At the foot of the slope, where the ground was wet from springs, marsh marigolds grew, and water avens, and white sheets of wild garlic. Bird life was plentiful and there were large colonies of rabbits. It was altogether a most satisfactory place for birds'-nesting and botanizing, and of course for eating the substantial cowboy-style

31

fry-ups which Johnnie and I so much enjoyed.

Noke Wood was to come into the family a year or two after Beckley Common, when my father decided to buy it for such shooting as it might provide. My parents, when it became known that they were considering that purchase, received urgent representations from people in Beckley, and from the neighbouring farmers, imploring them not to change their minds. The reason was that a band of gypsies, with the purchase price all ready in bags of greasy notes — or so the local rumour ran — were very much in the field as buyers. The local people foresaw nothing but trouble if the gypsies succeeded in buying the big wood, fearing for their poultry and other farm-stock, and even for their children, for some people — the older ones anyway — still firmly believed that small children might be 'stolen by the gypsies'.

At the time of those first picnic excursions I must have been about eight years old, and Johnnie twelve. At that period of our lives I would follow him anywhere, even into water up to my waist on winter shooting or bird-watching expeditions. He was my contact with the outer world, supplier of worldly wisdom, of precept and anecdote. He had things to tell about the preparatory school where I was to follow him which left me wondering how I should get on in that extraordinary-sounding society when, at the age of nine, I should have to forsake for it my safe, embracing home. Johnnie, by my standards, had travelled far, accompanying his father on stalking and fishing trips in the remote Highlands. Bizarre names such as Letterewe and Rhiconnich and Auchnacloich came easily off his tongue, together with stories of great fish caught or lost, and sketches of grown-ups, fierce or friendly, jovial, eccentric or alarming, whom he had met.

When I was eight my brother Alastair was in his sixth year. He was a bright, lively and adventurous child, but too young still to join in all the ploys which I made for myself and, moreover, being thought delicate, liable to be prevented by authority from attempting anything very taxing. Accordingly, my temperamental preference for being on my own took me farther afield than the grounds of home whenever the weather seemed right for wider exploration.

Southwards of the garden proper lay a big paddock called Pond Close. Here was to be found a well with worn stone steps, fenced, and surrounded by elder trees, into which, for centuries, people had thrown small coins before making wishes. That part of the demesne was reached through the green door in the stone wall, which opened on to a path, iron-railed on one side, leading past the back of Jack Allam's cottage, his vegetable plot, dog kennel, and coops for ducks and hens, to the walled garden and its extramural enclosure for soft fruit. Beyond that again Pond Close came to a point with, on the right, a wood called Pennywell — its name confirming the antiquity of the wishing-well near by — and the shallow basin of a half dried-up pond. At this point, with tall elms reaching for each other to make an arch, is (or was then) revealed that most perfect of all views of Oxford, with the dome of the Radcliffe Camera at its centre, a view of which I was to be reminded one day, gazing at the Duomo of Florence from the *podere* at San Francesco.

Another old print shows one of Francis Wise's more delicate conceits. The pond of Pond Close, in our time scarcely traceable, is there portrayed as a neat circle of clear water, stone-bordered, having at its centre a small structure in the Chinese taste, with a pointed, fluted roof on four slim pillars. The roof is hung all around with little bells, and a narrow bridge connects this pretty *point de repère* with dry land. It is pleasant to imagine Mr Wise and his friends, amongst whom, on more than one occasion, would have been Samuel Johnson, making a stately progress from the house to this far edge of the property, to exclaim at the elegance of the exotic structure and, once in its shelter, to cry out even more excitedly and in the best-chosen words, with probably a snatch or two of Latin thrown in, at the celestial picture of the University framed in its arch of elms.

Pond Close certainly had its appeal, especially in summertime, when I could slip into the fruit garden and take my pick of raspberries, in their steel cage, or gooseberries of every size and colour. If gardeners were out of sight I could also insinuate myself under the strawberry nets in the walled garden or, later on, pick plums off one of the espaliered trees on its outer wall. Once a gardener remarked to me, in a tone heavy with meaning, that something had been 'at' his raspberries. Did I know anything about that? I suggested pheasants. 'Ar!' he answered, 'I daresay! Two-legged pheasants!'

Most of my private explorations tended to be in a northerly direction, that is to say to the right of the house on its garden side. At the edge of the sloping lawn, opposite the Crow Wood, was a broad, serpentine herbaceous border, filled with all the varieties of perennials then in fashion, and behind it the yew hedge which my father had planted in 1920, and which grew surprisingly fast.

Beyond that again, and following the same steep slope as the lawn, was the second kitchen garden, bounded at its upper end by the grey wall of a stable building, and containing in my time a glasshouse never much used, but worth a visit for the fine toads which lived in its sunken, fern-shadowed rain-water tank. That garden grew such mundane things as potatoes, onions, leeks and various brassicas; it had also the mature beds which produced, in their season, a variety of bright green asparagus, nearly always fully edible from tip to tail, the like of which I have rarely had since, and never in such profusion.

At first that kitchen garden was separated from the orchard beyond by an open fence and some yards of an old red-brick wall at the upper end, along which ran a border containing flowers for cutting, and odds and ends of herbs and vegetables. A wicket gate led into the orchard by a path which skirted an ancient mulberry tree. Such trees are fragile and liable to split, or to drop their limbs when these become too heavy to hold to the main trunk; accordingly some of the lower boughs were supported on crutches of wood. In their season the mulberries, fat and juicy, covered the ground with a purple-black carpet, which turned to a bloody red when trodden on.

After a few years the orchard fence was replaced by a brick wall, with stone coping, going down in stepped sections to extend the existing one above. The wicket gate gave place to an elegant affair in wrought iron, designed by my sister. Peaches and nectarines of some maturity grew on the upper wall. There cannot have been many summers when it was possible to pick and eat ripe nectarines, but there were certainly one or two; that famous summer of 1921 for example, when I was five years old. For weeks the sun blazed unhampered; for weeks no drop of rain fell. In fields and woods great fissures opened in the ground and snakes became torpid, lost their shyness and slithered about in the brush making an unusual noise amongst grass and leaves dried to old paper by the heat.

It was probably in that same summer that I had an uncomfortably close encounter with an adder. Hungry (and also greedy) as usual, I was raiding the fruit garden, stuffing myself with gooseberries from some small old bushes which bore a garnet-red variety of great sweetness. Just as I was about to pick a berry from a branch low on the ground I drew my hand back sharply, for there, coiled like a spring, its scales shining yellow-brown, the V (for viper) clearly visible on its narrow head, was a small adder, apparently asleep. How it got up from the ground, even the few inches to its perch, I have no idea. Refusing to accept the appearance of sleep I made off quickly, and I am sure that I left gooseberry bushes alone for a long while afterwards.

Many years later, in Ceylon, I left the officers' mess one evening for my quarters, which were in a *kadjan* hut made of palm fronds some fifty yards away and on a lower level. It was a night of hard, glaring moonlight, in which all unshadowed objects were clearly discernible, even to a ghost of their proper colours. Steps of beaten earth, contained by wooden boards, led downwards to my hut. On the topmost step, neatly coiled but with its head up, looking at me, was a green Russell's Viper. That is a snake justly feared for two things; its fatal venom and the fact that it can spring four or five feet through the air if given a reason to attack. Once again I chose discretion, returned to the mess, had a drink or two, read a magazine, and did not venture out until I was sure that the viper had taken itself off. I think that I threw some stones from a safe distance, to make quite certain that my way back to bed was clear of snakes.

I do not know what has happened to grass snakes, for I have not seen one for years. In my childhood they were plentiful enough, and beautiful to watch as they slid from one shelter to another. They were harmless creatures, whose only weapon of defence, like the skunk's, was the exudation of an unpleasant-smelling liquid, if severely frightened. Johnnie, I remember, kept one for a long time in a box full of hay, letting it out regularly for exercise, and it was his grass snake which was to prove the singular mettle of Miss Smeaton, our governess.

Two gates led out of the orchard, one into a wide, steeply sloping field called Burnhams, and one into our own field, Manor Meadow. If I was bound for Long Wood or, more distantly, Woodeaton Wood, I would take the first of the two; if for Little Wood, the second, and then go on down, beside the tall hedge of our meadow to the small, solid hunting gate at its end.

They were accurately named, those two home woods. Little Wood was a hundred yards or so wide and deep, a neat square of fairly young trees. There was a narrow ride down the centre, at the far end of which another small gate opened on to a broad green alley. A further gate, directly opposite, opened into Long Wood. The perspective of green space between those two woods, which went from the unfenced lower end of Burnhams to the wide meadow called Lockels, had a continuing fascination for me. It was most particularly 'the right shape'; that is to say that everything about it was of balance and proportion; the level sward, the even thickness of woodland, and the sense it gave of not quite having happened by accident, but to have been planned by a discerning eye, were entirely satisfying.

Oxfordshire is not a spectacular county. Luckily, perhaps, it contains no famous beauty-spots, little in nature to attract tourists until it begins to march with Gloucestershire and the wide vistas of the Cotswold Hills. Nevertheless, its gently undulating landscape, where a small hill can assume importance from the proximity of flat meadows and level blocks of woodland, its hidden paths and small spinneys shading shallow brooks, its secret, enfolded places, are especially solacing to their devotees. There, nature is reticent, makes no demands, merely presenting its complete and self-sufficient cycle in ways which require close attention to be fully appreciated. There is nothing grandiose, nothing awe-inspiring, simply a pastoral scene and a continual activity of plants and creatures, a concealed purposeful busyness, throbbing with life. No landscape, both for comprehensible scale and abundant interest, could be more perfectly suited to an inquiring child.

When I was about six years old, and it was summertime, I would sometimes go for a picnic on my own, usually into Little Wood since that was well within earshot of the police whistle which, blown from the nursery window, was used to recall us from our local excursions. I possessed a small attaché-case, made from some precursor of plastic, and into that would go a corked medicine-bottle full of milk and a biscuit or two — perhaps, if I was lucky, one of the chocolate Bath Olivers now happily returned to commerce. I also had, slung round my neck, an oblong metal box for collecting flowers which, later, I would press. Thus equipped, I would set off down the meadow, at each step of the way using my eyes, as I had been taught to do, on almost every blade of grass, leaf and twig of the tall hedgerow which bordered it. I would note the abandoned birds'-nests with some regret but, if spring had gone, high summer had many compensations. Through tall grasses that would soon be cut for hay and, at the field's edge, through cow-parsley as high as my chin, I would force a path, my small height bringing me close to, and giving me a sense of inhabiting, an intensely busy world of insect life, of field mice and the young rabbits who had their home in the towering hedge, thick and billowing, long untrimmed.

Yet it is more of spring than of summer days that I think, when remembering those two woods. Long Wood was long indeed, stretching westwards towards the Cherwell river for nearly a quarter of a mile. It had straight rides cut through it for shooting, and winding paths at its edges, scarcely negotiable in summer by anything larger than a fox, a dog or a small boy. On an April day, however, in a fine season, all vistas were clear and open as the undergrowth, if thorn and bramble, was cut and burned, or, if something more useful, coppiced and laid in neat piles for faggots.

Then were to be seen the receding ranks of straight, slim tree-trunks, none of great age, silver-grey and brown, darkening with distance and hung with a blue gauze, the smoke of the brush fires which someone was making. The floor of the wood, where vegetation was beginning to spring which, in late summer, would be a riotous tangle higher than my head, was patched with wild flowers — violets, primroses, wood anemones, bluebells — set off by the dark green of dog's mercury and ground alder. The light spring wind which found its way through trees and hedges was tanged with woodsmoke, and every step that I took on juicy new leaves brought up to my nose that bitter-sweet vegetable scent which I have always thought of as a green smell, the very spirit of the colour green.

On days when fires were burning I would have company in Long Wood. As I crouched and burrowed, or examined the forks of trees, the depths of hedges, looking for nests, I would be aware that a man was at work somewhere in my vicinity, slashing brambles with a fagging-hook or cutting hazel rods into suitable lengths for faggots. Occasionally, as I followed a criss-cross course through the wood, I would come back to him, and stand for a minute or two by his fire and ask him questions. I remember no particular person from those early days, merely a generalized image which might be labelled 'countryman'; a stocky figure of indeterminate age (all grown-ups but the very old appeared to me to be more or less coeval) wearing corduroys held up by a worn leather belt and tied below the knee with string, and a collarless striped flannel shirt, its sleeves rolled up, held together at the throat by a brass stud. Strong brown arms, a ruddy complexion, tranquil eyes, thick short hair standing up in a crest, complete the picture. Such a man would pay little more attention to me than to a stoat or rabbit scuttling across a ride, unless I spoke to him directly, at which he would pause, looking at me with distant amusement, while he considered his answer.

Sometimes, if time was still mine because the police whistle had not yet sent its piercing, wiry note echoing over the fields, I would watch him as he laid aside his tools and settled himself to his midday dinner; watch with great interest as he undid the small bundle made of a spotted handkerchief and produced a thick sandwich of bread and bacon, or a piece of bread thinly smeared with margarine and a slice of yellow cheese, or a square of cold pudding glistening with grease. To go with those there might be a battered flask of hot tea or, more likely, a screw-topped bottle of the same beverage cold. After he had disposed of that, and if I was still there perched on a stump, watching with the beady, unblinking impertinence of a robin, I might see him pull out a pipe and go through an impressive routine of filling it from a tin box, and tamping the tobacco with a horny thumb, before striking a pink-headed match on the nearest dry piece of wood. Then clouds of good-smelling smoke would go up to join the filmy wreaths of blue still ascending from the embers of his fire.

Thus are fixed in our perceptions, at an early age, scenes or fragments of scenes which will continue to supply our need for a kind of poetry all the rest of our lives. For me that early appreciation of a wild nature no longer wholly wild, but brought under the prudent control of man for useful purposes, has stayed with me all my life and provided sudden irradiations of happiness in seemingly unpromising places. Meanwhile, there was always in my mind's eye a particular arrangement of things, such as I used to see on spring mornings in Long Wood: uncrowded trees receding into a distance, with flowers beneath — the components of a medieval tapestry, only lacking a unicorn — a movement of birds, butterflies and small animals; shafts of sunlight illuminating patches of colour or, as on a day of mixed storm and sunshine, straight-falling rain like threads of glass, lit from one side, bringing a wet glitter to new leaves and the bright bark of young trees. I was to find this effect again, many times: walking in the foothills of the Carrara mountains, for instance, through hanging woods of well-spaced ilex and cork, where the flowers were great clumps of hellebore, pale apple-green, seeming to light the forest floor with a luminosity of their own. Once, in the war, I was billeted near Acre in Palestine in what had once been a fruit store half-submerged in a vast orchard of citrus trees. The trunks of those trees produced the same effect of running away for ever to any imagined distance, and among them I found continual relief from the trials of a dull and exasperating period of service. The ancient olive groves of that country could make the same effect. The shift and shake of their leaves, grey-green and silver-grey, in a light breeze, the ripple of light on a long vista of them, could at once recall the springtime stir and glitter of my familiar woods at home. Again, in Bengal, during the war, at a time when the monsoon rains were only falling fitfully between bursts of hot sunshine, and the paddy-fields between my hut and the dark green feathers of the forest were swimming in steely water, I wrote:

> Yet I this respite have
> and this moist, seeking wind
> blows the green-fingered willows in my blood
> The rain-soaked distances
> are childhood's boundless Eden and the lawns
> and friendly fields I knew
> and may not know again...

One of the stranger effects of travel, I have found, is to confuse one's references, so that a summer day of intermittent sunlight and of rain falling straight down on to wet meadows can remind me of India; just as a certain kind of autumn weather, a particular clear yellow sunlight on golden-rod and pale blue asters, recalls New England.

Summoned back from woodland excursions by the shrill note of the whistle, I would climb the steep meadow at speed, eager for luncheon or tea and whatever else my day might have to offer. Leaving behind me the quiet woods, which might or might not have offered human companionship, I was hurrying back into, by comparison, a perfect hive of activity. As I made my way past pigs and hens and their strong ordurous smells into the smaller yard, Jack Allam might be at work in the woodshed where the sour odour of sawdust mingled with the oily smell of his petrol-driven circular saw. With the scream of the saw behind me I would hear further sawing sounds from the carpenter's shop, and then, in the stable-yard someone would be clashing buckets, or Amos Webb would be revving the engine of the car. There would be voices, murmurous or raised to carry over some distance, and perhaps a whinny from horse or pony which kept up a friendly champ and stamp and clatter in the stables above the yard.

Once inside the house I had to undergo a change from the solitary explorer of woods to the small component of a rather

complex ménage, to come once again into the orbit of people who
were not strange woodcutters but familiars, with claims, questions, criticisms, and many varied influences on my daily life. I
would make for the kitchen quarters, scampering down the stone
steps to the basement, then through the kitchen where cook and
kitchen-maids were too hard-pressed to pay me attention, and on
up the steep back stairs to the nursery, to handwashing and
hair-brushing and the expected meal.

More often than not, it seemed, there were visitors in the house,
either staying or come to luncheon, and their influence could be
felt in extra stress in the kitchen, and in the dining-room and
pantry which I passed on my way upstairs. Once arrived in the
nursery I might then set up with Alastair a litany of our invention
concerning 'nasty visitors', which grew steadily more hectic until
we were begged to be quiet. For us, most strangers in the house
were 'nasty visitors'. Our dislike of them was founded in
resentment at changes of routine, cautions about behaviour, and
the dreadful prospect of being shown to those large, growling or
cooing but generally patronizing interlopers for a quarter of an
hour after luncheon or tea.

4

THE SCOTTISH CONNECTION

Not all visitors proved to be wholly nasty, nor entirely without interest. Sometimes they came in cars of great splendour, their cockaded chauffeurs spending the nights of their stay as guests of the Amos Webbs. Mrs Pelly, an old friend of my parents, had been a benefactress to us during the Great War, sending butter to our nursery from her Hampshire farm. Her motor-car I can still see clearly, with its high-backed, morocco-covered seats, tall wood-framed windscreen and huge brass acetylene lamps. (A similar vehicle, with red leather upholstery and much gleaming brass, was still being driven by our neighbour, Hal Gaskell, in the 1930s, he wearing a deerstalker hat.) Such cars would now be what the French call *une valeur*, a capital asset, and perhaps those two are still to be found somewhere, in someone's prized collection.

Other visitors could be interesting in themselves, for possession of the rare ability to put themselves alongside children, to say strange and amusing things, to indicate reassuringly that being grown-up could, for some at least, be fun; and for being wholly free of condescension, or the false and semi-sarcastic jocularity which makes even the least sensitive of children shrink into themselves.

To some incursions we looked forward with real excitement. For example, our small Scottish family — Gran, Uncle Walter and Aunt Anna — came every year, more punctually than the swallows, in April, and their visits were productive of many pleasures. With Aunt Anna there would be outings to Stratford-upon-Avon, luncheon at the Shakespeare Hotel (where all the bedrooms were called after plays) and a Shakespeare play in the afternoon; to Oxford and intensive shopping which produced many spin-offs in the shape of presents and money to spend, and tea at Fuller's with poached eggs and walnut cake. Anna, whom my mother and sister called 'Olivia', because the O in 'O.Douglas', the name under which she wrote novels, was supposed to stand for that, was our father's only sister and one of our two genuine aunts. Her first novel, published in 1913 under that pseudonym, was called *Olivia in India*, and is a faithful and entertaining record of a visit to that country made in 1907 to stay with her brother Willie, then a rising young member of the Indian Civil Service. That first book, as is so often so depressingly the case with first books, was certainly her best, but by the time that I came to know her as more than just a shape of vague benevolence, which was all that most grown-ups seemed to be in my earliest days, she was a highly popular writer, especially in Scotland, who produced a book a year to the continuing satisfaction of a large and loyal public.

If one had only known Aunt Anna through her books one would have expected to find a personality decidedly cosy, gently humorous, contented, conservative and piously optimistic. One would have imagined a figure perhaps rather rotund, probably dowdy in dress, radiating kindness and robust common sense. The kindness and common sense were there, certainly, and in great measure, but the rest of the image would have been wrong. Anna was thin and alert, quick in her movements, with sharp blue eyes that missed very little. She cared much for clothes and took great pains with them. Her view of life was a thoroughly Scottish compound of high romanticism and practical shrewdness.

Anna and Walter had both been educated in Edinburgh, she at a young ladies' academy, and he at the university. Both, in consequence, had a light breath of Edinburgh east wind in their soft, agreeable Scottish voices. Sitting with them at Elsfield, and hearing them tell their news, was to be taken back to holidays in Peeblesshire which began when I was five and continued as a regular summer feature for six or seven years. Listening to them, I could see the long, strung-out Broughton village, with the family house, Gala Lodge, at one end, set on the steep flank of the Hill o'Man, and near by the shop, the post office, the garage and joiner's shop of Mr Plenderleith, who was also an undertaker, and then — an unfailing magnet for my brothers and myself — the railway station with its whitewashed stones, beds of brilliant flowers, advertisements enamelled on tin for Mazawattee Tea, Monkey Brand Soap, 'The Pickwick, The Owl, and the Waverley Pen'. Beyond the station, a quarter of a mile away, stood that other family house, Broughton Green, where Alastair and I, with our nurse, were usually put to stay.

It was lucky that my mother, in spite of misgivings and

objections freely expressed by my Scottish grandmother at the time of her son's engagement, had made immediate, firm friendships with the father, brothers and sister of her husband-to-be, and most particularly with Anna. Consequently, however ready Gran might be with criticisms on her visits to that foreign country, England, and however darkly she might foretell disaster where her grandchildren were concerned, Anna's and Walter's visits were no mere matter of duty, they were also a pleasure, and if they had criticisms to make they were discreet in voicing them. Furthermore they greatly enjoyed their forays into what Scottish people still, with a special intonation, call The South (so that you can almost hear 'the darkies' singing and see the bougainvillaea tumbling from the walls) which invariably included a week at Stratford and a week or so in London, as well as the fortnight spent at Elsfield.

I suspect that, for Aunt Anna, her niece's and her nephews' youngest years were the most satisfactory. Young children she could understand and spoil and put up with, unlike her mother seeing marvellous possibilities for them, possibilities which she had once seen strikingly realized in her gifted, tough and energetic brothers. Only when adolescence set in, with its quirks and contradictions, its bizarre emotions and concealments, she became a little puzzled, less wholeheartedly interested. She asked fewer questions, for fear, perhaps, of uncovering something which she could not like or approve, whilst remaining as sure a source as ever of munificent presents and the warmest hospitality when visited at Bank House, Peebles.

Between Anna and my sister Alice, in the latter's growing years, there existed a close and tender friendship. Both were passionately devoted to the theatre. Together, in Edinburgh, Stratford and London, they took in a rich diet of plays — rich, that is, in the terms of their time when nothing too subversive, too violent, too distressing or anywhere near obscene (Shakespeare always excepted) was permitted on the British stage. Anna was an enthusiastic amateur actress who, had her times and her upbringing been different (and her mother quite another person), might well have tried for the stage professionally, as at least one Scottish friend and contemporary, Jean Cadell, successfully did.

Anna's musical tastes were simple, and leaned mostly towards old Scots songs and light opera, and so, to supplement the prose drama, or to give light relief to an intensive course of Shakespeare, she loved to hear the works of Gilbert and Sullivan.

Neither Anna nor Walter ever married. Their lives were bound up, in the main, with the life of Peebles, his in his duties as Town Clerk and Procurator-fiscal — appointments into which he had stepped on the death of his Uncle William, who had held them for twenty-three years — and hers in caring for their mother and discharging a large number of functions for church and borough, as well as travelling all over Scotland to give the lectures, readings and recitations which were ever more widely demanded as her literary reputation grew.

I think, but can really only surmise since the evidence is scanty, that Anna, when young, loved and was loved by an extremely handsome and charming young minister, who went joyfully off to the 1914 war as an army padre, won the Military Cross, and was killed in action. There is some evidence of his affection for Anna and so, had he survived the war, life for her might have taken a different turn. For the young minister was brilliant as well as brave, and his future in the Scottish church would most likely have been such as to overcome the inevitable difficulties created by my grandmother, whose personal interests never failed to find elaborate scriptural grounds. As things were, Anna was to live to be the most admirable of maiden aunts, and we to be her beneficiaries.

Her rigorous sense of duty would not allow her to leave Bank House, and abandon her mother and Walter for the sake of a wider horizon. I believe that wide horizons, in any case, were things that she and her brother had decided, quite early in life, not to seek, knowing perhaps what a thicket of thorns they would have to go through with Gran if they developed any such ideas. So it was to be life in a country town for both of them, a life in no way as restricting as it sounds, for the Royal Borough of Peebles is a place of great character and charm, full of history and not unproductive of incident. Under the name of Priorsford it was to become a location for Anna's stories much loved by her readers.

I should never dream of charging my aunt with cynicism. That she wrote what a large number of readers, and by no means only women, delighted to read was largely because she had an immense sympathy with dutiful, straightforward people, with an educated, principled, well-conducted class of gentlefolk and with the significant trivia of their lives. She called one of her novels *The Day of Small Things* — ('For who hath despised the day of small things?' Zechariah 4:10) — and another *The Proper Place*. Each, in its way is a celebration of quiet living, traditional virtues, and home-centred family life. Being highly intelligent she was perhaps more fully aware of, and certainly better able to express anxieties about a quaking world than many of her readers; and so, as much to reassure herself as them, and from a determination to reaffirm clearly defined values of loyalty, courage, and 'doing the best one can' in difficult circumstances, she wrote of brave girls, honourable men, and older women courageously, humorously accepting the decline of a way of life which once they had thought enduring. A cynical writer might well have devised this approach, working backwards, as it were, from an observed state of affairs, and consciously supplying a need, but I doubt whether her success would have been so instant and so lasting. Such writing is next to impossible to do with tongue in cheek. If I have made it sound over-sweet or anodyne, I have done Anna a wrong. For one thing, her work is highly literate. Her style is deft and easy, and her humour engaging. Nor are all her characters paragons of virtue. When she deals with pompous, pretentious *bourgeoises* her pen sharpens remarkably, and certain characterizations of that sort are a delight. And of course, like her brother John and her hero Sir Walter Scott, she excels in the vernacular, wherever her characters are Scottish working people, whether Border shepherds or Glasgow charwomen. Indeed her writing about Glasgow, where my grandfather, a minister of the Free Church, had his last parish, is among her very best, both in descriptions of the lively, bustling Victorian city and in the observation, just this side of cruelty, of some of its more preposterous inhabitants.

It was in the life of a Glasgow manse that Anna acquired the overriding sense of duty which I have mentioned. From an early age she had to play her part in the many activities of a busy parish, teaching bible classes and Sunday School, visiting the sick and the poor. Since her father's church was in the Gorbals she had ample opportunity to observe misery and despair, the harsh effects of deprivation and, at the same time, to be delighted by the powerfully resilient humour of the Glasgow working class. Later, at Peebles or Broughton, in very comfortable circumstances, she never forgot what she had learned so young. In a sense the poor were always with her, and her charity was legendary.

James Walter Buchan, MA, LLB, on the death of his father's brother, William, had taken on the law firm of J. and W. Buchan which his grandfather had founded at Peebles in the 1840s. He also had the overall management of the Commercial Bank of Scotland's Peebles branch, the business of which had been lodged with

45

his grandfather's office, as was customary in former days. For that reason the old house on the corner of Peebles High Street was called Bank House, and I remember being intrigued by the heavy iron contrivance, concealed in a cupboard of my uncle's bedroom, which controlled the lock of the vast old safe built into the wall of the bank's premises next door.

Walter's book-plate is one of the best examples I know of that particular art-form. In it he is represented as a medieval scholar, robed and wearing a doctor's soft cap with square earpieces. He is judiciously studying a parchment, his face grave and calm. The likeness is very good. He sits at a desk, the lower part of which shows an open cupboard spilling out heavy books. The bench on which he sits has a panel with the Buchan crest of a sunflower; the family motto, 'Non Inferiora Secutus', occupies the top of the picture on a flying scroll. In the centre is a round arch through which can be seen Neidpath Castle, once a prison for Mary of Scots, on its bluff above the river Tweed. Behind his head an upright sword carries a sable escutcheon charged with a balance. On the desk is an hour-glass. The work is well organized, to take in so much symbolism and yet leave an impression of spaciousness and simplicity, of calm thought and ordered reflection. In it my uncle is an Erasmian figure, dedicated to justice and scholarship, with love of his native terrain and its history and a fondness of open-air pursuits indicated by the view through the arch. The sword and balance stand for his legal side, and the hour-glass is there, perhaps, to suggest a proper care for the use of time. The plate is signed HN. Whoever HN was he must have been either a close friend or a remarkable psychologist, for the book-plate gives a very fair idea of Walter's character, as well, perhaps, as an idealization of his own wishes for himself, a delightful compliment on the part of the artist. The whole conception could only belong to that period of the turn of the century, in which a romanticized view of the medieval world became, for some artists and writers, a refuge from the increasing clangour and complication of their own time.

Walter was a highly capable lawyer. In addition to the day-to-day business of the firm, his post as Procurator-fiscal meant that he acted as Public Prosecutor for the County of Peeblesshire. Like his uncle before him — he who was a French scholar, a traveller, a bibliophile, and a Fellow of the Scottish Society of Antiquaries, as well as the initiator of many schemes of public works, including gas lighting and a new bridge over the

Tweed — Walter had a turn for scholarship, and especially for history. He was fascinated by the life of Napoleon Bonaparte and over the years made a good collection of Napoleonic relics. Exhibiting the balance of his mind, he also wrote a biography of the great Duke of Wellington. He spent many years over his three-volume History of Peeblesshire, which is a wonderful mine of information, genealogical, historical, social and economic.

Walter may well have been a very happy man. He certainly seemed happy. In those days, he was always entirely healthy, brisk, occupied, maintaining a kind of masculine independence in a house full of women, attending to his duties scrupulously and with skill, whilst managing to cultivate his own tastes, particularly in reading, and to play golf and fish and go for long strenuous walks and climbs. Like my father, he moved about the place at great speed and, even in his leisure, never seemed to be idle. Like Anna, he must early have accepted his role in life which was to be guide and mentor to the town of his father's birth. Peebles itself, which always gave an impression of cheerfulness and pride, could be seen to be thoroughly well-managed, and much credit for that must surely go to my uncle.

Visits to our Scottish family, whether at Broughton or Peebles, held pleasures of a variety of flavours. Life at Broughton was open air, strenuous, with fishing in Tweed or its tributaries and, if my father was with us, long hill walks in any kind of weather. There were expeditions too, to St Mary's Loch, Talla Linns, and the Devil's Beef Tub, in Mr Plenderleith's hire-car; or whole days in Edinburgh, riding first to Peebles in our beloved train which puffed its way past Gala Lodge before turning east down the Tweed valley, and then changing from the Caledonian Railway to the North British by walking the quarter-mile which separated the rival stations. Coming into Edinburgh was a dark excitement, through the long smoky tunnel under the Calton Hill and the sheer walls of the Calton Gaol, a sinister approach to so much light and pleasure. Waverley Station seemed immense, noisy, insanely active after the peaceful, empty stations on the way. I always thought, then, that it smelt of mustard: to me it still does. Then would come the ascent by lift into the North British Hotel, and much sorting out and contradictory planning, before we set off shopping or sightseeing; to the castle, perhaps, and Lorimer's War Memorial, or to the old town, with its crumbling, tall, fantastic buildings marching so steeply down hill to Holyroodhouse, its towering walls, precipitous steps and narrow wynds still breathing pride and menace, and suggesting black secrets of bloodshed and betrayal.

For each of us Bank House was an image of order and peacefulness. The house, one of the oldest in Peebles, stood on a steep slope which dropped down to the shallow, swift-moving Eddlestone Water, known locally as the Cuddy. The kitchen quarters opened on to the garden, well below the level of the street, and the walls on that side were several feet thick. As in many Scottish houses of earlier centuries there was a round tower at the back which must once have held a staircase. That staircase had gone, to be replaced by an elegant Georgian example which went up in a dog-leg from the wide hallway. On the upper floor a lavatory, installed at the top of the tower, had a special character, being perfectly round and showing a fine view of old rooftops stepping upwards to the green woods of Venlaw.

Anna had decorated the house in the early 1920s, in a style much favoured at that period: grey and white striped wallpapers, royal-blue carpets, and everywhere, glossy white paint. Pictures tended to be contemporary engravings with thin black frames and very wide mounts. Interested, as ever, in my food, I relished the cooking of Mrs Cowan (referred to always by Elsie Charlett as Mrs Cohen), in which my grandmother, a first-class cook herself, took a possibly not always welcome hand.

The Scots in those days ate great quantities of sweets, as well as bakery products of many kinds. The sweetshops of Peebles were fabulously stocked and thriving, as were the bakers. Sweets were always on hand in the house for distribution after meals, and my grandmother's teas were lavish with a variety of scones and cakes, all home-made, very often by her own hand, and jams and jellies from the same source. A special delicacy among sweetmeats was 'taiblet' — thick rounds of flavoured sugar, supremely delicious, which were the secret receipt of Vallance's in Edinburgh, a firm now, with its product, quite disappeared. We had more sweets given to us in Scotland than ever at home, and I have no doubt that the lifetime's trouble that I have had with my teeth owed much to them, as well as to rationing (in spite of that extra butter) in the 1914 war. It may be that there was something — perhaps there still is — about the great Scottish consumption of sweets which had to do with the climate. In a harsh winter time or a chill, uncertain summer, calories were needed, which many men got from alcohol, something not possible for my aunt and grandmother or other good-living people, although Walter, still guarding his male territory, kept a stock of excellent matured whisky which I was to come to appreciate greatly in later years.

In the autumn of 1924 when I was in my ninth year and Alastair in his seventh, my parents went on a visit of some months to the United States and Canada. Our household at Elsfield was scattered for a time, and Alastair and I were sent to stay at Bank House. Walter had recently had a bicycling accident; knocked off his machine by a passing car, he had suffered concussion and was made to spend some weeks in a nursing home. So I had the pleasure of sleeping in his large bed, in the room which looked out on to the High Street, and comparing Peebles at night, so quiet but for a slow-chiming clock, with nights spent staying with my English grandmother in London and hearing the ceaseless oceanic rumble and swell of a great city which can never sleep. Beyond the blinds there was the green-white light of my great-uncle's municipal gas and no sound but the occasional tread of a policeman, one of 'Super' Dixon's trusties from the police station over the way.

Alastair and I attended a small mixed school across the river in a quarter of a large nineteenth-century house, where I learned — or rather went on learning — to make neat letters from a copy-book, while Alastair was petted and allowed every indulgence by the two elderly ladies who ran the school.

On Sundays we went to church in the big red parish church which stood a few yards from Bank House, where the High Street divided into two smaller roads running north and south. The church has an imposing, steep flight of steps and a crowned tower modelled on that of St Giles' Cathedral in Edinburgh. There services were shorter than at Broughton, perhaps because the congregation was busier, more metropolitan, more conscious of time spent, and the minister less of a marathon preacher than Broughton's famous Dr Forrester.

In my recollection, that odd interlude in our lives when, magically, a summer excursion was repeated in winter, was a time of pure pleasure. Gran must have been at her most genial, and Anna even more than her usual inventive self when it came to keeping us amused. Thus, for me, Peebles remains a complete small cosmos, safe, settled, productive of many delights. Sometimes we would go with Walter and Anna to the cinema. There was no picture-house in the town, in our earliest days there, but once a week a fit-up arrived, I suppose from Edinburgh, to show films in the Chambers Institution, the museum and library named for two of Peebles' most illustrious sons, the Chambers brothers, writers, antiquaries, publishers and founders of *Chambers's Journal* and of the well-known dictionary. There we saw serial dramas in several reels which stopped, each time, at a moment of high suspense; literally so when the heroine was left dangling from a cliff-top, thus originating the expression 'a cliff-hanger'. Could it have been Pearl White whom we saw? It is not that I cannot remember a name: I don't think that I ever knew one; nor do I remember the names of particular films. All that comes back to me is the excitement of the darkened hall, the flickering black and white light, the piano thundering, trilling or yearning to match the mood of the film, and the strange antics of the figures on the screen.

From Bank House I remember days of an unflustered busyness. No one in the house was ever idle, and there was much coming and going, so that the life of the family and the life of the town seemed to flow into one another. Very often my grandmother, in whom the Scottish spirit of hospitality was especially strong, would invite people to tea, generally ladies of a church-haunting persuasion. I remember having to form up, brushed and tidied, to be nodded over, pronounced upon, questioned. More than faces I remember hats, sometimes confections of great size mushrooming out in bows and ribbons and veils, and a strong impression of blackness, since most of the lady visitors must have been widows. There were many widows in Peebles, some of them rather rich. I was later to wonder whether the effort of working to leave them so splendidly provided for had driven some Scottish husbands to a needlessly early grave.

Although Gran did not think Anna's writing actually sinful, and although she must have been aware how much of her own comfortable and, in its way, influential existence was made possible by her children's efforts — since my grandfather, well-known as a divine, was also well-known for his inability to manage money — she considered that writing came second to social considerations. Thus she would interrupt Anna's hoarded moments of peace, when she wrote in her bedroom looking down on the Cuddy, to demand her presence because some unscheduled visitor had decided on a random call. As it is usually bores who are thus certain of their welcome, Anna's precious time — precious to her for quite other than financial reasons — was used up gratifying

50

the voluble curiosity of yet another black widow in a menacing kind of hat. Anna, like her brothers, for all her openness, her kindness and her great success in public appearances, had a deep-set core of reserve. I am sure that she found the continual quizzing and questioning of neighbours and visitors, which, although not usually malicious, was often indelicate (something to which some Scots are rather prone), definitely distasteful. After a time she made a gesture, uncharacteristic in its forthrightness; she rented a room in a house across the High Street, next to the police station, simply to have somewhere where she could not be so easily disturbed.

The life, then, of the household at Bank House pursued its established routines, year in, year out, in a fashion which came to be most appealing. Its characteristics were religion and literature, charity and public service and its foundation a comfortable amount of money. In later years, arriving somewhat frayed by school life and the difficulties of growing up, I found my visits there wonderfully calming. It did not take long to slip back into a remembered way of doing things, revisiting familiar houses, water, green spaces which never changed, going on errands up and down High Street and North Gate for things forgotten or suddenly found wanting; poring over casts and boxes of trout flies at Veitch's fishing shop, or pausing to sniff the marvellous waft of hot bread coming from Goodburn's bakery, which scented the street for yards on either side, the very spirit of the Scottish tea.

Then there would be the usual stream of visitors, solid citizens from the town for the most part, and I would be back again, answering, or more often parrying, searching questions about my current activities and what I intended to do with my life. Sometimes the visitors were from outside the town, from one or other of the big houses scattered down Tweed from Polmood to Elibank, and those were easier to manage. Noticeably different in dress and manner, they bore the evidences of a wider world; their conversation had a more extensive range, they were generally more amusing and notably less inquisitive.

My grandmother had had many sorrows and much illness, so that it was not surprising that her view of life was sombre. She had also, I think, a temperamental inclination to melancholy and foreboding, which perhaps her own misfortunes, the loss of a beloved husband and of three children, one dead in infancy, one at the outset of a brilliant career, and one killed in battle, had only served to confirm. Like many Scots of an earlier breed her

51

religious outlook was grounded chiefly in the Old Testament, quotations from which came readily from her on almost any occasion. She was never a British Israelite, but it did occur to me sometimes to wonder whether she half-believed that her people might be one of the lost tribes of Israel, so closely did she seem to identify her outlook with theirs. There are in the Scottish character certain traits which consort well enough with those of the chosen race: courage and endurance, a combative spirit, pride, touchiness, unwillingness to forgive past wrongs, great industry and skill in business affairs, strong tribal feeling, and with it all a mystical and poetical undertone, and a ready, if rueful, acceptance that all flesh is as grass.

Gran had an elder sister, whom I can just remember, who was as gentle and unemphatic as my grandmother was generally fiery and positive. Aunt Agnes, who wore widow's black satin and Shetland shawls, and had a long, pale, benevolent face, always reminded me of the sheep in *Alice in Wonderland*. She died when I was quite little, passing out of the world as unobtrusively as she had lived in it, leaving only a small stir in the atmosphere. I have to think, therefore, that Gran's special brand of militant Calvinism was a construction of her own, rather than the result of any great severity in her early training. Gran once told Alice that 'she believed in a personal Devil and an eternal Hell' — each of these conceptions deserves a capital letter — and surely such a belief, if it were not to plunge one into unilluminable gloom, could only be sustained by a private certainty of being one of 'the elect'. Reading her letters to my father throughout his life, I am appalled by her continual complaints, remonstrances, intimations of disaster, and a snuffling kind of deflation every time that his expanding interests and great ability led him to new projects or to success in some new field. There is no doubt that she had destined him for the church, and the secessionary Free Church at that, of which her husband had been an ornament. Not only had he not gratified that wish, but he had removed himself from Scotland, married an English-woman, and set up his home in the south. Never for one moment was he to be allowed to suppose that what he did in the world amounted to anything but a sad deviation from the one true path: that all glory, all worldly reward was tinsel compared with what, as a Minister of her Kirk, he might have had. Late in life, never-theless, she was to become more worldly; critical, this time, of others for not rewarding her brilliant son as she thought they should.

My father, who wrote to her very nearly every day of his life, was marvellously patient with Gran, only very rarely exploding when her jeremiads became too ridiculous. He loved her devotedly, and was perhaps glad, in a way, of her continual pinpricks, her almost sublime obtuseness about nearly everything that mattered to him most, feeling perhaps that she provided a kind of stimulus, although no one who knew him could imagine that he needed anything of the sort. Also, he had physically removed himself four hundred or so miles and, in mental and moral terms, to a distance almost immeasurable, and thus was, to some extent, armoured. Yet he treasured her, as did Walter and Anna, for the mother she had been to them when they were young. Whether she knew how great a strain she put upon their kindness and toleration, I cannot say. No doubt but that she loved them passionately in her own terms but, bred in the Scottish tradition of plain speaking, and the Presbyterian one of 'testifying before the Lord', she felt it her duty to keep up a fairly constant flow of precept, warning and reproof, coupled with much lamenting about her own life and frequent public examination (performed, I seem to remember, not wholly without relish) of her own shortcomings, of things done and things left undone.

Having to live with Gran, Walter and Anna, who were both naturally practical, humorous and energetic people, cultivated an extra breeziness to lift the frequent miasmas clouding the small black-clad figure of their mother. They had to spend a good deal of time and effort in cheering her up, when the repining moods were on her. To the rest of the world my grandmother was simply a wonderful old lady. Scots, like Americans, have a tendency to admire extravagantly rather dominating, forthright old women. Gran, with her clever and successful children, her insider's knowledge of church affairs, her manifest courage and very real charity, was a figure widely known in Scotland and greatly respected. I should have been thought poorly of had I ever so much as hinted to one of her host of admirers that I sometimes found her extremely trying.

The poor and the sick had every reason to love my grandmother for she was tireless in their cause. There were occasions when she took me visiting in the town, and we climbed, perhaps, an outside stone stair to a small room where some bedridden person lay, and I remember very clearly, being sensitive to smells, the fetid atmosphere of an airless room, unemptied slops, sick humanity, and a pervasive odour which I was later to identify as the smell of poverty itself. If my childish reaction, regrettably, was fear and disgust rather than compassion, Gran, deeply experienced in such ways of charity,

was perfectly in command of the occasion: and it was evident even to
my self-regarding eyes that her presence alone, apart from whatever
material comforts she might have brought with her, positively
brightened the day for the sufferer.

With time my grandmother's two unmarried children had
evidently come to adopt at least part of her rather limiting view of
life. For her, ideally, her sons and daughter would have made no
excursions into a larger world — to India, to war, to London, to
Canada. She must have longed to keep her brood as close to her
skirts as they had been in childhood, in a state of life bounded by
scriptural teaching, well-doing in a comprehensible community, the
rigid ring-fence of her church. In the end my aunt and uncle,
whatever their earlier dreams might have been, came to accept an
expanded, but still self-limiting, version of those terms. I never had
any wish to upset them, knowing how liable they were to be
disconcerted by anything radically different from, or opposed to, the
view of things which they preferred to hold. Although in all their
dealings full of practical sense and thoughtful kindness, they were
easily shocked by the world's lunacy and cruelty, evidence of which
became increasingly intrusive, the storms which raged outside their
happy ground. Walter affected extreme scepticism about almost
anything that happened beyond his immediate field of experience.
More often than not, when he heard some strange new thing, or
some anecdote about a public figure, he would make a grunting
sound which was not far from the 'Hoots!' which was once a familiar
Scottish expression of disbelief. Oddly, on the other hand, he seemed
to take for gospel everything that appeared in the 'serious' press.

Anna, quite simply, did not wish to be told of discouraging
aspects of human nature, or of evidence of humanity's destructive
side. Wholly innocent herself, and entirely, as Scots say, 'weel-
daein'', she had no wish to examine the darker aspects of the human
heart and behaviour and her faithful readers must have felt the same.
Sadly, when Alice reached the age of eighteen, 'came out' in London,
and threw herself with enthusiasm into the party-life of the period,
her ties with Aunt Anna began to weaken and fray away. One day
she must have recounted some happening or made some comment
about her English contemporaries which Anna found shocking, for
she said with vehemence: 'Understand, I do not want to *hear* about
what you do, now that you are grown up.' Not long after that, she
produced another novel in which a young girl shows signs of living a
'fast' life, but is ultimately redeemed, brought safely back to the

traditional verities which are the main theme of all her works.

Aunt Anna maintained an enormous correspondence with admirers in almost every part of the world. I don't think that she ever employed a secretary, but I do know, having so often carried them to the post, that her daily output of handwritten letters was very large, as were the sheaves which daily arrived for her. With the utmost patience, and a tolerance of sometimes foolish questions not usually found among writers, she answered punctually the voluminous screeds which arrived from far-flung fans; and if her reply elicited, as it often did, further letters, she would enter into an exchange which might last for years.

One stiflingly hot night in Calcutta during the last war I found myself being introduced to a civilian who, on learning my name, started off on what I thought would be the familiar line of questioning: was I, by any chance, related to, you know, John Buchan, author of *John Macnab* (or *The Thirty-nine Steps* or *Greenmantle*)? Not at all. What that man wanted to hear about was my relationship to Anna Buchan, who wrote under the pseudonym of O. Douglas. I looked with surprise at my questioner. He was, I had learned, a tea planter from Assam, down in Calcutta on a half-yearly visit. He was very large, craggy-featured, crimson-complexioned, drenched with sweat, drinking 'burra-pegs' of whisky as if they were cups of tea. He told me that he was a bachelor; from both his name and his voice I knew that he was Scottish. He told me that he led a lonely life somewhere at the upper end of the Brahmaputra valley and that his chief joy and sole literary recreation was reading and re-reading my aunt's books. Naturally, he was one of her correspondents, and it is certain that she had nowhere a more devoted admirer. Nor was his the only instance I have come across of tough, hard-living men, working in demanding or dangerous circumstances — soldiers, sailors, engineers — who perhaps found in Anna's books an assurance that somewhere there continued to exist a world of grace and gentleness, of high principle and plain dealing which satisfactorily counterpointed the harshness of their own experience.

Bank House was partly demolished in 1985 to allow for the widening of a road, and the last link of my family with Peebles has gone, but for the name of the law partnership which, happily, flourishes. Those who knew the house will probably remember it best for its sealing-wax red front door, a note of bright colour unusual in a

Scottish town, where taste leans generally to more sober tones. The door had bright brass fittings and a small brass plate which read 'Mr Buchan, Writer'. That must have been fixed when John Buchan, my great-grandfather, set up his practice in 1843, since 'Writer' is the Scottish word for solicitor.

During the 1914 war Walter had worked desperately hard on behalf of the town and of many war charities, and so had his sister. When war came again both threw themselves into wartime occupations once more. They were older by twenty years, however, and I think that the strains of war work, and anxiety for three nephews on active service, as well as for the children of so many friends, must have worn them down severely. Anna's health deteriorated. By the end of the war she was beginning to be seriously ill.

In 1948 I went to work in Glasgow, and took, as often as I could, the short but amazingly difficult journey to Peebles. I found Anna as indomitable, in her own way, as Gran had been, still rising early and performing all sorts of tasks about the house, still writing great numbers of letters, still keeping in touch with admirers of her work. But she was manifestly much reduced. In that year, she became gravely ill: cancer was found; she died, after much pain, in the summer of 1948. My last words to her were in the Edinburgh nursing-home where she lay, small and remote, no longer really interested in her visitors, already half overtaken by death.

Gran had died in 1937; and after her death the brother and sister at Bank House had seemed somehow at a loss, as if their lives lacked the focus, the sometimes excessively demanding centre, which she had provided. Anna had written one more book, her last, a volume of memories called *Unforgettable, Unforgotten*, which tells the story of her brothers' and her own upbringing in Fife and Glasgow, and their days of ecstatic release from city life at Broughton, in a glen of the Tweed valley.

Of the houses at Broughton one, Broughton Green, is still in my family. The little Free Church in the village, where, as a child, I suffered such pains of boredom and hunger during very long services, has ceased to be a place of worship. In 1984 it started a new life as the John Buchan Centre, a museum of the career, the works, and the various connections of my father. My grandfather came to that church to take the minister's place for some months in the winter of 1873-4. He first saw my grandmother walking in Peebles, in a crocodile with her schoolfellows, and was struck to his romantic heart by a cascade of bright gold hair. Gran was then sixteen. Shortly after her seventeenth birthday she married, at Broughton Green, the young clergyman of twenty-seven, and so began the expansion of a family which (since neither his brothers nor his sisters married) would otherwise have come to an abrupt end.

My grandmother's hair had long lost its brilliance by the time that I came to be aware of her looks. I can only remember it as a sort of flat cottage loaf, dark brown and streaked with grey. Yet that instant beguilement by a golden mane makes me feel close to a man whom I never knew, who died before I was born. The Reverend John Buchan had little of the world's goods and, if he ever had any money, he was apt to give it away, yet it was said that he could never be got past a jewellers' window, that he would gaze at the stones displayed for minutes at a time, in a trance of pleasure; and so, for all my grandfather's severely fundamentalist religion, his lifelong preoccupation with the spiritual life, I can feel that we had one lust in common, that of the eye.

I am telling the story of my Scottish family, telling it to myself, I suppose, because the two sides of my heredity offer such curious contrasts that I sometimes do not know quite where I am supposed to be. The voices are silent now which once propounded beliefs and certainties, framed rules of conduct and recalled the past with pride, whilst faltering a little over the future. If I stop to listen I hear echoes, affirmations of certain strongly held tenets, certain principles of right living, self-discipline, duty, and the need for achievement. Worldly success had biblical sanction (the Parable of the Talents), and was there not the example of my father and his siblings? In all, with every pleasure and comfort that went with our visits to Scotland, there remained to be felt an underlying severity, a conscious reference to religious principles, a mistrust of easy good fortune bred of bitter centuries of strife, suspicion of charm and prettiness, contempt for idleness and ease.

In later years, when I was in my thirties and struggling to make sense of the post-war world, I remember complaining bitterly and at length to my brother Alastair about some state of affairs, or group of persons, which had annoyed or disgusted me intensely. 'You have to get used to all that,' he said. 'You really can't go on expecting the world to be like Peebles!' 'Peebles' in that comfortable and gracious sense, a state of mind, almost, as much as a house and town, continued for a few years after Anna's death. Walter, whose health also was beginning to fail, arthritis having come on him rather suddenly and very severely, retired from business and his official duties and proceeded to take life more easily and to enjoy himself as

far as his half-crippled state would allow. He bought a large black
Austin Princess limousine, and had himself driven on numerous
excursions throughout the Border country, excursions which,
possibly, he had wished to make before, but had had, instead, to
bow to contrary wishes on the part of his mother and sister. But for
his wretched ailment I think that my uncle would have been perfectly
happy. In spite of his sorrow at losing a lifelong companion, for
Anna was older than he by six years, he must yet have enjoyed the
freedom to do as he liked, at home or abroad, and to be free at last of
comment, inquiry and exhortation, and the cross-currents of
domestic life. He continued to be looked after, cosseted in so far as he
would allow them to cosset him, by devoted servants, in great peace
and comfort at Bank House. My mother who, years before, had
made the Border country her own, and who was deeply attached to
Walter, went north every year to stay with him. She shared his long
motor-drives, visiting many scenes of past happiness, only complaining that he would have the wireless on all the time, choosing
programmes which she considered trivial, while she wanted to talk.

After a long lifetime of more or less enforced abstinence my uncle
amused me very much by his experiments with the demon alcohol.
He had an extremely good head, and therefore it was a pleasure to
watch him trying out various spirits, wines and liqueurs of which
hitherto and unlike, I am sure, the majority of Scottish lawyers, he
had been sadly deprived. Of one experiment however, I have a
terrible memory. We were dining at the Ritz, and Walter had
ordered a bottle of Château Yquem, to drink with dinner. That
precious and, I think, somewhat overrated wine had never come my
way before except in a minute crystal glass, with the pudding at the
end of a long dinner. The sweet, syrupy stuff seemed to encase my
liver in lead; indeed I had all the effects of a bad hangover while still
drinking it. Uncle Walter, however, did not turn a hair.

Walter did not confine his excursions to Scotland. He motored all
over England, seeing new places and sampling new hotels. From
time to time he came to London, where he put up at the Ritz. When
Aunt Anna and Gran were alive the base of operations during their
yearly visit to London was always the Langham Hotel, a grim grey
pile at the southern end of Portland Place, now, I believe, used as
offices by the BBC. I well remember the way in which Walter
asserted his independence at those times. He came and went without
announcement or explanation, appearing and disappearing throughout the day, sometimes going to the City to see banks and insurance

companies on civic business for Peebles, often to shop for clothes and make his routine yearly visits to the tailor in Conduit Street who was also patronized by my father.

He was always there in the evenings, however, to take us to the theatre, to such simple delights as a new Edgar Wallace play, or Robertson Hare losing his trousers in an Aldwych farce.

After Anna's death, Walter altered the pattern of his visits to London. I think that he must always have wanted to stay at some hotel grander and more exciting than the Langham. He loved hotels, and would, I believe, have been quite happy to spend his life in them. Perhaps he had always wondered what gave the Ritz Hotel its fabled reputation, but, because of the connotations of its name with expensive and, very possibly, sinful living, could never have persuaded his womenfolk to make the experiment of staying there. In the event, it suited him very well. He liked the décor, the food and service, although he was a little taken aback one day to find a dead mouse under his large brass bed.

After one of his trips to London in 1953, my uncle set off for Scotland on a looping itinerary, stopping at the city of Chester on the way. He stayed in the Grosvenor Hotel and there, wholly peacefully, in his sleep, he died. It is strange that it should have been in the very heartland of my mother's family that his seventy years should thus have come to their term. He was found sitting up in bed with his spectacles on his nose, an open detective story under his hand. His habitual nightcap, a tumbler of brandy and whisky, mixed half and half, stood untouched on his bed-table. He might have caused a fire, for a cigarette he was smoking had burned a hole in the sheet before extinguishing itself, but even in dying that good and sensible man had continued to keep his distance from disaster.

5

A WORLD OF AUNTS

One other genuine aunt was my mother's sister Margaret, known to us as Aunt Marnie. She was a few years younger than my mother and wholly different in personality and tastes. For one thing, she had inherited a musical gift from my grandfather, an inheritance which had missed my mother completely. She was different also in physique, larger boned, taller, but with the same mass (before 'shingling') of fine fair hair. Temperamentally the sisters were almost at opposite poles. Whereas my mother was gentle, inclined to shyness, studious, indeed bookish, Marnie greeted the world and all its possibilities with open arms. Hers is one of the key voices of my childhood: musical, with the same nineteenth-century pronunciation as my mother and her cousins, and the same die-away inflexions, the same touch, at times, of humorous mock-despair, but more usually a vivid enthusiasm, a fullness of life. She and I got on very well. Being something of a rebel herself she could detect the rebel, or at least the awkward non-conformist, in me. My tendency, never quite outgrown, to act without reflection and so, sometimes, cause scandal, led me to be regarded — and I believe that I was aware of this quite early on — as something of a problem, unpredictable, unconventional and, very probably, likely to grow up wild.

Sisters have a strange, and sometimes strained relationship, especially sisters who have no brothers and also, from an early age, no father. Bound together by shared memories differently accented, experiences shared but differently interpreted, their affection does not go unmixed with criticism. I do not suppose that either sister always resisted the temptation to criticize the other's offspring or way of living, if only obliquely, and I am sure that her sister's admirable marriage and the general feeling at Elsfield of outstanding worldly success, may sometimes have irritated my aunt whose life, in some respects, had not been so fortunate. If, then, one of her sister's children showed signs of being difficult, Aunt Marnie who, in her day, had herself caused some family upheavals, probably felt a sympathetic interest in that child, and not only from a perfectly human wish to find some flaw in the seemingly flawless front which my parents presented to the world, but from a genuine intuition and a personal knowledge of the difficulty of being, for whatever reason, 'odd man out'. I know that I admired my aunt for her beauty, her unconventional style, and a delicious sense of humour which never left her through the ups and downs of a very long life.

Aunt Marnie had had a career different in many ways from that of my Aunt Anna, but common ground for them could always have been what are now called the performing arts. As soon as she was out of the schoolroom Marnie declared rebellion against the accepted pattern of life as a débutante, aimed at the hoped-for marriage after a couple of Seasons. She wished to be a singer; she meant to be a singer, and nothing, nobody was going to stop her. My grandmother, even if disapproving, and moreover under great pressure from my great-aunts to make her younger daughter toe the line, gave in and allowed her to go to Munich to study. I am hazy about this period of her life, kicking myself as usual for not asking more questions while there was still time, but I know that she made friends with Wagner's son Siegfried and his family, and that she greatly enjoyed the relatively unfettered existence of musicians and students in a Munich still beautiful, still untouched by totalitarian insanity, still unscarred by war.

Marnie was no stranger to Germany or to German life. When my grandfather, Norman Grosvenor, died in 1898, he did not leave a great deal of money. This is something which I have found hard to explain to people for whom the very name of Grosvenor, like that of Rockefeller in the United States, is synonymous with great riches. People generally seem to be hazy about the principles of primogeniture, except those younger sons who moan continually about the wretched accident which has prevented them from being the first-born. Wealth and property, in this country, have always been maintained by passing on the major portion from eldest son to eldest son or nearest heir. My grandfather was the younger son of a younger son and, although the family fortune was sufficiently vast to allow a reasonable competence to its remotest members, his own circumstances were never more than comfortable. Indeed, after his marriage, he went to work in the City, something which I find difficult to equate with his love of music and the arts and his romantic devotion to the ideas of William Morris and his school. After his death my grandmother took to doing what many people did in those days. She let her Mayfair house to someone anxious to spend the Season in London (probably 'bringing out' a daughter) and took herself, her maid, and her two children to winter in Italy or Germany. So, at an early age, Marnie knew Munich and Dresden and had some grounding in the German tongue.

My aunt's ambition to be a professional singer was never to be fulfilled. Perhaps her voice was simply not good enough. I cease to be at all sure of chronology in this history, but I think that her return from Munich must have coincided with the appointment of her uncle as Governor of Victoria. Great-uncle Reggie Talbot had married my grandmother's elder sister, Margaret, after whom Marnie was named. I can imagine how many family conferences there must have been, of the 'what to do about Marnie' variety, before it was decided that she should accompany her aunt and uncle to Australia as a kind of extra lady-in-waiting.

Australia was to have a strong and lasting influence in Marnie's life. I cannot believe that she did not enjoy her stay at Government House, Melbourne, because, even if the official protocol were irksome to her, the natural ebullience and good nature, at least of the younger Australians whom she would have met, would surely have suited her very well. In addition there was music, and a particular kind of music at that: Melbourne was the home of Nellie Armstrong, the singer, then middle-aged, who was known to the whole listening world as Melba. Her soprano voice, matchlessly clear and pure, was said to have been the finest to be heard in Europe since Adelina Patti.

Melba is a name one cannot think of without associating it with a confection of peaches and ice cream, but what is usually passed off as *pêche Melba* is a sad travesty of Escoffier's original creation, where a great swan, carved in ice, held ice cream and fresh peaches masked with his own special crimson sauce.

I do not know whether Marnie met Dame Nellie actually in Melbourne, the latter's home town, or whether, armed with an introduction she went to see her in London, on her return from Australia. However it may have been, the meeting was successful, for Marnie was offered, and accepted, the post of secretary to Dame Nellie. I have often wondered how two such powerful characters got along: swimmingly, no doubt, but with intermittent explosions.

When war came in 1914 Marnie once more took a line of her own. She learned nursing, seriously — not simply the rolling of bandages at afternoon gossip-sessions in London drawing-rooms — and went to Paris to work in a military hospital. There she met and fell in love with a young Australian, Jeremy Peyton-Jones, who was working in France for his country's Red Cross. Marnie and Jerry were married in December 1916, when I was eleven months old. Their wedding took place, quite conventionally, at St George's, Hanover Square, the Grosvenor family's church where my parents had been married in 1907. After that they settled in Buckinghamshire near Amersham, at a farm called Wendover Dean, about thirty miles from Elsfield. They had three children of whom the eldest, Carola, was a year or so younger than me. Then came young Jeremy, and lastly Peggy. Both Aunt Marnie and her husband were particularly interested in furniture and pictures. Marnie's taste, to my eye, was nearly faultless, her knowledge considerable. At one time, in my prep-school days, she and Jerry put their knowledge and skill to work running an antique business of a necessarily rarefied kind from a house in Park Street, Mayfair, provided by the Grosvenor Estate.

I used specially to enjoy expeditions to Wendover Dean which, with its farm and interesting buildings gave plenty of scope for games or exploration. I was fond of my cousins and sometimes thought that they, in a less strictly ordered establishment, had a freer hand than I had at home. The more formal routines of Elsfield were, of course, designed to give as much peace and freedom as possible to my father for his writing, and to facilitate the rather large amount of entertaining required by his ever-expanding political career. Life at Wendover Dean was lived at a different tempo, with different aims and, while Jerry was alive, a particular briskness which he had the power to impart. I remember him — here this is again — chiefly for his voice. I know that he was not tall, that he was dark with a small moustache, quick in his movements, a man of great charm. His voice was deep, very deep, a kind of friendly growl, and I now suppose, with hindsight, that there may have been something morbid about that because, far too soon, after only thirteen years of marriage, he died of tuberculosis, leaving Marnie to a widowhood even longer than that of my mother.

The Peyton-Jones children were our only first cousins. We also had two Scottish cousins in a rather odd relationship. Ian and Tommy Masterton were of an age with myself and Alastair and yet they were first cousins to our father, whose mother's much younger brother had married late. Feeling shorter of cousins than most people, we adopted the second and third kinds as close relations, as we adopted aunts, something which, in so cohesive a family as my mother's, was both easy and rewarding.

One of the most notable features of the time into which I have lived is the decline in the aunt-population, particularly of the maiden sort. Aunts actual and honorary, and particularly great-aunts, had a strong influence on the lives of families such as mine. Their many appearances in literature bear witness to the import-ance, the influence, the ubiquity of the aunt-world of earlier days.

When I think of aunts it is particularly of five great-aunts, four of them my grandmother's sisters and one her sister-in-law. I shall write further of the eldest, Aunt Mary Lovelace, known as Mamie, a commanding character if ever there was one. Each of her sisters, nevertheless, had a very distinct personality of her own. Next in line came Aunt Margaret Talbot, and after her Aunt Blanche Firebrace. The youngest, after Caroline (Tin), my grandmother, was Aunt Katharine Lyttelton. They were all the children of the Rt.Hon. James Stuart-Wortley, MP — brother of Lord Wharncliffe and Solicitor-General in Lord Palmerston's first administration — and when young had lived with their parents and brothers in St James's Place, in an eighteenth-century house which was the goal of many young men keen to see and converse with 'the girls at James's'.

If music itself can be a powerful mnemonic, so too can the music of voices. All the women of my mother's family, on both sides, had unforgettable voices, bearing inflexions that were partly of their period and partly the product of an idiosyncratic view of life, and long practice in conversation, in the art of saying apt and entertaining things. It is a great pity that those voices were never recorded, I should so like to hear them again; even though I should have thought more than twice about approaching Aunt Mamie with a tape-recorder.

All the Stuart-Wortley daughters had benefited from that Victorian young ladies' education which now seems so impress-ive: literature, languages, music — both Aunt Margaret and her brother Charles★ were notable pianists — painting and, of course, serious social work to leaven a nicely graded programme of pleasures and privileges attendant on growing up in Society. Mary and my grandmother studied drawing and painting under Sir Edward Poynter PRA. Both exhibited at the Royal Academy,

★ Lord Stuart of Wortley (1851–1926).

Mary large canvases, pre-Raphaelite in feeling, and Caroline really admirable miniatures. Painting was to be a favourite occupation of my grandmother throughout her life.

Margaret and Katherine both married soldiers, the former Reginald Talbot★ who, amongst other distinctions, had been chosen by the War Office to attend the American Civil War as an observer, and the latter Neville Lyttelton★★ who commanded the British Second Division at the battle of Omdurman and was later Commander-in-Chief in South Africa and from 1904 to 1908, Chief of the General Staff.

The aunts were strategically disposed over the centre of London. At the end of his career Neville Lyttelton was made Governor of the Royal Hospital and so there was Wren's great building to visit, where Aunt Katherine gave splendid children's parties. Hilda Grenfell, her daughter, also known to me as 'Aunt', was my mother's dearest friend, lovely, elegant, impassioned for many causes, and on occasion wonderfully funny. Aunt Margie lived in York Terrace, Regent's Park, and Aunt Blanche in Buckingham Palace Road, then much less of a howling hell of traffic than it is at present.

When we went to London, therefore, we had no need to stay in hotels. If Upper Grosvenor Street could not accommodate all of us there were other welcoming households not too far away. My grandmother and her sisters had all married men somewhat older than themselves and so suffered long widowhoods. All had delightful servants who always seemed pleased to see a young person in their house. Their welcome was warm and, I believe, sincere. Some time in the thirties I remember staying at York Terrace and finding that I had left my evening collars behind. I have not forgotten the alacrity with which an elderly housemaid offered to go and buy one for me in Marylebone Lane. She seemed so eager that I let her go, wondering whether perhaps it gave her pleasure to go shopping for such masculine gear.

At one point in a varied and distinguished career Reginald Talbot had been military attaché at our Embassy in Paris, where Aunt Margie's beauty and spirit had great success. She was indeed a celebrated beauty, although today's fashions might not agree. Hers was a beauty of a high-bred, now antique kind, her profile somewhat hawk-like, in repose severe. Today we expend our admiration on the looks of girls who, in my great-aunt's time,

★ Major-General the Hon. Sir Reginald Talbot, KCB.
★★ General the Hon. Sir Neville Lyttelton, PC, GCB, GCVO.

might have been thought 'actressy' or even 'plain-headed little things'. One photograph remains of Margaret dressed for the famous Devonshire House ball, wearing what looks like a steel breastplate and carrying a spear: something Wagnerian no doubt, possibly Brünnhilde. In that picture the gentle, humorous woman that I remember looks distinctly forbidding.

It seems that she took Paris by storm. A great friendship with Comtesse Greffulhe and another, possibly less comfortable, with Comte Robert de Montesquieu bring her on to the stage of Marcel Proust. Only a providential headache, one hot summer day, probably saved her from being burned to death in the terrible fire at the Bazar de Charité (4 May 1897). Admiration of Margaret's looks took practical form when the three most fashionable portrait painters of the time queued up to paint her portrait. They were Helleu, Boldini and Jacques-Emile Blanche, the last of whom, not surprisingly, produced far the best result.

All the sisters were fond of animals and birds. At Government House, Melbourne, Aunt Margie kept many dachshunds and several cockatoos. Aunt Mamie had a cockatoo called William of Ockham who used to lurk beneath the dinner-table and nip the diners' ankles. If anybody shrieked Aunt Mamie let it be known that she despised people who were afraid of cockatoos. Tin nurtured a series of pekinese, their long succession only once broken by a Dandy Dinmont. Aunt Blanche's house in Sussex was home to a number of dachshunds.

Thus it was, with so much beauty, wit, gaiety and kindness in a much older generation, that it never really occurred to us to belittle our elders, even when we disagreed with them, or to imagine such a thing as a 'generation gap'. I treasure most of all my memory of Tin, my grandmother, for her affection, her perceptivity, her humour forever breaking through seriousness, the sure taste of her surroundings, her very personal style.

What the Ebury and Wharncliffe families possessed materially in such large measure has been as largely dispersed. Of the family houses none remains in family hands. Wortley, in Yorkshire, now belongs to British Coal as a kind of rest-home for trade-unionists and is, I am told, beautifully restored and maintained. Escrick, also in Yorkshire, home of Lord and Lady Wenlock, parents of Tin's mother, is now a school, and Simonstone, in Wensleydale, which my own mother loved so much, has likewise gone. Part of the estate of Moor Park is now a rather expensive suburb; the rest is a golf course and the house its club-house where tired golfers relax at the nineteenth hole under the romping gods and godesses of Cipriani's ceilings.

The sisters were much travelled. At one time Reginald Talbot was Commander-in-Chief in Egypt, where Tin and my mother went to stay one winter. It was a memorable visit, full of varied pleasures which included watching Howard Carter uncover a tomb. It also gave my mother a lifelong fear of bats which, she had been told, might tangle themselves inextricably in her long fair hair. Even after that hair was cut short, in the twenties, the fear remained, and I was often called on to evict bats from her bedroom on summer nights.

The most cosmopolitan of all those remarkable women was Great-aunt Sophie, widow of my grandfather's brother Thomas. Tommy Grosvenor, a diplomat, was secretary of Legation, and later chargé d'affaires at Peking from 1879 to 1883. Two years before going to China he had married Sophie, daughter of Mr S. Wells Williams of Boston, Massachusetts, who had been American Minister in Peking some years before. In 1885 Tommy Grosvenor was posted to St Petersburg as secretary of Embassy and there, in 1886, he died. I was lucky enough to see something of Sophie, who lived quite long into my life. In 1895 she was married again, to Sir Albert Gray, brother of Ruskin's (and Millais's) Effie, and so I always knew her as Aunt Sophie Gray. Her house in Carlyle Square, Chelsea, was full of fine Chinese things.

Aunt Sophie was small and slim and always exquisitely dressed. She had a fund of sound Bostonian common sense and an attitude of somewhat ironical affection towards her adopted country and her first husband's family. If she found the highly formal life at Moor Park sometimes stupefyingly dull she managed to be very funny about it, teasing her brothers-in-law about their devotion to cricket, tennis and field sports, and writing a couple of sketches gently ridiculing the rituals conducted by butler, valets and Groom of the Chambers around her father-in-law, or her mother-in-law's devotion to fresh air, religious instruction and homoeopathy. Once again, as to voices, hers was an enchantment for its gentle New England drawl, which gave a special flavour to her often sharply amusing remarks.

I have one more aunt to think of who was no aunt at all but my godmother. Aunt Sylvia, as I called her, was married to Lord Edward Gleichen, whose unusual name bore strange foreign and royal connotations. He was grandson of Queen Victoria's half-sister Princess Féodore, who had married Prince Ernst of Hohenlohe-Langenburg. Edward's father, Prince Victor, tersely described by the *DNB* as 'admiral and sculptor'★, had a distinguished career in the British Navy and chose, for most of his life, to be known as Count Gleichen, that being the family name of the Hohenlohe. Then, by the most masterly exercise of British compromise Edward, in 1917, having renounced his German titles, became overnight the younger son of a British marquess; hence Lord Edward.

Aunt Sylvia was no stranger to royal circles. As a young girl she had been a maid-of-honour to Queen Victoria. She had many wonderful stories of staying with her husband's relations in Germany and Austria, in the kind of castle where the drive wound through thick forest for twenty miles between lodge-gates and front door. She spoke beautiful French and, in that language, was an unforgettable *raconteuse*. She was also an admirable godmother, never failing with presents on birthdays or when she came to visit us at Elsfield. After her husband's death in 1937 she went to live in one of the new small houses in Burnsall Street, Chelsea, where I saw her quite often. She was then, I suppose, in her fifties, yet the impression she has left with me is of an undimmed youthfulness, of a spirit humorous, positive and deeply interested in many things and people, including myself. Her special cosmopolitanism was reflected in her surroundings, so full of fascinating objects. I particularly remember, on her dining-table, a Fabergé bell-push, a square base of white onyx mounted with two small elephants, one green and one pink — jade and rose-quartz perhaps; not something of great aesthetic moment, but wonderfully typical of the taste of its time and place.

It is a lasting regret for me that I never knew my grandfather, Norman Grosvenor, who died eighteen years before my birth, since he seems to have been much loved and admired. Of his father, my great-grandfather, Robert Grosvenor, I think often with a mixture of respect and amusement. Pictures of him done in later life make him appear stern and extremely serious yet in his youth he had been the life and soul of many parties, so much so that his family called him 'Reveller Bob'. Born in 1801, younger son of Earl Grosvenor who was soon to be the first Marquess of

★ He made the statue of King Alfred which stands in the centre of Wantage.

Westminster, he seems to have done pretty much as he pleased throughout nearly the whole of the nineteenth century. After his father's elevation to the marquisate, he received a peerage of his own and became the first Lord Ebury.

In 1826, at the age of twenty-five, Robert Grosvenor became Member of Parliament for Chester, very much a family seat, and remained thus until 1847 when he changed to Middlesex which he represented for the next ten years. He began as a Whig, like his forebears, but later joined the Liberal party. His younger son, my grandfather, was also at one time Liberal MP for Chester, not, I feel, from strong political conviction but simply because there was no other member of the Grosvenor family available at the time.

My great-grandfather was made Privy Councillor in 1830 and, from that year until 1834 was Comptroller of the Household to King William IV and Queen Adelaide. Later he was to be Groom of the Stole to the Prince Consort. I have often wondered about that appointment, which ranked high at Court, directly after the Vice-Chamberlain. My encyclopaedia speaks of it as 'an office only in use during the reign of a king', in which case what about Queen Victoria and her Consort? It goes on: 'He has charge of the vestment called the stole worn by the Sovereign on state occasions.' Not too hard a job, one might suppose, requiring little more than a sharp eye for moths. Brewer, however, offers a more down-to-earth origin for this post: 'Stole here is not connected with Lat.*stola*, a robe, but refers to the King's *stool* or privy. As late as the sixteenth century, when the King made a royal progress his close-stole formed part of the baggage and was in charge of a special officer or groom.'

According to the *Complete Peerage* Robert Grosvenor at the end of his life was regarded as 'a dear old gentleman, very much the Frenchman's idea of an English Milord'. He was, by then, decidedly set in his ways, and the whole stately mechanism of life at Moor Park was pivoted on his comfort and peace of mind; for he was easily put out and, whenever some small crisis, whether domestic or familial, threatened his orderly day he would retire to his library murmuring resignedly: 'Well, we must just do the best we can!' He felt, I think, that his life was as much borne on by trouble and anxiety as the lives of his tenants and retainers. I suppose that he was a millionaire in our terms, yet would certainly have thought such a description an impermissible vulgarity.

That dear old gentleman, so stern and burdened-looking in his later pictures, was once a lively and adventurous young man. The 'reveller' in him is detectable in George Richmond's portrait, done in Rome in 1839 when he was thirty-eight, and there is little in his looks there to suggest the Privy Councillor, courtier and serious Liberal legislator. What, I wonder, had taken him in 1830 to the Barbary Coast: was it a grave political inquiry or a possibly rather dangerous lark? Somewhere there exists a small book entitled *Extracts from the Journal of Lord Robert Grosvenor: being an account of his visit to the Barbary Regencies in 1830.*

The last was not his only excursion into debatable territory. In 1825 he went to Russia to represent his country at the coronation of Czar Nicholas I. It is said that he astounded the Muscovites, themselves not unused to display, by the splendour of his horses and carriages and the elegance of his entertainments.

In 1831 he married Charlotte Arbuthnot Wellesley, daughter of Lord Cowley and niece of the great Duke of Wellington, and proceeded to settle down to family life. A slight mist of scandal, in no way her fault, hung over Charlotte, for her mother had run away with the dashing Lord Anglesey — he who lost a leg at Waterloo — and there was just the faintest uncertainty as to whose child she might be. She had lived with her father in Vienna when he was Ambassador to Austria (1823-31), and had brought home with her a Viennese pastrycook called Joseph who supplied incomparable rolls for her husband's breakfast.

The Eburys were extremely Low-Church, and churchly matters seem to have preoccupied my great-grandfather increasingly after his marriage. He became impassioned for the cause of Protestantism. 'He viewed with alarm,' says one reference book, 'the development of High Church views in the Church of England.' It was not long before he became President of the Society for the Revision of the Prayer Book, which post he held until, in 1889, disappointed by almost total lack of success, he resigned. Nevertheless, by pulling a number of political strings, he succeeded in having removed from the Prayer Book the Service in Memory of Charles I, the Service of Thanksgiving for the Restoration of Charles II, and the Service of Thanksgiving for Deliverance from Guy Fawkes. He often spoke, and published articles, on liturgical reform.

Homoeopathists have reason to be grateful to Lord Ebury, for it was his influence which got through Parliament the bill legitimizing their practice; and, Milord though he might be, he was a staunch ally of Lord Shaftesbury in his efforts to limit the hours of work in factories. For all his conventionality he must have

70

preserved a spirit of open-mindedness and an admiration for the brave and desperate because, in 1864, we find him presiding over a banquet for Garibaldi when the latter visited London.

I have another portrait of my great-grandfather, done about 1860, a little in the manner of later political cartoons, in which his black frock coat, his shepherd's-plaid trousers just breaking over narrow polished boots, his high collar and white-spotted blue stock, his gleaming silk hat, all bear witness to the care of those two valets and, no doubt, a final once-over from that Malvolio-figure, the Groom of the Chambers.

Some time in the early nineteen-forties my mother's cousin Maudie Glyn, daughter of the second Lord Ebury, wrote a short set of reminiscences of life at Moor Park during her childhood. This enchanting work has not been published: perhaps it should be, since the solace it evidently gave its author in those dark days to write it might work as well for others who care to read of a way of living which could be that of two centuries ago, rather than simply of one. Here she is on some of its delights: 'The kitchen garden: acres of it. High walls covered with plums and pears and the crowning glory of apricots,★ strawberries, raspberries, gooseberries, all in unbelievable profusion. The fruit house where Munden the head gardener always kept bunches of Muscat grapes with the stalks in bottles [of sugared water] the last to be eaten on April 24th, Grandpapa's birthday.'

Of the Palladian house, sometimes attributed to Leoni, she writes: 'I always loved the unhampered approach; no gates or railings to divide it from the park, and the animals, deer, sheep and even cart-horses would sometimes come close up to the steps in damp weather. The sheep loved the flagstones and even lay on the steps sometimes, and on many a morning I've been woken up by the does bleating under my window.'

Of the life of the house: 'It was a strange mixture of grandeur and discomfort. Very lavish in the way of food — masses of fruit, and cream in enormous jugs; butter in golden pats with the family crest on them — but I don't suppose we should think it comfortable now.' And of her grandfather: 'Grandpapa, the benevolent nobleman. When I knew him he had begun to be intensely interested in just seeing how long he could keep alive and that rather obscured his native good sense. He had lived a full and interesting life and had known everyone and done most things. A

★ The Moor Park Apricot, mentioned in *Pride and Prejudice*, and still to be had from nurserymen.

wild young man in the fashion of the day, living, as they did in those times, to the full: not intellectual but, I imagine, with a certain power of taking advantage of his opportunities ... He told me once that, in his youth, he had always, or nearly always, been carried up to bed by his valet, but his constitution was quite unimpaired and he said it never interfered with his riding to hounds. I suppose it was just a fashion of his youth. He was wonderful on a horse and there are legends about his prowess — he and his brother Lord Wilton once jumped a canal lock side by side, and I myself remember that he came to Brackley at the age of seventy-five and pounded the Grafton field on one of my father's hunters.'

Lord Ebury succeeded in his aim of outliving most of his friends and contemporaries. He died in 1893 at the age of ninety-two.

My mother had especially happy memories of Moor Park where she spent many summers as a child. I think that she found her grandfather remote and rather intimidating, but dearly loved her grandmother, who was known to the family, I have no idea why, as Greekie. I think that no house or pleasure garden encountered later, however wonderful, quite succeeded in matching her golden recollection of Moor Park.

I remark elsewhere that there sometimes seemed to be too many women in my life. There was certainly a large number of them. The lack of a dominant masculine presence in my mother's family, at the time of my growing up, was due to the fact, already mentioned, that most of the women had married men much older than themselves, who had left them widowed for a long time. However, I remember well one of my godfathers, Arthur Grenfell★, married to Aunt Katharine's daughter Hilda, who, when I attended with Alice the Eton and Harrow match, always made room for us on his coach at Lord's. He was a delightful man but, during all the time that I knew him, almost impenetrably deaf.

My other godfather, Brigadier-General Cecil Rawling, was a professional soldier and explorer, discoverer of the source of the Brahmaputra, who was killed in France when a shell landed on his headquarters. As that was not long after my birth I have no recollection of him, but I revered his memory for he had left me his Westley-Richards 16-bore, his Greenheart trout-rod and a silver cup which he had won at polo. Great-uncle Reggie Talbot I

★ Lt-Col. A.M. Grenfell, DSO.

can remember, tall and straight and beautifully dressed. His memory is coupled with that of his ex-soldier-servant and coachman, Fripp (Mr Fripp to me). He too was tall and soldierly and the two of them acted in concert to shield Aunt Margie from any discomfort or shock. I can remember the trio arriving at Elsfield one hot summer day, having driven from their house near Henley in an open victoria, and being particularly impressed by Fripp's recommendation of spit as a remedy for nettle-stings and the beauty of his shining cockaded silk hat.

There it is, then, my somewhat curious heredity, which might easily have been difficult to live with; and yet never, in childhood or youth, did I find the least difficulty in assimilating my parents' two such strikingly different worlds. If family life in Scotland, as I have described it, lacked great houses, grapes as big as golf balls, or Fabergé knick-knacks, it had many other valuable things to offer, and indeed the two different atmospheres quite neatly complemented one another, having as common factors kindness, intellectual keenness and constant affection.

6

FIRST STEPS

Some boys, even before they are ten years old, know perfectly well what they want to do in the world, whether it be soldiering, going to sea or flying jets. Others, quite early on, develop a resistance to doing what their fathers do, sometimes going to great lengths to find an occupation as radically different from theirs as possible. I had no such rebellious sentiments, at least in one respect. My father was a writer, and I wanted to be a writer as well. This chronicle will illustrate, if nothing else, the obstacle-course, largely self-made, which hindered my achievement of that ambition.

At Elsfield there was no shortage of writing materials. I was always well supplied with pencils and paper, ink and pens. I even had a tall, ledger-like book with ruled lines, large enough for a novel or at least a novella. Every so often I sat down, looking serious, and wrote a word or two. There were many old-fashioned books in the house, some of them instructive, some works of fiction, probably of an improving kind. The novels often began with a preface or an introduction; the instructive works invariably did. So, before considering what I meant to write, I usually put 'Preface' in capitals on the first page. Sometimes I wrote 'Introduction' in the same way, but it made little difference because at that point I almost always stuck. I am thinking of attempts at writing made between the ages of seven, by which time I had learned reasonably well to write and spell, and twelve, when I was beginning to find something to say. I should have been more discouraged by my lack of inspiration — for, after all, many people have written whole romances, complicated fairy stories, even plays, at a very early age — but for the fact of poetry. If I was getting nowhere in prose I could generally produce a poem. The great charm of poems was that it did not seem to matter how short they were. When my sister gave me a rhyming dictionary I believe that I abandoned prose, for the time being, completely.

I read a great deal of poetry, of all kinds and of many different dates. Originality, as a conception, had not yet begun to trouble me, and so, stumping up the nursery slopes of Parnassus, I was content, in those days, to place my feet where others had trodden before. I wrote odes and sonnets and a number of short pieces entitled 'To ...', since such discreet declarations of love had a powerful, mysterious attraction for me, as well as the merit of also being mysterious to other people. I alone knew that the divine being at the far end of those dots existed only in my imagination.

One day I put a few of such effusions together into a small book, being innocently, or rather ignorantly, proud of my work. My mother showed this to my Scottish grandmother one holiday time at Broughton. When Gran came to one of my 'To ...' poems she looked over her spectacles. 'Is he not a wee bit young to be writing love poems?' My father stepped in quickly with, 'Oh, he's a versatile sort of lad, you know.' An awkwardness was passed over, but probably not without leaving a seed of doubt in my grandmother's mind, which later would grow sturdily alongside certain others.

Poetry was much in the air at Elsfield. My father, an accomplished versifier himself, and something better than that when he wrote in the Scottish vernacular, took an interest in my poetic efforts. We read poems, learned poems by heart, sometimes recited them. Poets came to visit us, and Alice, when a child, had verses addressed to her by Henry Newbolt and Walter de la Mare. Shakespeare was quoted continually by Aunt Anna, not only in her books but in daily life as well.

My reading was omnifarious, from robust and rousing or nobly mournful ballads — 'Ivry', Browning's 'Cavalier Lays', 'The Loss of the Royal George' — to Shelley, Keats, Cowper, Coleridge, Tennyson and, of my own time, Kipling, de la Mare, Noyes, Binyon and Masefield. It would not be until much later that Blake would mean more to me than his brightly burning tiger, and Yeats and Hopkins were to be discoveries of my adolescent years. At that early, pre-school age, untroubled by critical theories, unaware of fashion, I gobbled poetry without discrimination, even spending a whole day, whilst in bed with a cold, taking in Scott's 'Lay of the Last Minstrel' from a very old edition set in diamond type.

There was nothing remarkable about such a poetic diet for a child of my time and place, little that could not be found in most school poetry books or popular anthologies. I suspect that today's children are given less of the martial, the glorious, the proudly boastful, always so enjoyable to declaim or hear declaimed. I wonder whether 'Drake's Drum' and 'The Fighting Téméraire' are still thought proper for the infant psyche. Newbolt being so old and valued a friend of our parents it was natural that we should be introduced to his work at an early age. It is a pity that his reputation should have been allowed to collapse on to such items as 'Vitae Lampada' and 'Clifton Chapel', when there are several much better things never anthologized. He was, as my father said, truly a minstrel, a maker of ballads, born out of his time. He should have followed armies, to sing of their triumphs, or spent his life extolling the actions of some great king.

When not occupied with the stories in verse of high deeds, battles of men and angels, storms at sea, the loss of noble causes, I would turn to the pastoral, to the sunlit orchard of Herrick, Marvell and Suckling, and to Crashaw in secular vein.

> Who e'er she be,
> That not impossible She
> That shall command my heart and me ...

had a special magic for me. Surrounded as I was by obviously possible 'shes' of several varieties I had, from the age of eight or so onwards, a tendency to brood happily on one as yet unrevealed. A Jungian might say that I was really communing with my own *anima*, the invisible but ever-present complement to my masculine nature. Although the thought never occurred to me at the time, I now believe that the possession of a sister near my own age, preferably a twin, might have supplied something critically lacking in my life. My real sister, because of the difference between our ages, was already, in my early childhood, and through no fault of her own, a little remote. She was much occupied with learning and with various feminine ploys to which the usual adult mystifications seemed to cling. When I was nine years old and in my first year at a preparatory school, Alice was rising seventeen, already a young lady, already (and however unwillingly) being prepared for 'coming out', for presentation at Court, the London Season and the right true end, as Tin and the great-aunts saw it, of a desirable marriage. It was not until I was in my late teens that Alice and I became great friends, combining enthusiasms artistic and literary, reinforcing one another's tastes and prejudices, sharing innumerable jokes.

If you are the third of four children it may be unusual to think of yourself as the one in the middle, but I managed it just the same.

My sister was the eldest of the four, being three and a half years older than Johnnie who came second. There was then a gap of more than four years between my elder brother and myself, and a further one of three years and nine months between myself and Alastair; and so, if I thought only in terms of my two brothers, the middle position was mine.

Between what seemed a perfect shower of grown-up pleasures and privileges bestowed on Johnnie, and the (in my view) excessive admiration and attention given to Alastair, I frequently felt left out, slighted even, and that feeling I expressed in aggression of one kind and another. As a very small child, resenting no doubt, in classic terms, the birth of a younger brother, I was often extremely fierce and difficult to manage: so much so that I earned the nickname of 'the tiger toddler'. As time went on my spleen was sometimes reawoken, especially on visits to Scotland where Alastair was always made a great fuss of, being frequently referred to by Gran as 'the flower of the flock'. Gran came from a line of Border sheep-farmers and must be supposed to have known what she was talking about when it came to flocks.

There were days in my childhood when I thought that there were too many women in my life. Unlike my 'not impossible She' they were very much there, on the spot, positive, critical, demanding, and wielding various kinds of authority over me. All the servants in the house were female except the butler. As butlers changed rather often, and were of variable temper, they could not always be counted on as a refuge from petticoat government.

Old Nanny was heavy-handed and inclined to be grumpy. She also used certain infuriating expressions. For example, if I asked when something was going to happen, she usually answered, 'presently'. Children like clear-cut answers: 'presently' was maddeningly vague. If I begged her to do something which she did not feel like doing, she would say that she had a bone in her leg. A proper little gentleman would never, of course, have asked her age. I did ask from time to time, only to be told that she was as old as her tongue and a little older than her teeth. It seemed to me that grown-ups spent a lot of their lives making unnecessary mysteries, and so I most respected those like my father who gave serious and lucid answers to reasonable questions. From my mother and Nanny, and from Alice and Alice's governesses, each one in her way a very definite character, I had much kindness but also a continual scrutiny. I disagreed with all of them in turn, and sometimes all at once, fairly frequently.

It may have been at a really early age, say five years, that I began to be secretive, to resent persistent questioning, to keep my thoughts, wishes and intentions as far as possible to myself. As I grew older I could escape from sight fairly often to talk to the always friendly and equable Amos Webb, our chauffeur, or follow the gardeners about, learning as I did so a little about gardening, without knowing how much of a passion for me it would one day become. Also, if I felt that too much was being demanded of me, or if I simply wanted to make myself scarce, I had the whole range of stables and lofts, and my favourite grooms' rooms to disappear into. Only a mounting hue and cry and frantic blowing of the police whistle would bring me, blinking, into the daylight, expressing mild surprise at the idea that I had given anybody any trouble.

I cannot think of myself as a nice child, certainly not as an easy one, but I did provide my elders with entertainment from time to time. Aunt Anna put me into one of her books, *Pink Sugar*, and since she preferred, where possible, to draw from life, I don't think that the activities of 'Bill' in her novel, horrifying though they may be, are anything but the truth. For instance, I do remember biting a Scottish parlourmaid in the ankle. (I can still seem to taste black woollen stocking.) I happened to be under a tea-table, the cloth of which touched the floor on all sides. My presence there was unsuspected until announced by a squeal from the parlourmaid. My explanation was simple: I was being a crocodile.

On another occasion Alice, Johnnie and I had been told to play a 'Bible game'. That was also in Scotland, and on a Sunday, when ordinary games were forbidden by our grandmother. We chose to play the story of Adam and Eve. My sister and brother (Barbara and Specky in the book) were our original parents, partly undressed and adorned with ivy leaves, since there was no fig-tree about. I had most of my clothes on but had chosen a highly significant role. My elders had collected a lot of plants from the greenhouse to make a garden in the attic:

> ...there in the 'garden', among the flowering plants, on a high chair from which his legs stuck out stiffly, sat Bill... He wore the pale blue jersey and blue trousers that he had worn at church, but on his gilt head was laid a wreath of tropaeolum. His sea-blue eyes were sternly fixed on vacancy; his lower jaw was thrust out, making him look extraordinarily like Lord Carson or a bloodhound; he was heavily scented.

'What is he?' Miss Carter asked.

Barbara gave a frightened giggle. 'We didn't want him to be it...We told him we would just pretend something was moving in the bushes, and pretend we heard a voice — but he *would* do it. First he was the Serpent, and went on his stomach (look at his new jersey) and now he's — he's...'

'He's God,' said Specky.

The heavy scent with which I had enhanced the solemnity of my part was something called 'New Mown Hay', a small phial of which I had bought at the Broughton village shop. In those days, before the establishment of a great industry in 'toiletries', village shops carried cards of very small bottles which had names like 'Ashes of Roses', 'Ashes of Violets' and, of course, the 'New Mown Hay' of that occasion. I imagine that I poured the whole contents of the bottle over myself, and probably went about for several days trailing clouds of synthetic coumarin which grew staler and more nauseous with time.

Aunt Anna apologized in the most practical way for, as she called it, taking away my character in *Pink Sugar*. She announced that I was to have a royalty of one farthing on every copy sold. As an interesting indication of what a moderately popular writer might expect in the way of sales I can say that my portion, as finally computed, was twenty-five pounds. Even supposing that Anna rounded out the sum to that very satisfactory size, the sales of her novel, after half a year, must have been more than twenty thousand copies.

Few people read O. Douglas nowadays, except an ageing, faithful band who still possess sets of her books; and that is a pity, for every one of them contains scenes and situations accurately illustrating aspects of Scottish life over the past eighty years, told, as I have said, with literacy and real humour. O. Douglas and John Buchan between them contributed handsomely to the prosperity of Messrs Hodder & Stoughton and also, no doubt, to the upkeep of the large Rolls-Royce in which Percy Hodder-Williams, the firm's proprietor, used to come and stay.

Sometimes I read the expression 'planned parenthood' and wonder at the misnomer. What is really meant, I suppose, is planned procreation, the management of fertility so as to control the size of a family. Parenthood is quite another matter, for who can plan for the unknown and the unguessable where character, brains, moral sense, responsiveness to others, approach to living itself, are concerned? If children, as Bacon said, are hostages to fortune, they are also in themselves a considerable gamble. When two people unite in marriage they may know, or think they know, themselves and whatever influences may come through them from immediate forebears. They cannot, however, know what the interaction of their genes may produce, what throwbacks may not appear to ancestral quirks or motives unapprehended by either of them. Sometimes a child will arrive in the world trailing, not clouds of glory, but a small fog of dissatisfaction, of melancholy or anxiety or mistrust. It is hard to see how any young father could be adequately prepared to deal farseeingly with such evidence, since he naturally expects his child to be a reproduction of himself, if a boy, or of his wife, if a girl; and if the child's character begins to seem noticeably different from his own or his wife's, or from what they hoped that it would be, he and his partner are likely to be at a loss as to how to proceed. Hence comes friction, both with the child and between the parents.

('*Your son*, Charles, has gone and let us down again!'

'*My son* indeed! He's simply your awful Uncle Edred reincarnated!')

Something for which no parent is likely to be prepared, and for which an explanation might be impossibly hard to find, is the fact that certain children, despite every appearance of care and affection all around them, will yet grow up with a sense that their lives have somehow been lacking in love. What causes this feeling of deprivation in children who, to the outward eye, are the very opposite of 'deprived', I should not be able to say. Weighing the evidence as scrupulously as I can, and considering over a long stretch of time certain clear images and persistent thoughts which have come on with me from an early age, I have to conclude that this particular sense of a lack, no doubt neurotic, formed part of my makeup from the very beginning of my life. I have no wish to insist upon this, nor to lay any kind of blame, merely regarding what I now believe to have been a fact with the same remote interest and mild mystification that I should feel if confronted with a stone of unusual colour and shape, or a rune inscribed in a language to which I had no key. It could, however, be made to explain satisfactorily a pattern of action, of rather violent ups and downs in the affections, which was to occur in later life.

When I was about five, Old Nanny left us to look after a little girl, an only child, in London. This is an amusing example of the odd and sometimes striking designs which show up occasionally in the generally inchoate pattern of a life. The parents of that little girl were Sir Kenneth and Lady Swan, great-uncle and -aunt of Sauré, whom one day I would marry, but who would not be born for another fifteen years.

At the departure of Miss Frances Earl, which was not much regretted although she had served my parents faithfully for a dozen years, Elsie Charlett took over the nursery. The Charlett family were a benign influence in our lives. At one time there were four of them working at Elsfield: Mrs Charlett as cook, Elsie as nurserymaid, her younger sister Gladys as parlourmaid, and her brother Sonny as groom. They were a remarkable family, and not less remarkable was the way in which their mother, left a widow and pretty well penniless many years before, had managed to keep them all together while she went as cook to a number of posts. At first they had lived in London, where Mrs Charlett cooked for a well-to-do Jewish family in Hampstead. By the time that my mother came to hear of her she was working at a country house in Suffolk belonging to people known to my parents.

After a year or two with us Gladys left to be married. Sonny died suddenly, and much too young, of something I can only see as mysterious, since no one told me the nature of his illness at the time. When Old Nanny left us, Elsie was promoted to full charge of myself and Alastair, and she and her mother remained at Elsfield for some years. When Alastair was sent off to boarding-school Elsie left to be married. Mrs Charlett came back to cook for the family after my mother had returned from Canada early in the last war, and stayed there almost until the end.

The nursery was at the very top of the house on its gabled Victorian side. So high up was it that a small child standing on the floor, or sitting at the big table under the window, could see nothing but sky and the weaving patterns of rooks. Most of one side of the room was taken up by a wide, white-painted cupboard, the top part holding linen, the bottom part stuffed with toys. Opposite was the fireplace with its tall fireguard of wire mesh, brass-railed at the top and with a pull-out rail for drying clothes on, the one I remember from Portland Place. In winter there was always a hot coal fire. Beside the fireplace stood a creaky basket chair upholstered in green rep. The window curtains were of the same material. To the right of the fire, and also upholstered in green, was a 'box-ottoman', a kind of overstuffed *chaise longue* with one raised end, of which the seating part could be lifted up to

81

reveal a further selection of toys, liable to be squashed shapeless or broken if carelessly put away. The floor was covered in dark green linoleum, and in front of the fire was a parti-coloured rag rug.

My earliest recollections of the nursery are of warmth and light, (a hard white light from a bulb in a glass shade shaped like an oriental hat), and of considerable activity. In our earliest days the room must often have been rather crowded, before my elder brother and sister graduated to the schoolroom and thence to eating with the grown-ups downstairs. On the table where we younger ones ate our meals there was a brass reading-lamp with a pleated shade of green silk which gave a softer light, in welcome contrast to the searching glare of the one overhead, and next to it, quite early on, the wireless.

The first two wirelesses that I remember were crystal sets, boxes of varnished wood, their topsides of black vulcanite sparsely set with knobs and switches and something resembling a miniature Japanese bridge, the 'cat's whisker' and its attendant crystal. The former, a fine, short wire with a vulcanite handle, mounted on a universal joint, had to be manoeuvred with extreme delicacy so that it touched the crystal beneath it at the point where a broadcast could be intercepted. Since I never began to understand the principle of that contrivance I cannot attempt to explain it. The excitement lay not so much in what finally came through in the way of a programme, as in the nervous, probing search with the cat's whisker for the exact spot on the crystal and the sudden, magical release of sound.

The radio industry, however, was growing even faster than I was and, in a very short time, we were able to have a new set containing valves, with a separate black loudspeaker horn shaped like a question mark. The crystal and its whisker, by then, had been left behind and there were condensers and a rheostat for finding wavelengths and controlling volume. My interest in electricity, which was strong, never extended to the air-waves, being wholly concerned with light and motive-power. Later, at my preparatory school, I found real enthusiasts who could go off into flights of scientific language, using rather poetical words like 'superheterodyne'. ('I longed for roses, virgins, wine / And pleasures superheterodyne.')

Elsie had more pleasure out of the wireless than I or Alastair, from the popular songs of the time. How flat and tinny-sounding those songs would seem today, and yet they must have struck the ear with a special force and significance for the very reason that they were plucked from the ether through the agency of a small square box. 'It ain't a'gonna rain no more', 'Show me the way to go home', 'I'm one of the nuts of Barcelona', 'Ramona', are among the earliest that I remember, and they are good enough examples, since popular songs of that period tended to be either quite nonsensical or soupily sentimental.

It is a truism that old tunes, with scents and particular sounds, are reliable triggers of memory. One or two can fix for me, immediately and invariably, a place, a gathering of people, even a kind of weather, a time of day, or a state of emotion. In the drawing-room at Elsfield was a middle-sized grand piano, by Collard & Collard, which probably came to my parents as a wedding present, since neither of them was sufficiently interested in music to be likely to consider a piano a necessity of life. That instrument was regularly tuned but rarely used, except when my sister or I wanted to pick out on it something which expressed a feeling or underlined a wish which we were incubating. A music-stand beside the piano contained books of songs including, naturally, 'Songs of the North' and some sheets of forgotten drawing-room ballads, which makes me think that the piano, in earlier London days, may have had more use, when people who were known to play or sing were sometimes invited to perform. There was also a bound book of old French songs, exquisitely illustrated by Boutet de Monvel, from which I learned 'Frère Jacques', 'Au Clair de la Lune', 'J'ai du Bon Tabac', 'Fais Dodo…' and 'Cadet Roussel'. Those songs were among the many impulses nudging me towards all things French.

The only time that the piano really came into its own was when Alice organized the entertainment which we offered every year to our Scottish family during their regular spring visits. For that performance it was played by Mrs Cox, who came on her bicycle from Woodeaton for rehearsals, as she did every Sunday to play the mothy old harmonium in Elsfield church. If, now, an up-to-date and rather complicated Japanese radio comes through with some favourite of those days — 'Who is Sylvia?', say, or 'Plaisir d'Amour' — I am back at that piano, tinkling away with my right hand, seeing late-afternoon summer light coming through three tall westward-looking windows, their blinds lowered to protect from fading the grey and rose and pale blue of an Aubusson carpet.

When not cleared for meals the nursery table had many uses: as laboratory bench, builder's yard for Meccano, solid surface for

83

drawing and painting, bed for a stationary steam–engine, or space for sorting silkworms into paper cornets which, filled with mulberry leaves, were then pinned to the curtains. (The mulberry leaves decayed with a sickly vegetable smell; the golden cocoons looked pretty but resisted all attempts at spinning; it was not long before grown–up protests led to their removal.)

Sometimes we had to yield the table to Elsie when she needed to cut out and sew together some dress material. Then it would be covered with pale brown paper patterns, and the sewing–machine on the cast–iron trolley which housed its treadle mechanism would be wheeled out to stand near by. Sometimes Elsie trimmed hats, removing some faded glory from a basic straw and covering it again from rolls of trimming which looked like the paper garnish of shop–bought cakes. I cannot read a passage in *Le Grand Meaulnes* where the narrator's mother hides herself away and 'makes over some humble dresses' without seeing Elsie at work reviving and refurbishing her own.

When Old Nanny left us Elsie must have been about eighteen, and so youthful an influence made a great difference to our lives. Like all her family she was brown–complexioned, with coal–black hair and fine dark eyes. Her personality was an exceptionally calm one, and her manner warm without effusion. She was gentle, discreet and wholly reliable. It took a great deal of anxiety or distress to disturb her equanimity. With it all she was cheerful, open to ideas, and deeply interested in the lives of her charges. Compared to Old Nanny, at all times too ready with sharp word or blow, she ran her nursery on liberal principles, for which reason I still think of it, in spite of the quite frequent rows between my younger brother and myself, or myself and the rest of the household, as a light and comfortable place.

If, of nursery food, I seem to remember chiefly rabbit and rice pudding, I am probably not far wrong. For a reason which may have been moral, because few children can ever actually have declared a liking for rice pudding, we seem to have been given that dish rather often, together with its unlovely relations tapioca and semolina. In those days little fuss was made about children's food; indeed, children and servants tended to be fed much the same things. Rabbits were plentiful and cheap, so the household ate plenty of rabbit. There are several delicious ways of cooking that particular animal, but boiling it and covering it with gluey grey gravy is not one of them. Mrs Charlett, on her day, was a truly excellent cook, but I think that her artistry was directed mainly towards the dining room. For the rest of us the fare, although no doubt wholesome and plentiful, was decidedly plain. When, however, there was entertaining downstairs and a surplus of something interesting, Elsie usually managed to secure some of it for her charges. Ice-cream, for example, made of strawberries from the garden and cream from the dairy, has left a memory and a standard of comparison difficult, nowadays, to match. Making it certainly meant a lot of hard labour for the kitchen-maid, turning the handle of a cylindrical machine packed with freezing-salt and ice, but the result came very near to the sublime.

I only once saw Elsie severely shaken, and that was on the day when she lost Alastair. Coming up the front stairs one morning, past my parents' bedroom, I heard crying and at once rushed in to see what was the matter. There was Elsie in tears, trying to explain to my mother how Alastair had slipped her hand in a crowded Oxford shop and had then completely disappeared. This story illustrates very well the practical and determined nature of my younger brother. While an anguished Elsie was searching for him among the crowds of shoppers, he was also looking for her. After a time, not having found her, he might well have succumbed to panic, howled, implored the help of passers-by. Nothing of the sort: he simply decided to walk home. He knew the way out of Oxford perfectly well. He set off down the High Street, over Magdalen Bridge, and along St Clements, a wide street then divided at its far end by a line of small shops before the road forked, going right for Headington and left for New Marston, Old Marston, and Elsfield nearly five miles away. Recounting his adventure later on Alastair was calm. 'I knew the way,' he said. 'I just turned left at the ham-and-beef shop.' He was then six years old. When she realized that Alastair was not to be found, Elsie, with Amos Webb, tore back to Elsfield to set all possible wheels in motion. Somehow, and probably because he was hidden among the shoppers of St Clements, they passed Alastair, without seeing him, on their way.

Elsie had won my affection and, indeed, respect from the moment of her first appearance. As time went on I came to feel for her an emotion, part dependent, part protective, which could only be called love. I loved her, in fact, more than anyone else in my world and when, at the age of nine, I was torn from familiar surroundings to face the vast discomfort, racket and competitive scrimmage of a preparatory school, it was leaving Elsie that I minded most. She was the guardian of my childhood's secrets, the wise, kind friend whose fine intuition and delicate understanding of a child's sensibilities had allowed me to feel safe, unirritated, reasonable with her as with nobody else. I needed her good opinion and did more to win it than I would have done for most others, my parents included.

When I first went away to the Dragon School in Oxford, it was, as it had been for Johnnie and would be for Alastair, on the principle of weekly boarding. I suppose that my parents, or at any rate my mother, had insisted on this. It was, I think, a great mistake. The majority of boys were boarders, and some were very far from home. As far as I can remember my brothers and I were the only weekly boarders throughout our time at that school, and we were apt to have the worst of both worlds. A full boarder was obliged to say goodbye to his home and family for the whole length of a term. Living among the full-time boarders we were bound to be objects of envy, for being able to get back to our own homes, our own things, every Saturday afternoon. The passions of small boys do not allow of a broad view. In the shifting, unpredictable alliances of schoolboy existence we held a precarious place. One could leave, on Saturday, a diplomatic situation apparently satisfactory, with all allies in place and professing loyalty, one's own gang seemingly well-established, only to find on Monday the whole scene changed out of recognition, friends turned to foes, friendly forces depleted, enemies in gleeful control. Ignominy, ostracism even, had to be faced. Then came the laborious rearrangement, the parleys, the overtures, the bribes needed to regain a respectable position in the power game. And so, although it could never be anything but a pleasure to go back to Elsfield, that pleasure was sometimes more bitter than sweet. The stable point in those homecomings was Elsie, who never changed, whose welcome never varied in its restrained affection, whose personality had the power to soothe anxiety and put worries into perspective. Only, there was Monday morning to come, too often bringing with it a hollow feeling of apprehension, as though one were setting out for the scaffold rather than simply for school.

There was a narrow pantry between nursery and night-nursery where tea could be made and washing-up done. Elsie's life, therefore, was nearly as isolated as our own, at the top of the steep house. She went down to the servants' hall for supper, but had her other meals with us, trays being brought up the almost vertical back stairs by a panting maid. In spite of her special position in the household she seemed always to be on good terms with the other servants, even with butlers who were, in the truest sense, 'odd men out'. She was fond, as we all were, of Annie Cox, who doubled as housekeeper and lady's maid to my mother, and who had her bedroom at the top of the older house, next to the long, low attic with its three windows facing east and south, which was a dormitory for the younger maids. That attic must have been nearly as cold in winter as the dormitories at my first school, and I don't suppose that there was much, if anything, in the way of heating. However, two of its windows looked down into the village street, and into the upper branches of the big elm tree which served as the village notice board, and so some amusement for the young ones may have been possible. In the last year of our occupation of the manor, which was also Coronation year, we gave a fête in the garden. While I was dashing about trying to deal with the many problems which arise at fêtes, I was stopped by two elderly ladies, strangers to me, who asked if they might be allowed to see inside the house. Both were well-dressed, well-mannered, with soft Canadian voices. They told me they had worked as housemaids at the manor for our predecesors, the Parsons, and that they would dearly like to see again the room in which they had used to sleep. Later they had married and gone to Canada where clearly they had prospered. I took them upstairs to the attic and stood at the door while they exclaimed with pure pleasure at the sight of the place where once they must have tumbled so gratefully into bed at the end of a gruelling day's work. They turned to me, sparkling with happy recollection, and told me how, when 'the family' was away, the village boys used to climb the elm tree to the height of their windows, and of the larks and flirtations which then went on.

For reasons attributable to Tin and the great-aunts her sisters, my sister Alice was never sent to school or university. In earlier days, in London, she had had a French governess who, it was said, 'shrieked like a peahen' when put out. Things steadied down after our arrival at Elsfield, when Alice was eleven, and between that time and her coming out at eighteen there were two governesses in succession, Kathleen Claxton and Harriet Smeaton, each a remarkable woman in her way. Accordingly my sister received as good and varied an instruction as was possible under a system which old-fashioned people thought the only one suitable for a girl of her sort. It is greatly to be regretted that Alice was not given the chance, if not of boarding-school (which she would

surely have disliked as deeply as I did myself) at least of a
university education, something from which she would have
derived vast benefit. She was the victim of a rigid conservatism
which was, even then, by no means general in our world.

'Don't be clever with men, my dear,' said Tin. 'Men don't like
clever girls.' In her view marriage was the only proper career for a
girl like Alice, and nothing must be done to baffle or discourage
those highly nervous trousered creatures, unless, of course, they
were without background or prospects, in which case they could
be treated kindly or otherwise, but never in any way which could
possibly lead to marriage.

All that was understandable if, in its results, unfortunate. My
grandmother and her sisters had been brought up in and had
married within a small world, the social pre-eminence, the very
cohesion of which depended on its members making the 'right'
marriages or eschewing marriage altogether. 'Marrying at random' (her own phrase) was something of which Tin could not
bring herself to approve. In every other respect she was a free
spirit, intelligent, accomplished, an excellent writer, a painter, a
linguist, highly cultivated and much engaged, especially in
charitable terms, with the affairs of the larger world. She was not
above encouraging her younger relations to rebellion, but never
her own granddaughter. With all her cleverness and knowledge of
the world, and in spite of the liberal-minded and even radical
views which she had once shared with her husband, Tin clung still
to a belief in the immutability of social position and the right to
continued existence of the traditional governing class. Yet she had
lived through all the changes and upheavals which had so fatally
damaged that class, from Harcourt's death duties legislation of
1894 through the Liberal landslide of 1906, Lloyd George's
'people's budget' and the ensuing defeat of the House of Lords, to
the final crippling blow of the Great War and the hecatomb of sons
from which so many families never fully recovered. By the time
that Alice would have been old enough to attend a boarding-
school Tin was already in her sixties, the Great War only two
years past, and all of her acquaintance, bereaved in most cases, in
many newly impoverished, must have thought longingly back to
things as they were, and to have resolved boldly, fiercely or
simply wistfully to maintain what was left to them and pray for a
long, long rest from any further change. I am not disposed to
blame those who allowed sentiment or nostalgia to overrule
reason and obscure what, to their clearer sight, was unpleasantly

evident. They had really been through enough.

So, for Alice, it was to be the schoolroom rather than school. The educational system used by our governesses was that devised by the Parents' National Educational Union, or PNEU. This highly original body had been founded by Miss Charlotte Mason in 1887, with the idea, I believe, of giving a systematic education to the daughters of country squires and others living remote from towns or centres of learning and unwilling to commit their offspring to the schools for girls then not long come into existence. It could also serve for their brothers before, at the age of nine or so, they were sent away to boarding-school. In a way the PNEU performed something like the function of the Army & Navy Stores, supplying, instead of mixed biscuits and whisky and shotgun cartridges, a varied and well-chosen regime for the young mind and hand. Not all governesses, I daresay, had been taught the PNEU method; but we were lucky that ours were amongst its warmest devotees.

The whole proceeding was most efficiently managed. Neat tables were drawn up to show which lessons were due on which days, and at what times. The teaching was divided into terms, just as at school, and at the end of every term there were examinations. Papers arrived from the headquarters at Ambleside and were opened with some ceremony at a prescribed date and time. After we had laboured over them they were sent back to their place of origin, to be marked. The resultant marks would then govern the degree of emphasis to be placed on each separate part of the curriculum in the following term.

Our first governess, Kathleen Claxton, was (I now see) quite young and rather handsome when she came to us. Hers was an enthusiastic spirit and she had, generally, the power to arouse enthusiasm. Her aesthetic tastes were derived, I think, from the optimistic simplicity of the Arts and Crafts movement, and so she did her best to build Jerusalem wherever she found herself. Under her tutelage I learned to read and write, and absorbed my country's history as represented in such works as *Our Island Story* without, however, coming to any lasting comprehension of dates. Arithmetic, from the very start, was to be a real difficulty for me, but that should not be blamed on governesses. Mathematics teaching all over the country, at that time, was, it can now be seen, old-fashioned and strangely inept; so much so that only the abnormally gifted could hack their way through a jungle of boredom and irrelevance to enter what I have always thought must be a world of exquisite clarity and excitement for those who can inhabit it.

The boys of the family had a mere portion of the full PNEU feast, a grounding only in subjects which would be gone into more thoroughly at school. For Alice education was to be continuous and increasingly demanding, until the day when she would be sent, at sixteen, for a year's 'finishing' in Paris. Her work in the schoolroom was serious and wide-ranging. History, for her, went far beyond *Our Island Story* into the works of Burke and Motley, Macaulay and John Stuart Mill. No one needed to urge Shakespeare upon her; she had been a passionate devotee from a very early age. With her schoolroom companions she learned and performed scenes from his plays; showed, indeed, every sign of a leaning towards a theatrical career, subtly encouraged in this by Aunt Anna who, as I have suggested, might have felt the same inclination when she was young. As Alice grew older her instruction included attending lectures in Oxford on many subjects including theology.

I have written of schoolroom companions. It was usual, in those days, for the employers of governesses to gather children from their neighbourhood, or even farther away, to share the instruction and help to defray the cost. Of those who stayed in the house and took part in the schoolroom life I remember best Susan Feilding and Beatrice Spencer-Smith. Susan was the only daughter of Percy and Clotilde Feilding, both architects and connoisseurs of old houses, who had bought and put to rights remote, romantic Beckley Park, which lay at the end of a long, rough drive, amongst woods and water-meadows, on the edge of Otmoor below Beckley village. I could hardly know, at the age of seven, how much Susan, then a calm and graceful fourteen-year-old, would come to mean in my life at a future date, nor how good a friend Beatrice would one day become. For the time being those two brought light and colour to the life of the house, providing a kind of intermediate territory, neutral but kindly, between the small children and the not always fathomable grown-ups. Beatrice was niece to the redoubtable Mrs Pelly, provider of butter and owner of a splendiferous motor-car. At Holyrood, during my father's two stints as Lord High Commissioner (1933, 1934), she would act as a Maid of Honour and, shortly thereafter, go with my parents to Canada for a couple of years as lady-in-waiting.

7

PARTIES AND PLOYS

For myself and Alastair party days were apt to be days of mourning and remonstrance. It must have been an effect of our enclosed, busy and absorbing life at home that we seldom seemed to want anything different. It is possible that this attitude resembled our mother's, since she was never very socially inclined, indeed quite happy to remain where she was, doing what she did, surrounded only by close friends and her own family. Nevertheless there were, in Oxford and the county, people she liked to see, and houses to visit which gave her pleasure. One or two country neighbours were real friends, and it was natural, since most of them had young families, that there should be coming and going between the houses, whatever we children might have thought about it. Every so often a perhaps conscience-stricken recall to social duty would cause my mother to accept invitations to children's parties on our behalf.

We went to parties by car. The first car that I remember was American, an Overland, with what was then called a touring body. This meant that it was open to the air, and only to be partially enclosed by means of a canvas hood and side-screens of talc. On a winter afternoon — and, since most of the children's parties took place around Christmas, it is winter driving that I chiefly remember — the cold in that car could be ferocious. There were too many chinks between the screens letting in blades of draught for internal warmth to be possible, and cars in those days had no heaters.

Quite early in the afternoon Alastair and I were rounded up from some outdoor occupation, washed, brushed, brilliantined and buttoned into our party clothes. Once dressed we were told to sit down and do nothing to dirty clothes or hands, which meant an hour or so of fidgeting, questioning and complaining, or, at a later stage, reading and becoming so absorbed as to be thoroughly cross when the time came to set out.

We left the house well swaddled in coats and voluminous

91

shawls and were packed into the back with Elsie under a thick fur
rug. Sometimes my mother came with us, when we would crowd
into the back with her, while Elsie sat, also rugged, beside Amos
Webb, himself a solid figure in heavy topcoat and peaked cap,
seeming to give off a genial warmth of his own. Sometimes the
drive was a long one, or seemed so, for the Overland was hardly
speedy, thirty-five miles an hour being about the best it could
manage on those as yet untarred country roads. Long drives were
to Thame or Bletchingdon, Middleton Stoney or Weston on the
Green; sometimes we only had to go the few miles to Beckley or
Islip, Wheatley or Stanton St John.

   Whether it was a matter of temperament, a kind of wild
shyness, or simply an effect of what we felt to be our complete
self-sufficiency, and consequent resentment at having to break out
of it, to suffer the abrasion of strange personalities, the possible
dangers of the unfamiliar, we certainly set up a great resistance to
any kind of social event arranged for us in the world outside.
Invariably the grown-ups told us that we would enjoy ourselves
when we got to the party, and quite often they were right. Quite
often we did enjoy ourselves and so, typically, produced a
mirror-image of the previous fuss when the time came for us to
leave.

   Splashing along under driving cold rain, stealing through white
fog, crackling over iron-frosted macadam, or picking a way
between cliffs of piled-up snow, we forged on to the pleasures
awaiting us. The engine hummed loudly, the headlights made a
yellow tunnel walled by dark, tangled hedgerows or roofed with
the skeletal arches of elm and beech. The steady engine-hum, the
yellow-lit roadway unreeling away from us, the warmth inside
our cocoons of rugs and shawls, induced drowsiness, a sense of
suspension. By the time that we came to our destination, a
white-painted gate, perhaps, or a pair of stone piers between
matching lodges, and entered a drive lined with dark trees, to see
the lights of another car sweeping the ground ahead of us, I was
usually half asleep. Alastair and I, peeled of outer wrappings and
urged to run quickly indoors, stumbled out of the car, yawning
and grumbling. (A flight of steps: tall figures proclaiming
welcome; the black bulk of a house soaring upwards, its lower
windows brightly lit: a high doorway letting out light from a
scene of movement and brilliancy within; a sinking of the heart
and a strong wish to rush back to the car and hide under the rug.)

   Alastair was always a more sociable creature than I. Once put to it I think that he enjoyed the shock of new acquaintance, went out to meet it with his chin up. He was a singularly appealing small boy. All that he really had to do was to smile and look expectant, to be immediately inducted into the social scene, where he continued to smile and respond cheerfully. By contrast, I may often have looked affronted or glum. Once at a party, Alastair would let himself be pulled hither and thither by kind hands, smothered by kindly voices, whereas for a while I would hang back, and thus often find myself isolated, presenting a familiar problem to my hostess who, deeply experienced, would soon set in motion some reserve plan for dealing with awkward small boys.

There were usually a lot of grown-ups in control, or more or less so, of those children's parties; the hostess, her family and servants, all doing their best to make things go with a swing. Once one was inside the unfamiliar or little-known interior there were smiling people to send the boys in one direction, the girls in another, to take off their coats and change into dancing-shoes brought along in linen bags by nurses. Music, generally a piano but sometimes a small band, would be playing in the middle distance. If one had arrived amongst the first guests the dancing space would be empty, those children already prepared to dance peering into the room and ducking out again, laughing, gasping, exclaiming, unwilling to be the first on to the floor. At the earliest parties, those given for the very young, when my contemporaries and I were still at the splendidly solipsistic stage of proceeding to any desired goal in a direct line, barging into and surmounting obstacles, human and otherwise, like small tanks, we were rather bemused by lights and noises but, on the whole, interested, excited and, barring accidents, ready to be pleased. At a later stage all kinds of self-consciousness would have developed, from my own brand of stony non-cooperation to the developing signs of social piracy, the thrusting, molesting self-conceit of the extrovert boy or girl.

The truth was that my brother and I were not used to other children, nor did we feel any need for them in our lives. When strange boys and girls came to tea we often disgraced ourselves, refusing to part with favourite toys, even for a few minutes, as though they might lose some particular virtue in alien hands. But I, if I was obliged to entertain little strangers, definitely preferred them to be girls. Boys usually meant competition, febrile boasting or clam-like silence, and rough handling of precious things. For

93

many aspects of line and colour, for softness, a delicate difference in rounded bare arms and knees, a touch of audacious showing-off in the shaking of bright curls or the glossy thickness of a short 'bob', girls had a fascination never to be wholly diminished by sulks, or hauteur, or ill-temper, or tears.

Oxfordshire in the 1920s still kept many characteristics of the previous century. Some country houses were without electricity; few had central heating. For parties great efforts were made to dispel a centuries-old chill in stone-flagged halls and high, many-windowed rooms. Log fires blazed in every fireplace, but still one sometimes shivered, bare arms showed gooseflesh, games and dancing were extra strenuous from the need to keep warm. One day a neighbour, a middle-aged bachelor who lived in a large classical house, took it into his head to give a children's party, and that was unforgettable. We entered a splendid chiaroscuro, gold light and umber shade, and smelt wood-smoke and paraffin and hot wax. In the hall a great fire in a Cyclopean fireplace sent sheets of flame, red, blue and yellow, streaming upwards from logs five feet long. Oil lamps and candelabra made areas of light, soft-edged, which died into a velvet dusk, just showing the feet and legs, or the sculptured skirts, of tall portraits. Stoves, set here and there to reinforce the fires, gave off the hot paraffin smell which was so pleasantly familiar from visits to cottages and farms. Children climbed a broad staircase which soared upwards into darkness, took off their outer clothes in bedrooms wavering with candlelight, and were at once awed and exhilarated by the antique strangeness, unaware that they were at the threshold of an older world which they would not often enter again.

It had been many years, probably, since that old house had resounded to fiddle and piano, to the scamper of feet and the laughter of children; and if the children, ceasing to be subdued by the half-lit vastness around them, seemed happy, so too did the old servants who looked on, beaming, at the fun, glad to see, for once, young life in that sad place. Their daily lives, I think, were shadowed, for their master was a man given to melancholy, for some particular reason lonely, who one day would take his own life.

History, measured by even a moderately long lifetime, telescopes easily. When I was, say, six years old and going to such parties as I have described, my elders, if aged more than twenty-two, must all have been born in the reign of Queen Victoria. My own mother, for example, was eighteen at the turn of the century: accordingly, all the important early influences on her life, together with some of its most joyous or poignant recollections, belonged to the Victorian age, as did many fixed conceptions about living and rules for its conduct.

Given an upbringing in the days of Queen Victoria and King Edward, it was not surprising that my hostesses at children's parties should have perpetuated games and dances, food and drink as they had known them in their own childhood. Servants, too, such as cooks and nurses, liked to see reproduced what they thought traditional and proper for childish entertainment. Present-day children, I suppose, by reason of a more varied and interesting general diet — no rabbit and rice-pudding for them! — do not fall like starving wolves on any sweet thing, as we did. When we were shepherded into somebody's dining-room for tea, our eyes were met by such a display of colour and enticing shapes, such a prodigality of sweetness, as to seem like something out of the *Arabian Nights* by comparison with our nursery teas at home, where such rules obtained as 'No jam on the first piece' and there was strict rationing of cake.

Often the party scene was brighter, less romantically atmospheric, more up-to-date, when we were invited to some house which had been recently modernized, full of warmth and light, but lacking in mystery. In our earliest days when dancing, if carried on for too long, was liable to degenerate into a riot, and the attention of the very young had to be concentrated for the sake of peace, there might be a conjurer, with a Punch and Judy performance, or even a film show, in black and white, of comedy 'shorts' featuring Chaplin or the Keystone Kops, or that earliest of cartoon characters, Felix the Cat. Anything to do with light, real or artificial, had always fascinated me: I was happy enough to watch the static coloured pictures of what was still called the 'magic lantern', but was quite carried away by the moving variety, not much caring what came on to the screen, since the whole thing seemed so miraculous.

Sometimes — although not, I think, very often — we were obliged to put on fancy dress. Planning and making this gave great amusement to the female members of the household; our own feelings ran from indifference to a gloomy sort of embarrassment. Fancy dress of another kind was also to be found at home. My sister's passion for the theatre, which has never abated to this day, expressed itself in quite frequent bouts of acting, either semi-

95

impromptu or rather elaborately rehearsed and staged. Consequently a large, deep, white-painted box, which stood on the top
landing just outside our bedrooms, was often in commission.
Known as the 'acting box', it contained a remarkable assortment
of garments, belts, beads, scarves and trimmings, most of them
items of some former importance, cast out of one or another
grown-up wardrobe. There were silks and velvets, capes and
cloaks, which had once been evening clothes. One sumptuous
dress of burgundy-coloured silk, its skirt a mass of minute pleats,
had been a teagown of my mother's, a Fortuny model. It is strange
to think — and this is surely something which it would then have
been impossible to predict — that the Fortuny creation, relegated
to the acting box in the category of cast-off, would now fetch a
great deal more than its weight in gold, so impassioned have
people become for the elegancies of even a quite recent past.

For the annual springtime visit of our Scottish family Alice
devised and produced the entertainment which, starting with
traditional songs, and the reciting of poems, and a duologue or
short play by Anthony Hope or Maurice Baring, grew with the
years increasingly sophisticated, taking in Noël Coward, the
Sitwells, Betjeman and Jean Cocteau. The audience, apart from
our parents, our aunt and uncle and grandmother, was supplied by
the domestic staff with, occasionally, someone staying in the
house. Nowhere should we find again such indulgence, for the
family contingent were eager to discern talent in all of us,
although most obviously in the author, producer and leading
vocalist, our sister; whilst the servants and anyone invited from
the village were so glad of a chance to sit down and stop working
for an hour or so that they would probably have heartily
applauded a recitation from the London telephone directory, with
or without music.

The stage for those events was the end of the drawing-room
farthest from the door and nearest to the piano. It would not have
been possible to rig up a curtain without driving nails into the
eighteenth-century panelling, so we were early pioneers of the
open stage. Wings, or spaces at the side for concealment of those
not 'on', and of the piano and Mrs Cox, were achieved with
screens. In those days of draughty houses, before central heating
and double glazing had become commonplace, there were a
number of screens about, mostly in bedrooms; rather dull
threefold screens covered in green or blue stuff, I seem to
remember, except one which had a chinoiserie print of little red

figures performing acrobatics against a black background which, put beside my bed in the night-nursery so that I should not see Old Nanny dressing, gave me nightmares imagining what lay in the black void behind those figures so intently balancing in the middle air.

I was in charge of lighting, for which my ambitions were boundless, but I was constrained by the nature of our first electric-light plant to limit them severely. That plant, although efficient enough, could only stand so much load. If overloaded, the system simply cut out, plunging the whole house in darkness, and putting Amos Webb to fearful trouble getting it going again. That made whoever was responsible feel guilty since, if the overload happened at all late on a winter evening, Webb would be at home enjoying his rare leisure, and should not have been made to turn out of his warm house to fiddle with screwdrivers and find fuses by torchlight.

Alice, also, was a great improviser when it came to providing properties (swords, crowns, shields), or costumes, or chain-armour made of knitted strings painted silver. All such things came under the heading of 'handicrafts', and upon these the PNEU had very strong views. So, for Shakespearian excerpts, we cut out crowns from thin sheet brass, and attached to them jewels of faceted coloured glass backed with gilt, which could be bought at a theatrical supplier's and which were sewn to the brass with fine wire.

Handicrafts: I think that this word, with its suggestion of time usefully employed and satisfaction obtainable without any commanding technical skill, has gone out of currency in favour of 'crafts' pure and simple, so that nowadays we are invited to 'craft centres' and even see the word used as a verb, when something is presented to us as 'finely crafted by skilled workmen using traditional methods'. I suspect that the PNEU's (and our governesses') reverence for handicrafts stemmed from the late nineteenth-century revolt, amongst 'artistic' people, against the industrial world, so that hand-made, like home-baked, was to seem to guarantee a kind of integrity, wholeness, individuality unachievable by the machine.

As far as we children were concerned, the time spent in the schoolroom on handicrafts was, quite simply, great fun, whether it was painting jam-jars with sealing-wax dissolved in methylated spirit, which gave fine, clear colours, or fabricating wastepaper baskets from flexible wicker strands, a large flower-pot being used

97

as a former to provide the shape; or mats of dried rushes, coloured by nature a satisfactory yellow-green like my favourite toads.

As I have observed, my surroundings and Alastair's, in childhood, were under a strong feminine influence for most of the time. Although I rebelled against it often, and had dreams of solitude, that influence was in no way stultifying, almost excessively the reverse, in fact, being a perfect corruscation of energy, ingenuity, imagination, all sustained by moral, intellectual and aesthetic principles of the most admirable kind. Only, it all must sometimes have seemed to me rather too brisk, too strenuous, too open, and lacking perhaps in the sort of light and shade which appealed to my nature; and so, if nothing but bright thoughts and constructive intentions were to be the general order, I would create for myself some mystery, some dark corners to explore on my own, indulging a taste for melancholy and the more passionate, woeful or tragic aspects of the human condition as they came to me though books and poems.

Unlike Harold Nicolson, who clearly found his 'Miss Plimsoll' (in *Some People*) unsympathetic and rather ridiculous, and whatever impatience and even resentment we may have felt at the time, all four of us owed Miss Smeaton much in our approach to the world and its mysteries. For example, I have never ceased to be glad that I was taught, very early in life, to use my eyes on all sorts of natural phenomena, and I know from whom that teaching came. One element of the PNEU curriculum, for country-dwelling pupils, was the 'nature walk'. Those walks I enjoyed without qualification, licensing me as they did to pursue a favourite hobby of nosing about in fields and woods and hedgerows for birds' nests, the haunts of animals, and rare and astonishing flowers. When Professor (later Sir George) Clark, sometime Provost of Oriel, produced, at my father's request, his monograph *The Manor of Elsfield*★, he added two appendices, one by Johnnie on the local fauna, and one by Miss Smeaton on the flora. Her list of plants, all found and recorded by her within a radius of about five miles, contains more than three hundred specific names. As we went along together I learned from her to identify some of these, and was solemnly informed of the extreme rarity of the *female* Dog's Mercury. I wonder how many of her plants have survived the onslaughts of chemical farming. For instance, she lists eight separate varieties of orchis: Green Winged,

★ Privately printed by the OUP, 1927.

98

Marsh, Early Purple, Spotted, Butterfly, Frog, Bee and Pyramid-
al, most of which I myself have found at different times but might
now look for in vain.

I should like to quote from Johnnie's contribution which has a
flavour of its own. He records, from a conversation with our
predecessor, Herbert Parsons, that the last polecat was seen on the
place in 1881, and that the hobby nested for several years in
Pennywell before the wood was cut down; and 'an old farmer, Mr
John Greaves, who used to be at the Home Farm, remembered
that, when he came to Elsfield about 1840, the Kite was plentiful
and the Bittern not unknown'. Johnnie hardly needed to be taught
to use his eyes: a born naturalist, he had eyes for everything in
wild nature, and still has.

In all her educational activities Miss Smeaton had the full
support of our parents, who both liked her and respected the
quality of her mind. Particularly in the matter of using one's eyes,
of assessing, appreciating and comparing one's observations, she
and my mother were at one, but whereas Miss Smeaton's
instruction referred mostly to the natural world, my mother
encouraged me to be interested in architecture: houses, churches,
villages of Cotswold stone; in furniture, pictures, china, and
objects of art in general, and their human history. When I reached
an age to be really responsive to such teaching, and went with my
mother to visit houses in the county, she would always tell me
what to look for, whether it might be a feature of the house itself,
or of its history, or some item of its contents. Sometimes, if she
knew our host and hostess very well, she would ask that I be
allowed to examine something, a picture, say, which was a special
treasure, or a collection of books, and, seeing that it was she who
asked, the people concerned were usually glad to satisfy my
curiosity which, in someone unvouched for, they would have
found unacceptable.

Obviously such inculcations would have been useless had I not
had an innate feeling for all the things, from willow-wrens' nests
and badgers and orchises to Inigo Jones gateways and *famille rose*
china, which were displayed to my young eyes; but such feeling
was really only the expression of an eagerness to embrace the
physical world in all its variety, and those particular manifestations were the first to be found by myself or to be shown to me by
people of knowledge and educated taste. Left to myself, and given
certain temperamental needs and leanings, I should probably have
made such discoveries piecemeal, and over a long period, of my

own accord. As things were, I was off to a good start. One way and another, throughout a fairly stormy passage on this earth, the contemplation of the durable works of both men and nature has brought me good, not least because they asked nothing of me but that I should look and listen and accept whatever message they might seem to offer. Very often, finding contact with my fellow creatures either stultifying or abrading, I have been deeply grateful for something silent but eloquent — a picture, a piece of furniture, a spring cloudscape beyond an office window, a building seen from a rocking taxi on the way to a dire appointment — which, by the integrity of its statement, has compensated for the lack of that quality among the people with whom I was having to deal.

I should not go so far as to say that I was fond of Miss Smeaton: I was too much in awe of her for simple affection to be possible. She had a very noticing eye and a psychological perceptivity too acute for comfort. Yet I admired her for her many accomplishments, had great pleasure from some of her inventions and, as I have said, benefited largely from her guidance to the use, not only of my eyes but of my time.

Hers was a strong nature, and one extremely difficult to rattle, although each of us, at one time or another, tried hard to disconcert her. I have written of grass-snakes and of the pet one which Johnnie kept in a box. One day when Miss Smeaton was in bed recovering from flu — a rare occurrence since she seldom showed weakness of that kind — Johnnie and I had the idea of frightening her by introducing the grass-snake into her bedroom. Miss Smeaton never turned a hair. She cast a cold glance, first at the snake and then at us, and said: 'Take the poor thing away: you're only frightening it.'

When the time came for her to leave we believed ourselves jubilant and made many plans for a send-off which would show how pleased we were to see the last of her; but when the day came our bright schemes lost their lustre. We were abashed and rather sad, since we were not only saying goodbye to a good friend, but to a significant part of our childhood as well.

I think it worth recording, in favour of the PNEU system, that I went to my preparatory school at the age of nine with a fair grounding in Latin verbs, French grammar, English history and literature, and even, thanks to one of the periods in the weekly curriculum known as 'picture study', some familiarity with the names and best-known works of English, French, Dutch and

Italian painters of the past three centuries.

As to handwork, after the nursery ceased to be the lair of small children, it became a kind of studio workshop, where Alastair and I practised various techniques of art, chemistry and mechanics. Lino-cutting, wood-engraving, poster painting, mask-making — at all of these we tried our hands, but my principal interest lay in my model theatre, in which I could try out effects of décor and lighting, the permutations of the latter being something of which I could never grow tired. As to the dramatic use of model theatres, that is to say puppetry, I found puppets unhandy. I had not the skill to carve them for myself, and dolls of the right size for the stage were wrong for looks and lacked proper articulation. In any event it was then, as later, to be the technique of stage design and lighting which interested me most. I was prepared to leave the drama, the plot and its characters, to others, being quite content to lose myself in imagination within the scenic effects and the play of coloured light which I created.

The model theatre had its special appeal for me because of a fascination by the miniature, which I imagine that I shared with all children not wholly devoid of imagination. My forts and temples and funeral pyres in the garden, my toy armies and their battles, my dreams of model boats and trains more elaborate and technically advanced than my limited manual skill could ever encompass, all these were expressions of the need to reduce the huge, hectoring outside world to manageable proportions, to a state where I could be the controller instead of the controlled. Years later I was to be both cheered and amused to read of C.G.Jung★ constructing in his garden, at the age of thirty-seven and during a bad period of disorientation, a model village complete with church, as a means of establishing contact with his creative eleven-year-old self.

★ C.G. Jung, *Memories, Dreams, Reflections.*

8

RUMOURS OF WAR

My father was an intensely busy man: he had to be, I have described the somewhat complex edifice of our life at Elsfield, that life of family and employees interdepending which, although on no vast scale, was nevertheless expensive enough to maintain. Born without material fortune but having discovered, through his highly popular novels, a notable capacity for earning money, my father could never contemplate slackening his pace, since what, in human and practical terms, he had conjured into existence required perpetual financial support. Obviously, in those happier days for authors, he had been able to accumulate capital, which was managed for him by his capable lawyer brother, and although for many years, and in spite of continual ill-health, he made a sizeable income, he was never rich as other popular writers sometimes were. Had his poor health taken a bad, a really crippling turn, or had death overtaken him early, in the full flight of his writing career, his family's fortunes would have suffered a very serious blow.

It was a marvel that one man should take on so much, and accept each new burden so equably, and possess so profound and unshakeable a belief that, ill-health or no, he would always be able to do so; a marvel, too, that we his children accepted without question all the good things he brought to us, never pausing to consider the strain to which our sole provider was put. That fact reflects no credit on any of us but, since we were not wholly callous or self-seeking, must largely be put down to the extraordinary unquestioning confidence which our father was able to inspire.

He was, indeed, intensely and impressively busy for, quite apart from his writing, which he achieved with perfect regularity and apparent ease, he had straightforward business commitments demanding time and thought, not to mention the quantity of unpaid work of a charitable or academic nature. After 1925, when he entered Parliament as member for the Scottish Universities, he had the proceedings of numerous committees to attend to. In the early 1920s he was deputy chairman of Reuter's and until 1929, a director of Thomas Nelson and Sons, the publishers. It can be seen, therefore that his appearances at Elsfield were sometimes irregular. At first he went to London every day and, even if we scarcely saw him, since his return was usually after our unalterable bedtime, his presence in the house could be felt in a general heightening of atmosphere, a kind of pleased excitement.

After entering the House of Commons, he took to spending most of each week of the session in London, returning on Friday to use every available hour consideredly, unwastefully, on writing, looking over his property and, on long walks or other excursions, seeing something of his family. In the evenings, if no visitor was staying in the house, or come to dinner, he would sometimes read aloud from a work in progress or just punctually completed. I remember how in the earliest days, when garden and woodland were being pulled round from the effects of recent war, he was much occupied — all of us helping to the best of our capacities — at work in the Crow Wood, clearing and felling, and in the garden supervising the planting of beds and the re-laying of turf. As time went on, and the claims of the outside world and of his blossoming career became ever more insistent, he devoted his rare hours of leisure to long walks, which he found good for planning his books, and an increasingly heavy schedule of writing on the historical works which he hoped would be his true literary monument; none of which prevented him from producing, at least once a year, one of the novels for which a faithful public was always eager, and the profits from which were so essential to the upkeep of his private world.

The only times when we really saw much of our father were in the family holidays, which were taken each summer, first at Broughton, then for two years running in the Isle of Mull, and later at Ffrwdgrech, near Brecon, in the Welsh marches. Those were strenuous holidays, with much fishing, shooting, riding and many long, challenging hill-walks. Something strongly masculine was thus brought into our lives, and for that we were grateful, being, as I have indicated, generally somewhat overwhelmed by a very positive feminine influence. Johnnie, the first to be sent out into a strictly masculine world, must have feared a developing namby-pambiness in his two young brothers for, in the earliest days during our holidays he saw to it that we had a full programme of athletics — hurdling, sprinting, and high-jumping

103

on the terrace, undertaken in a highly competitive spirit — or long
excursions into the woods, or the depths of Otmoor, looking for
birds and their nests, or tagging along with our airguns while he
went ahead with his first sporting gun. He taught us a lot about
guns, and much about gunmen, having a strong romantic
attachment to the histories of violent men, from Jesse James and
Billy the Kid to such contemporary practitioners as Babyface
Nelson and Dutch Schultz. As we grew older, the games which he
devised for us became more and more exciting. Having learnt that
old gamekeepers' remedy against poachers of the milder kind, a
shotgun cartridge in which salt was substituted for the lead shot,
he introduced this to liven us up. It would make any policeman's
hair stand on end to know that long-barrelled pistols firing .22
rounds could, in those days be bought without a licence. They
were made in Belgium, and were very cheap. Of these we
possessed one example. I had my .410, Johnnie his twelve-bore.
The salt technique was applied to the various cartridges and war
was declared, there being only one strict stipulation, that no shot
should be fired above the knee. We also used airguns, and air
pistols for the same purpose. According to the shifting alliances
between the three brothers, either we stalked each other separate-
ly, or two of us would combine against the third. Ambuscade was
usually the aim.

Sometimes, returning dreamily on my bicycle from a summer
afternoon's ride visiting such favourite places as Noke Wood or
Woodeaton Church, and quite forgetful of the dangers I might
expect at home, I would receive a well-directed blast at my bare
legs from two villains hidden in the elder-bush which grew
outside the grooms' room windows and overhung the road.

By the time I first went to school, the Great War would have been
nine or ten years in the past. All over Europe and America those
who had fought and survived had tried, with varying degrees of
desperation, to forget its miseries, and either to construct a future
as little like the immediate past as possible, or to re-create the
pre-war past in all possible details, or to drown memory in the
oblivion of drink or overwork. We played our games of siege and
ambush, set out our lead soldiers in exciting battles which were
chiefly satisfactory, perhaps, because death on the battlefield was
only temporary: recumbent soldiers could be stood up straight
and made to fight another day. We knew of war (our elders had
seen to this), only what was gallant and glorious. Older people

were not to be blamed for this deception, thinking, I am sure, that no good purpose would be served by sharing with us their nightmares, giving us too early an insight into human baseness and folly, or death in its more horrifying aspects.

Those who lived around us in the country were trying with all their might to settle life back into a remembered pattern, to revive social and communal events, traditions and duties while at the same time remembering the young men who had gone away to war so uncomplainingly, never to return. Throughout the land public tribute was paid to them in war memorials and memorial halls, tablets in churches, and commemorations of all kinds. That done, it was generally felt that life must go on.

Looking over the time between my birth and the year in which I am writing, one theme more than any other asserts itself again and again, and with a kind of rhythm, and that theme is War. Like a recurring thread of sharply different colour in a patterned stuff, or more, perhaps, like the outcropping of granite rock in a green valley, reminding the spectator of the harsh substratum upon which a delectable landscape may rest, war and its references were constantly present throughout my growing up until, once more, they became facts of life and death. It was perfectly possible, of course, to forget all about warfare for long stretches at a time, especially for the very young but, by the early 1930s, anxiety about another war was affecting even such self-centred and unpolitical adolescents as myself.

By the year 1925, the year in which I went to the Dragon School at Oxford, the Great War had been over for nine years. The Treaty of Versailles was six years old that June (in terms of the Second World War comparable, perhaps, to going to school in 1954, also, like 1925, for many people a season of some hope).

Certain reminders and legends of wartime were to be found at school. One master had half his face hollowed and scarred by shrapnel and one sightless eye; another limped from a wounded leg. One old boy had won the VC. For reasons which may have been particular rather than general at that date we were still made to eat dried egg. Even at a distance of nearly a decade the war came very close to us on Armistice Day, when we clustered round the school's war memorial, which stood at the far end of the playing-fields, above the Cherwell river. At that time no one would have dreamed of shifting the date of the ceremony away from 11 November, as has since happened, to suit anyone's convenience; the two minutes' silence was observed with a solemnity which even a nine-year-old could tell was deeply felt; for not only had the grown-ups family tragedies, or personal experience of horror, to recall, but many boys had lost a father or some close relation in the conflict. We sang: 'O valiant hearts, who to your glory came', and someone spoke Binyon's lines: 'They shall not grow old as we that are left grow old...', but none of us had any thought of growing old, and death in action had no more reality for us than some old print we had seen of stiff, shakoed soldiers falling backwards, looking surprised, at Austerlitz or Waterloo.

There were many and various reminders of the late war in the house at Elsfield; as there were in our elders' conversation, and in our father's writings. There hung in the hall, to the left of the front door as you entered, a strange picture which was not wholly a picture, being partly a map. Incised on a panel of yellow wood it showed, in black silhouette, a French château where Haig had had his headquarters, with black lines raying from it to various points of the compass indicating the chain of command to the divisions of his army, and the names and locations of villages and towns between. My father had spent part of his time in France on Haig's staff, and this production had been given to him as a souvenir of that service.

During his visits to France, which were frequent from 1915 to 1917, he also saw much of, and greatly admired, the French army commanders. I do not know where he acquired them, but he possessed portraits, good coloured reproductions of oil paintings, of the French Marshals Foch, Joffre and Mangin, and these were given a place in the library, not hung, because the books allowed no wall-space, but standing on a broad shelf above the lowest ranks of books on one side of the room, alongside a signed copy of Sargent's portrait of Field-Marshal Haig. When he took up his work as Director of Information in 1917 my father saw at once the value of pictorial representation of wartime events and situations, and was responsible for recruiting a distinguished team of war artists, and for the use of film cameras actually on the battlefield. One of his war artists was Eric Kennington, and a number of reproductions of the latter's work — including *The Kensingtons at Laventie* — were hung in the nursery passage and in other parts of the house wherever space could be found. My father's difficulty with pictures was that he cared for them chiefly for their associations, and so was unhappy not to be able to find room for them, even where space was at a premium. Hence the overflow of

Kenningtons into the nursery quarters.

There were solid souvenirs as well, such as must have brought their grim associations into many British homes: a German bayonet, a gunmetal watch half-smashed by a bullet, a pair of Zeiss binoculars taken from a dead German officer. One day, from I do not know where, my father produced an electric signalling lamp, with three lenses, red, green and white, a number of port-fires and one heavy flare with a wooden handle, all which he gave to Johnnie and me. Obsolete they might be, but the port-fires still worked, burning with dark smoke and vivid flame for a long time. Of the big flare we made a bomb, by adding to its ingredients a few more, such as sulphur and charcoal and sodium chlorate. When we detonated this with some ceremony and many precautions, it went off with a pneumatic thump rather than a bang. It was as well that we did not know enough to confine its explosion properly, or worse than flame and smoke might have eventuated.

For some years, in my early childhood, and until, I suppose, the things fell to pieces, one or two men in the village continued to wear their army boots and brass-buttoned tunics when they worked on their allotments. Clothing on a narrow budget was too great an item for anything to be lightly discarded. I think that such young men of the village as went to war — and they were not many since the age level there in 1914 was high — joined the county foot regiment, the Oxford and Bucks. In other places grooms and stable-boys and huntsmen, all those who worked with horses, probably joined the Oxfordshire Yeomanry, as did their young employers. Elsfield was not a horsey village. Farm animals apart, on which children were sometimes allowed a ride, the only riding horses were my father's Alan Breck, a sober creature, once a US Army charger, our ponies and the big chestnut from which Farmer Watts, wearing a high-crowned bowler hat, surveyed his land.

Those men who, I imagine, had set off to the war with such excitement, such hopes of a swift and glorious conclusion, must have shared with my father a vast disillusion, the sense of a security lost and irrecoverable, which was that war's chief legacy to those who had had a part in it. Into the enthusiasm with which so many young men, in 1914, greeted the declaration of war against Germany, I was given an insight at a later date. Brian Fairfax-Lucy, who married my sister in 1933, had gone straight from Eton into the Cameron Highlanders and so, as a very young subaltern, to France where he was severely wounded. He had been brought up at a great house in Warwickshire, Charlecote Park, and had a clear recollection of the effect of war on the young men who worked in the house or on the estate. To a man, he told me, they were jubilant, quite simply delighted at the chance to escape from a rigid traditional routine, an established hierarchy in which a footman, or groom, or under-keeper had only the slenderest chance of significant advancement in life. War meant to them adventure, excitement, travel abroad, a break with family ties and heavy convention, perhaps even a change of fortune, above all change, and a chance to see the world.

At first the war was a very recent fact not easily set aside. Bereavement had struck both my parents, in the loss of friends loved and enormously admired, all representative of the very best in their world — gallant, funny, poetic, unconventional, high-minded, high-spirited, honourable, they had gone down into the dust of deserts or the mud of Flanders, leaving what seemed unfillable gaps. Of these, on my mother's side, were the two pairs of Grenfell twins, cousins to one another, Julian and Billy, Francis and Riversdale, and her favourite cousin, Jack Stuart-Wortley. My father had lost nearly every one of the Oxford companions to whom he had been so deeply devoted, among them Raymond Asquith, Bron Lucas, Auberon Herbert, besides his dearest friend and fellow-publisher, Tommy Nelson. For them he wrote and had privately printed a volume of brief memoirs, *These for Remembrance*. Most tragically of all, his young brother Alastair, was killed at Arras, in 1917, aged twenty-one: 'Mhor' (the Great One), the lively and insouciant boy, adored by his whole family who, had he lived, might have done so much to lighten his mother's persistent gloom. My Scottish family's yearly visit preceded, for several years, a journey to France, to lay flowers on his grave.

To a child's ear, then, grown-up conversations must often have held a sombre, sorrowful note, a tone of bitter and unassuageable regret, which was profoundly disquieting. Worse, as one grew older, and perhaps quite unjustifiably, an idea might gain ground that, in parental eyes, the best had gone for ever, that the children growing up after the war would never be seen as anything but second best; that there was little hope of their equalling, let alone rivalling, the chivalrous, brilliant figures which had gone before.

War and its tragedy was one aspect of a weighty past, always present, very often in elegiac terms, which, although we should

have been shocked to find ourselves resentful of it, did keep
continually before us standards which sometimes seemed impossibly high. Idealism can be dangerous, when it parts company with
practical considerations and observable fact. Children, I believe,
have to learn to set their own sights. It is in no way wrong to
indicate to them the highest examples — of courage, say, or
selflessness or mental brilliance — but it ought never to be
suggested that should they not manage to match these, or that,
should they seek a set of different, not necessarily less worthy
standards to emulate, they would cease to be seriously considerable. Those true stories of splendid beings who had gone before,
lit from all sides by lights of affection and admiration and, with
time, increasingly romanticized, sometimes gave me a hollow
feeling of inadequacy.

An expression much used nowadays is 'culture shock', and this
might be taken to mean the unsettling effect of confrontation by
totally strange ways of thinking and acting, and wholly unfamiliar
people, in a hitherto unknown environment. If that is so then it
describes very well what I underwent at the age of nine on my first
acquaintance with a preparatory school, the Dragon School at
Oxford.

I have no right to claim any particular hardship in this respect.
Most children, I imagine, exiled from their families and the
familiarities of home and sent, at the age of eight or nine, to live
among strangers in somewhat spartan surroundings, must suffer
what I suffered in more or less degree. Only a raging extrovert, an
incorrigible competer, or a boy from an unhappy home might be
expected to modulate easily from the one set of circumstances to
the other.

The first shock came from the surroundings. Accustomed to
grey Cotswold stone I was unprepared for red brick. Although
brought up in a fairly large house I was intimidated by
institutional buldings much larger, more strictly utilitarian, and
certainly uglier than I was used to. As I have noted elsewhere I was
always to be greatly influenced by the architectural quality of my
surroundings. That first school, to my eye, was forbidding.
Buildings put up at the turn of the century seemed gaunt and
unfriendly, in some lights sinister. Only the playing fields,
guarded by tall trees and stretching to the willows by the Cherwell
river gave, tamed meadows that they were, a point of reference to
my favourite fields at home.

The school, now universally known as the Dragon School was, in my time, more generally referred to as Lynam's, from the name of the family which had founded and still managed it. Lynam's was considered advanced for its time. At all seasons we wore open-necked shirts over dark blue shorts, usually combined with a blue blazer which bore a heraldic dragon (actually a wyvern) on the top pocket. Discipline was definite but elastic; religious instruction generalized and unemphatic. The school was cautiously co-educational, with a handful of day-girls, daughters for the most part of members of the university. The catchment area for pupils was wide, and tended to supply rather unusually bright children, many coming from the families of academics at Oxford or other universities or from professional backgrounds.

I was not the only one to have an author for a father. Michael Carey's was to become well-known as a novelist, particularly for *The Horse's Mouth*; Tolkien's father invented the Hobbits; Crystal Herbert was a daughter of A.P.Herbert, then a very well-known writer. It should be mentioned that the teaching was first-class, and that the school's record of scholarships was probably second to none. Most of my contemporaries had been brought up with books, and quite wide reading was general. We were inclined to pride ourselves on our vocabulary, which we embellished continually with recondite words. All that suited me very well; only my instinct for non-cooperation made me refuse to take part in 'crazes' — for clubs, badges, cant phrases and so on — which from time to time swept through the school. My one exception was cigarette cards, then a staple interest of schoolboys, which I greatly enjoyed collecting.

Our backgrounds were highly varied. During my time at Lynam's there were two French boys at the school, two or three Americans, several from the Republic of Ireland. A number of boys had far-flung parents, serving the Empire as soldiers or administrators, or working abroad for international concerns. The school's reputation for intellectual distinction and progressive methods must have spread very widely and thus attracted particularly the sons of able and liberal-minded parents.

What the Dragon School was not was smart, in the accepted social sense of the time. Nowadays I have the impression that it has become very smart indeed, that it is pressed on from all sides by parents of every rank anxious to provide their children with the very best in preparatory school education. Conservative parents of my time may possibly have thought Lynam's cranky, insufficiently traditional in its ways. That has all changed, and whatever may have happened to other prep schools once thought the best, the Dragon School has reached an eminence which its founders may not, in their most sanguine moments, ever quite have envisaged.

Another element in my culture-shock lay in the sheer numbers of my fellow-pupils. Most of the better-known prep schools of the time confined themselves to fewer than a hundred boys. Lynam's had something like three hundred boys and girls, not all of whom, of course, were boarders. With the numbers went noise, impossible to escape, and a bewildering amount of movement, of shuttling, running, jostling, strolling to and fro. All that had to be accommodated together with the learning of a variety of different personalities amongst the boys, and a wary assessment of the masters in all their individual peculiarities. I, who had never had to deal at close quarters with more than a dozen or so strangers every year, now had twice as many to sort out, name, judge, attach myself to, propitiate, or try to avoid, every single day.

Early friendships entered into from sheer anxiety, the need of a buffer against the encircling mob, very often faded rather fast, to be replaced by something steadier based on a consonance of tastes. Of all the more or less enduring friendships made at that time only one has survived.

Of those schooldays, various frictions with school and school-fellows apart, I chiefly remember great heat and fierce cold. Those summers between 1925 and 1929 seem to have been, on the whole, brilliant: that, at least, is how I remember them. The winters were correspondingly cold. We shivered in our iron beds in the big dormitories, and trying to warm those beds with stone ginger-beer bottles filled with hot water did not help much, since the water from the bathroom taps was never very hot. On winter mornings we would inspect the ice in our tooth-mugs before being herded to leap, naked, into a lead-lined indoor pool of cold water known as The Plunge.

In spring the gardens of the Banbury Road and of all the polite suburban roads surrounding the school burst into clouds of blossom. Later the chestnuts came out all over the city and along the side of the playing-fields, which were soon baked yellow-brown by the sun. Outdoor swimming-pools were scarcely heard of in those days, and so we were taught to swim in the River Cherwell, which bounded the school grounds on their eastern side. That performance was penitential. Perhaps I am wrong

111

about the fineness of those summers, because I remember days of biting cold or pouring rain, when we were still required to jump — apprehensive, shivering, reluctant — into the river, held round the middle by a webbing belt attached to a pole held by a master on the bank. Nothing could have been better designed to put me off swimming for life.

All that I could say in favour of the Cherwell, green and sluggish where it passed the school, was that an upper reach of it ran half a mile below my home, a stretch of water with happy associations of fishing, botanizing, bird-watching and excursions by punt.

What I have written is no reflection on a truly excellent school. The truth is, simply, that some people are born schoolboys, and I was not one of them. I particularly resented organized games; not the games themselves so much as the organization. In winter, playing the two kinds of football sometimes gave me pleasure, even mild kudos, but I did not wish to play them every day. So I took to absenting myself, sometimes with an accomplice, to explore the City of Oxford and especially its museums. Occasionally I was caught and punished for doing this. Liberal in many ways as the school undoubtedly was, unilateral activities were not encouraged. (In one report it was said of my elder brother: 'He goes his own way. It is not a bad way but it is not our way.' That remark seems somehow to reflect credit on both parties.)

It was perhaps a good thing to be early inured to discomfort and communal living. When, in 1940, I joined the Royal Air Force as the lowliest kind of airman, many of my colleagues were from working-class homes where capable mothers had looked after their every comfort. Some of them made a great fuss about the rigours of barrack-room life, but not I. As far as I was concerned I was simply back at boarding-school.

9

TOO LITTLE LEARNING

Yesterday was Midsummer Day, and it turned out a sinister travesty of its traditional self. For most of the day it rained remorselessly from a sky of smudged charcoal, and a malign south-east wind tossed everything about in the garden, causing much breakage. It is small wonder that the weather should be a pre-eminent topic in England: its caprices seem, sometimes, of an unparalleled perversity, demanding comment and complaint. I cannot remember a worse 24th of June from all my recollection of spoilt summer occasions, ruined picnics, washed-out garden fêtes, holiday plans knocked endways by a vile inclemency.

One effect of a disappointing summer is to send memory harking back to better days. In 1929 I went to Eton, at the beginning of the summer half. (One of the first things to be learned about Eton College is that little in it resembles the customs or usages of the world outside. Thus 'half' is the Eton word for a term which, being one of three, is actually a third.) I arrived with my mother on a hot afternoon in early May. I said goodbye, almost tragically, to Amos Webb, as though I might never see him again, outside a gaunt, red house on the corner of Common Lane and Eton High Street, directly opposite the tall stone bulk of College Chapel. I was in a thoroughly strung-up state, a compound of anticipation, homesickness, curiosity and sheer terror, and ready at any moment to be unstrung. Together we inspected my room, my mother and I, and disposed about it such small things as we could carry up the almost vertical stairs. My heavy new trunk would, we were told, be brought up later by one of my Tutor's men.

My furniture, a wicker armchair with a cushion, upholstered in a dim cretonne, a tall bureau (which I must learn to call a 'burry'), a couple of hard chairs, a small table, and a box-ottoman covered in the same stuff as the armchair, was neither pleasing nor the reverse, but merely serviceable and hard-wearing. A dark carpet, some nondescript plain-coloured curtains, and a wholly

113

forgettable patterned wallpaper, gave a tired colour to the surroundings. The bed I discovered behind another curtain, folded
flat against the wall and hinged to the floor. There was a grate of
Victorian make in cast iron, with a shelf above it.

That room could have been said to lack character, or rather
possess a character identical to that of most other boys' rooms,
but, after dormitory life, to have a room all to oneself was
something of a wonder. The window looked out on the old dark
red brickwork of Upper School and the grey-white stones of the
chapel. In between ran the road, the main way between Windsor
and Slough and London, then comparatively uncluttered.

By a kindly dispensation new boys were invited to arrive before
the whole school reassembled so that I had some hours of
comparative peace in which to try and settle down before the
shock of the returning hordes. I was one of two new boys in the
house that half and when my mother and I, after losing our way
several times in that rabbit-warren of a house, finally came to rest
in Miss Byron's cheerful sitting-room, we were joined for tea by
my fellow-victim, Freddy Fermor-Hesketh.

Miss Byron, who was to be at Eton for many years, and to
become a celebrated Eton character, was in many ways well fitted
for her duties as a Dame. Her physical appearance was comforting. She was decidedly stout, with an open, humorous countenance, and a deep and hearty laugh with a wheeze in it which was
a constant subject for imitation by her charges. She was also
shrewd and kind, in a brisk and unmaternal way, and she ran my
Tutor's house with great efficiency. Almost anywhere else in the
scholastic world Miss Byron would have been known as Matron;
the title Dame referred to the days, about a century before, when
certain lodging houses for Etonians who were not Scholars — still
known as Oppidans — were kept by women who were known as
Dames. Norah Byron was of the poet's family, by a cadet branch.
I think, in those days, that it was still thought essential that Dames
should be dames, in the old sense, that is to say ladies. I would at
once learn to address Miss Byron as M'Dame, in the same way as I
should call Mr Lambart M'Tutor, and speak of his house as
M'Tutor's. Fortunately, thanks to Johnnie, I was already well up
in Eton lore, and so I arrived there knowing how to avoid the very
worst mistakes. Poor Johnnie: I may have envied him his position
as the eldest son, and the privileges which this brought him, but
the reverse of that medal was that he had to go quite alone into
unknown territory, and find his own way about a world of school

which gave him no more pleasure than it gave me. It was thanks to him that I went to both preparatory and public schools thoroughly primed with instructions for avoiding being danger-ously conspicuous.

Whatever manly resolutions I might have made, the moment of parting undid me. Later, my mother said: 'You cried when I left you, but I didn't!' She seemed to be proud of this. I had nothing to be proud of: the whole thing had been altogether too much, beginning with leaving Elsfield, then the fifty-mile drive, making conversation interspersed with pauses which, as we passed through Henley, and then Maidenhead, grew longer and more packed with gloomy speculation; the heart-lowering approach over Dorney Common, with Windsor Castle hanging in the middle distance, and the first sight of the newer houses, as ugly and forbidding in their utilitarian red brick as the buildings at Dragon School had been. Trees there were, and gardens, and playing fields with white goal-posts; nevertheless the effect was raw. As we turned into the narrower, older part of Common Lane, between high houses, there was a jumble of buildings to our right, one ecclesiastical, and some red-brick structures with tall windows which I was to know as Lower Chapel and the music and science schools. The apparently enormous extent of the place was awe-inspiring: even so, by the time that we reached Mr Lambart's house, we had seen less than half of it. I could not know at the time just how much trouble the scattered nature of the school's buildings would one day cause me; how often I should have to run, in something like panic, to cover the distance between two widely separated establishments, in danger of reprimand or punishment for being late.

I remember the summer of 1929 as especially beautiful; and that memory coupled with the fact that everything for once went well with me, both at work, which I found easy and appetizing, and in my first acquaintance with the River Thames, has left a sense of glow and satisfaction, never, I fear, to be achieved again. All was new, all a mixture of awe, pleasure and danger: awe before august antiquity, complex tradition, majesty of style; pleasure from a degree of freedom, even within an iron framework of restrictions, never experienced at my former school; danger from the possibility of retribution, often in the form of beating, which lay round every corner as the penalty for forgetting, ignoring or simply being unaware of some inflexible rule or time-hallowed

115

custom, or for committing some perhaps not quite specifiable offence against accepted form.

Outside my window was a long box, full of dry earth and the brown sticks of my predecessor's wallflowers. Here I put a Camembert cheese in its round wooden container to ripen in the summer heat. Purchase of the Camembert was a suggestion of Lyulph Stanley who, much more sophisticated than I, soon introduced me to several new aspects of good living. Even the names of exotic cheeses, apart from some antique jokes about Gorgonzola, had not come my way. The Camembert was something new. One day, when thought ripe enough, it would appear on the tea-table in flattened shape, its crust no longer holding the creamy ooze in place, and smelling extremely strong. Foie gras was another introduction of Lyulph's, and I think that we must have clubbed together to buy it, for, although nowhere near so expensive, even relatively, as it is now, it cost more than could be managed on pocket-money of five shillings a week. Boys in the house messed together, normally to the number of four, and, although a full half ahead of us in his experience of Eton, Lyulph graciously allowed Freddy Hesketh and myself to mess with him. And so, amongst the many new prospects opened to me that summer, there was a vastly increased interest in food. At my prep school meals had been regular, rarely interesting, and impossible to supplement in any substantial way. The fierce hunger of schoolboys was stayed, but never completely, by what the school tuck-shop had to offer, and that was only open for a short while every day.

We seem to have spent a great deal of time at my public school in eating. Lavish teas, or teas as lavish as funds would allow, were part of the traditions of the place. In the two tall houses successively occupied by Mr Lambart's young gentlemen, the individual rooms were arranged on either side of long corridors. Between doors, on one side of that corridor which I best remember, there stood a row of large gas stoves, which from an early hour in the evening, after school or games, were in hectic use for the cooking of sausages, bacon, eggs and for the reheating of food sent in from the town. Amongst the advantages never mentioned to parents in any prospectus was a rough training in cookery. Lower Boys — that is to say those in Lower School, which naturally included new boys like Freddy Hesketh and myself — were liable to fagging in two sorts: firstly, we were attached to some senior boy, a member of the Library, as a kind of

116

personal servant, with the likelihood that we should also have to help fag for that person's mess. Hence the need for a crash course in cooking, since anything might be demanded of one, from scrambling eggs to grilling ham to uncovering and serving any roast game which might have come up, still warm (but only just) from Rowland's, with its concomitants of potato chips, bread sauce and gravy, all of which would need reheating. In the event, my early cooking experiments with Johnnie on Beckley Common served me fairly well. On a winter evening, following an afternoon of cold and wind on the football field playing violent games in driving rain, everybody was ravenous. The scene in the corridor was positively infernal, with the gas roaring away, and desperate fags fighting to get their masters' food cooked, in hot competition with various 'uppers' intent on satisfying their own hunger in the shortest possible time.

For a while I fagged for four people who, I must recall with gratitude, were extraordinarily kind and forbearing, even when I burned their sausages or scrambled their eggs to damp flannel. Officially I belonged to Bernard Fergusson* and the messing took place in his large study. He and his friends had (and deserved) my sincere respect, for their good nature, good manners, and an apparently easygoing attitude to life which, I could see even then, disguised great ability and which was most restful to contemplate. Bernard, as a fellow Scotsman, and a Borderer as well, took a kindly interest in me. He frequently asked me questions about my religious views, since we both belonged to the Church of Scotland, but got, I fear, only the vaguest of answers. He was very tall, with a lightly worn but definite air of authority which would intensify later, when as General Wingate's chief of staff, he would go through that amazing campaign in Burma, wearing an eyeglass, replacements for which would be the subject of special air drops from time to time. All that, and a difficult time with his regiment, the Black Watch, in the Palestine of 1948, together with his appointment as Governor-General of New Zealand, and his marriage to my delightful cousin, Laura Grenfell, Aunt Hilda's youngest daughter, lay concealed in the future. In the meantime Bernard composed very funny light verse, and generally managed to maintain as light a touch in all his dealings. He and his friends all seemed singularly mature. Like some Etonians of the eighteenth century, they might have decided to grace the school with

★ Later Lord Ballantrae (1911–80).

their presence, bringing with them clear-cut attitudes, an elegantly ironical demeanour, as though it were they who were conferring distinction on the school, rather than the other way about.

The word 'fagging' and the practice it describes go back a long way and have a possible connection with the word 'fatigue'. People outside the schools which allowed the fagging system used to rise up from time to time, to condemn it as out-of-date, barbarous, feudal, undemocratic, and much else besides. Once in a while there was talk of 'fag suicides'. I have to say that my friends and I took it fairly calmly. More tiresome than having to tidy a senior's room and cook his tea were the calls for 'boy', which could be heard at almost any time of day up until the evening closure of the house, known as 'lock-up', and which obliged any Lower Boy who heard them to scamper up or down a lot of stairs, to form a line (if there were several respondents) and try to avoid being last in it. The latest comer was given the commission, whatever it might be: to carry a note, perhaps, to someone in another house, or hurry to buy something at the shops. To shirk a call of 'boy' and be discovered, was a certain road to a beating.

The King's College of Our Lady of Eton beside Windsor, founded by Henry VI in 1440, bore on its shield, in addition to the English leopard and the fleur de lys of France, three lilies, couped proper and, below, for motto, 'Floreat Etona' — let Eton flourish. An ideal of purity was thus established under the symbols of regal power. Throughout the older buildings of the school austere aspirations could be sensed, from the splendid soarings of Lupton's Tower, to the stony, pale perpendiculars of College Chapel, itself a model perhaps, a preliminary maquette, for the airy magnificence of the Founder's later achievement at King's College, Cambridge. At every turn, and in many subtle ways, boys were reminded that much was expected of them; that each step they took on pavement or playing field covered some illustrious footprint from the past.

I have written of my tendency to be influenced, happily or otherwise, by buildings and their arrangement; and by gardens, parks and natural features in relation to them. For me, therefore, even at my darkest moments, there could usually be some solace to be found in a happy conjunction of old bricks and grey stone, the vivid green of a field running up to the dark red-brown of a Tudor wall, the massing of huge leaf-laden trees, the glint of the river through fruit blossom in spring.

One of the bedrooms at Number 30 Upper Grosvenor Street. Built in the mid-eighteenth century by Sir Thomas Grosvenor as part of his Mayfair estate, the house was sold with Grosvenor House in 1929, to a developer erecting an hotel.

The front drawing-room of Number 30. To the right is a painting by Sir Edward Burne-Jones, 'Hill Fairies', which my grandfather bought at the sale following the artist's death in 1898.

At the age of four, not long after our move to Elsfield, 'a compact and sunny small boy'. Watercolour by Charles Gere, RA.

With my younger brother, Alastair (*left*), and an early toy motor-car. We are playing in the road at Elsfield, something that would be too dangerous today, for the tiny lane now bears an indecent amount of traffic.

My elder brother, Johnnie, aged about thirteen, in full rig for the Eton and Harrow Match, with Alastair, then about six.

Elsfield Manor (*above*). Part Jacobean, with eighteenth-century additions, and part Victorian, it provided the frame and setting for much that was formative in our lives. The entrance hall (*below left*), looking through to the drawing room. What remains of the Temple (*below right*), one of the conceits of the scholar and cleric Francis Wise, and where he and his friends – including Samuel Johnson – used to sit.

An appreciation of photography as an art was not one of Uncle Walter's many excellent qualities, in spite of his ownership of an expensive and complicated camera. This, taken in 1924, is one of his more successful family groups – all serious and none actually scowling. *From left to right*: JB, Alice, Alastair (in front), Johnnie, our mother, and me.

My grandfather, the Reverend John Buchan, with his wife Helen – the girl whose cascade of bright gold hair struck to his romantic heart – and John and Anna in about 1879.

William Henderson Buchan (1880–1912) – my Uncle Willie. A rising star in the Indian Civil Service, he contracted some undiagnosed disease in India and died in a Glasgow nursing home while on leave. His bearer wrote to Anna: 'Further I beg to pray that there will not be in the world such a master as my master was'.

J·WALTER·BUCHAN

My aunt, Anna Buchan, as the popular novelist O. Douglas, looking, as she self-deprecatingly put it, 'like a sly hen'. A highly popular writer in her time, especially in Scotland, she depicted traditional virtues and quiet living. Her admirers, from all over the world, included, to her surprise, the toughest of men.

Uncle Walter's bookplate (*above*). In it Walter Buchan is represented as a medieval scholar seated at a desk studying a parchment; the likeness is very good. The end of the bench is decorated with the Buchan crest of a sunflower, while the scroll bears the family motto.

The Stuart-Wortley sisters in the late 1860s, my grandmother and great-aunts. *From left to right*: Aunt Mary Lovelace (Mamie); Aunt Margaret Talbot (Margie); Aunt Blanche Firebrace; Caroline (Tin), my grandmother; and Aunt Katharine Lyttelton.

'The English Milord' – Robert, 1st Lord Ebury (1801–93). Pictures of him in later life make him appear stern and extremely serious, yet in his youth he had been the life and soul of many parties, and was known to his family as 'Reveller Bob'.

The lime avenue at Moor Park, the home of Lord Ebury. The figures are those of the Hon. Victoria and the Hon. Albertine Grosvenor, goddaughters respectively of the Queen and the Prince Consort.

Great-Aunt Margaret, the Hon. Lady Talbot. She was a celebrated beauty, although perhaps not in today's fashion; it was a beauty of a high-bred, now antique kind, her profile hawk-like, in repose severe, belying her gentle, humorous nature.

Lord Wentworth (Byron's grandson, and later Earl of Lovelace), on honeymoon in Florence with his wife Mary Stuart-Wortley (my Great-Aunt Mamie). No one would have dreamed of calling her eccentric, for her actions and pronouncements followed a personal logic of a consistent, if uncompromising, kind.

My grandfather, the Hon. Norman Grosvenor, with his daughters Margaret (Aunt Marnie – foreground) and Susan (my mother), on a bicycle tour of Brittany in 1896.

My grandmother, Caroline Grosvenor, known as Tin, in the late 1870s.

One of my godfathers, Brigadier-General Cecil Rawling, CMG, CIE; a soldier and explorer, he discovered the source of the Brahmaputra river, and planned an attempt on Everest with John Buchan. I never really knew him, for he was killed in action in France a year after I was born, but I revered his memory for having left me a 16-bore Westley-Richards, a greenheart trout rod, and a silver cup he had won at polo.

Adolescent attitudes – myself at seventeen (*above left*), and aged twenty (*above right*).

Michael Asquith, grandson of the Liberal Prime Minister Herbert Asquith, and a close friend of mine at Oxford. Tall and strong, with a clear-cut profile and auburn hair in unruly waves, he walked very fast, with his head thrust forward as though it were trying to reach a destination before the rest of him.

The lost view of Oxford: as serene and eye-catching as a celestial city in the background of an Italian primitive. John Buchan's bookplate by E. H. New, 1926.

My father, by now Lord Tweedsmuir, in Canada, probably in 1936. One of the rare informal photographs of him as Governor-General, in one of the few private moments he managed to make for himself.

My mother, from a portrait by John Morley that now hangs in Government House in Ottawa, and painted when she was well into her long years of widowhood.

Johnnie in court dress for a levée in London, a photograph by the late Francis (Franzi) Goodman.

The garden front of Casa Brewster, once the monastery of San Francesco da Paola, on the slopes of Bellosguardo, above Florence.

In Florence, 1938: a self-portrait, the anxious expression because of the timing device on the camera. This was, in fact, one period of my life which was in every respect golden.

The mysterious villa in the hills above San Francesco. I could not have imagined a villa so original, so entirely satisfactory.

Stir and glitter – an olive grove I photographed in Palestine during the war.

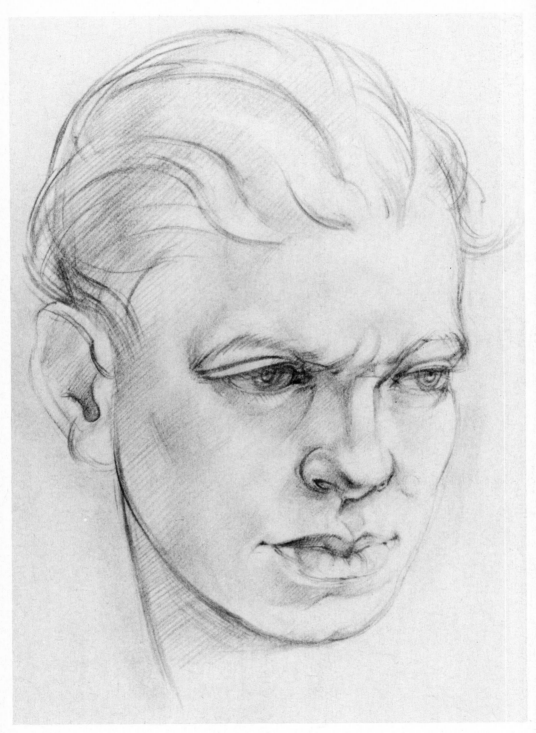

At the age of twenty-three: a drawing by Leonard Huskinson. I have always thought that the drawing makes it clear that the artist did not much care for his subject.

The strangeness of it all! In the early days of my first half I was brought up short again and again by something, some sight or sound or simply emanation which had no parallel in my experience. My prep school had been rather consciously democratic, undenominational, breezy and up-to-date. Nothing there had prepared me for such astonishing flourishes, not only of architecture and dress and hieratic formality, but of personality itself in both masters and boys.

The school lay, not exactly in the shadow, but for ever under the eye of Windsor Castle. There was, at all times a strong, if deeply respectful and never alluded to, sense of a bond with the family for which the castle was sometimes home. Eton had received much favour at the hands of George III, who had had a special affection for the place. At his death in 1820 the school went into deep mourning — and stayed there. Hence the uniform of black clothes and silk hats still, in my day, narrowly prescribed and rigidly adhered to. If I had been tall for my age which, at thirteen, I was not, I should have been put into 'tails', the classical morning coat, worn with striped trousers, which I still find myself wearing, occasionally, for funerals and weddings. Those not thought tall enough had to wear what was known throughout the land, and not only to Etonians, as an Eton suit. This consisted of a short jacket which stopped at the base of the spine and so was known, naturally enough, as a bum-freezer; below came striped trousers which were generally a rather tight fit. (My mother was much amused when the tailor fitting me for those trousers remarked approvingly 'very snug!'.) Above the jacket, and overlapping its collar, was another turned-down collar, six inches wide, of starched and shiny linen. The ensemble was completed by a black waistcoat, a white shirt, and a black tie, and crowned with the gleaming cylinder of a top-hat. All this gave an oddly peg-top effect to the appearance of any but the stoutest small boys, particularly if, like myself, they had rather large heads and, consequently, hats which were noticeably out of proportion.

In a kind of perpetual royal mourning we might be, but there were changes to be rung, all of them connected with prowess of one kind and another, either athletic or intellectual. Meanwhile my eyes soon became accustomed to the surely very unusual spectacle of hundreds of young people, aged roughly between thirteen and nineteen, moving purposefully among the college buildings, or up and down Eton High Street, each in some way wearing his uniform with a difference, either, at one extreme,

with a self-conscious elegance, a careful gloss, or at the other a
squalid untidiness, with crumpled collar, stained waistcoat,
cracked shoes and a hat much creased and battered, its silk rubbed
all the wrong way. Too great scruffiness, if persisted in after
warnings, could lead to punishment, sometimes severe; I never
heard of an extreme of dandyism being similarly rebuked.

Eton's special relationship with royalty was given prominence
once a year when King George V and Queen Mary came to
Sunday morning service in College Chapel. They came attended
by equerries and ladies-in-waiting and their visit was preceded by
that of two enormous detectives, correctly dressed in morning
clothes with top-hats and spats. We thought rather comical their
ferreting about under the stalls at the west end of the chapel where
the royal party would sit beside the Provost. Later events have
made such precautions routine, and no longer the least bit
amusing. We should have remembered that the street in Eton, just
outside the chapel, had been the scene of a serious attempt on
Queen Victoria's life. A man with a pistol had fired shots (which
missed their mark) and had been swiftly overpowered by the
Etonians lining the route.

At a certain point in his progress up the school a boy would
graduate from Lower Chapel, the uninteresting architectural
exercise by Sir Arthur Blomfield which I had noticed as we drove
into Common Lane on my first day. He would then attend a
morning service each day, and two services on Sunday, in Henry
VI's lovely building, whose soaring stones could give, if anything
could, some notion of spiritual aspiration to even the crassest of
boys. There the magnificent organ was played by Dr Ley,
sometime President of the Royal College of Organists, who, as
Precentor, supervised all musical teaching or performances at the
school. To hear him play was to gain a good grounding in the
more interesting church music, particularly Bach. Dr Ley was a
delightful man, full of humour. How he managed to play as he
did, with one lame leg, when so much of organ-playing is
pedal-work, I do not know. The school maintained a professional
choir, and a long-established choir school for its training. Of the
anthems so beautifully performed I remember best 'Jesus Joy of
Man's Desiring', then much less often heard than it is today, and
S.S. Wesley's 'Love one another with a pure heart fervently',
which had its special appeal, naturally, since I was so much beset
with the need to love, and could give the anthem, perhaps, a

personal interpretation. I was not alone, I should add, in being obsessed by love. Many of us passed a good deal of our time thinking about it, aspiring to it, falling in and out of it; sometimes a young face of great beauty could be studied in chapel, become the subject of a kind of idealization, more protective than passionate even at that age of fast-developing sexuality, and anyway impossible of approach, because school-life was organized, by no means unintentionally, to prevent the development of tender feelings between growing boys.

Dr Ley had many musical treats up the sleeves of his voluminous gown. For example, once a year, a trumpeter would come down from the castle garrison and be stationed in the organ loft. As its anthem for that day the choir would sing 'Let the bright Seraphim in burning row...' and when they had sung '...their loud, uplifted angel trumpets blow', the trumpeter would repeat the phrase, his glorious notes of triumph swelling and filling that tall stone lily of a church.

A Victorian headmaster, on being asked what kind of product he expected from his teaching, is said to have replied: 'We aim to produce Christian men, since Christian boys is a contradiction in terms.' And so, to wean our lower natures subtly but purposefully away from their natural habitat, there were inspiring tapestries behind the high altar, designed by my grandfather's friend Edward Burne-Jones and woven at Merton Abbey, and in a corner, G.F. Watts's towering portrait of Sir Galahad, moustached and pensive, and giving, at least to me, not an impression of a sublime and steely virtue, but of a certain feebleness.

More intriguing were the frescos on the north wall of the chapel. Quite recently some canopied stalls, a later accretion, had been cleared away and Professor Tristram set to uncovering the *grisaille* paintings concealed beneath whitewash behind them. Not all Tristram's restorations have received equal praise, but these, I think, are successful. The young dandies, whose counterparts I should one day see in Florentine frescos, in their flower-pot hats, trunk hose and cod-pieces and their air of careless arrogance could be imagined as portraits of fifteenth-century members of 'Pop', the Eton society.

Everything about the College Chapel services was organized to the smallest detail, from the allotment of places, the checking of attendance (non-attendance for anything but an official reason would result in dreadful punishment), even to the provision of tickets for Sunday evensong to parents and other members of the

121

public. It was the Anglican church at its elegant best: fine diction, superb singing, everything ordered to obviate tiresome human vagaries; a little frosty perhaps, but splendidly disciplined, religion as theatre in a specifically English mode with as little 'audience participation' as possible. There was only one stumbling-block to perfection, and that lay in the personality of the Conduct, the school's resident chaplain. The Conduct of my earliest days, no doubt an excellent clergyman, was a notable wool-gatherer. On one occasion he upset decorum severely by turning to the east at the wrong moment in the service, and starting on the creed. 'I believe...' he intoned, then checked himself, said crossly and very loudly, 'Oh no, I don't...' and faced his front again. Light relief of that sort was a joy, the more so for its rarity. I do remember another joyful occasion when some visiting preacher had been carefully installed by the verger in the high, free-standing pulpit at the top of a winding stair, with its low door apparently bolted behind him. He was a powerful orator and all the more boring, we felt, for that. Ranting, particularly on religious matters, was not something of which we could approve. When he came to his peroration he waved his arms, thundering '*That*, boys is the thought with which I leave you today,' and threw himself back in the pulpit. Either the bolt was not home, or his weight simply tore it off, for he went spinning away down the stairs, wildly clutching at the rail to save himself; altogether a most enjoyable perform-ance, the thought of which remained with us for many days.

Our way into College Chapel was through the arcade below School Hall, and up a broad staircase to the ante-chapel at the western end. We did not use the north door, at the head of its precipitous steps, between the tall, slim buttresses which had been the inspiration and the first trial ground for the game of Eton Fives, one of the few games which I have ever greatly enjoyed playing. Along the wall of the arcade were carved the names of those old Etonians who had died in the Great War. Beyond them were names going back many years, of former members of the school, some famous enough to thrill by their familiarity. A gravelled space on the road side of the old school buildings was bounded by a low wall, known as Pop Wall, on which members of Pop would dispose themselves of a fine Sunday in all their magnificence. Unthinkable retribution would come to any non-member of Pop who should be rash enough even to lean for a moment, let alone sit, upon that wall.

On weekdays of reasonable weather, at eleven in the morning, the masters in their caps and gowns and white ties would meet, outside the chapel, for Chambers which, as the name implies, could also take place indoors. That was the moment for brief, pointed discussions between house-masters and others, and the chance perhaps of a word with the Headmaster himself. Bargains were made in respect of various pupils and their futures, favours claimed or offered, points raised, suggestions taken or scouted; a spectacle at once intriguing and alarming to those of us who walked by, for those black-robed figures had us in their power and, whilst some were benevolent, careful, far-seeing where their charges were concerned, others were spiteful, irrational, neurotic, soured by jealousy and ancient grudges, not really to be trusted at all. Standing taller than most of his colleagues, in black cassock and white bands or, sometimes, in the scarlet of a Royal chaplain, the Headmaster carried his own special isolation with him. The Reverend Cyril Argentine Alington, DD was a commanding figure, handsome, powerfully built, with an air somewhat disdainful, impressive beyond question, and seemingly none too easy of approach. Yet later, when I got him to do some work for a magazine that I was editing, I was to discover how much of openness, of kindness, and even of humility, that rather forbidding presence concealed. His wife, born Hester Lyttelton, was a distant relation of my mother's, which meant that we sometimes went to tea at the Headmaster's house; a superb tea if only I could have been left alone to enjoy it, but quite spoiled for me by too close proximity to one august and imposing person, even though Hester had the same wild and unpredictable sense of humour as her first cousin, my Aunt Hilda, and was kind and amusing, expert at putting small boys at their ease.

The education offered at Eton was probably as good as any to be had in the world at that time, for those who knew how to make the best use of it. Until the beginning of the nineteenth century the curriculum had been purely classical. With the scientific and industrial advances of that century much had been added, and certain subjects adopted into the general teaching which would once have been considered peripheral or eccentric. So, in addition to science schools (chemistry and physics), there was an engineering school, frequented by certain silent, concentrated boys who, presumably, already knew quite well what to do with their lives, and an art school near by.

123

Formal education apart, however, there were many other things to be learned at Eton. One of them was shopping. Going towards Windsor, which is separated from the town of Eton only by the river Thames, the school came to an end, with the last of the boys' houses and Messrs Spottiswoode's stationery and book shop which supplied everything required both for learning and for its rewards, from school books, pens, pencils and the special kinds of papers required for exercises, to books for prizes stamped in gold with the college arms. The High Street proper began on the Windsor side of Barnes Pool, an oblong pond crossed by an iron bridge. Just before that were the School Stores, still known to everyone by their original name of Rowland's. The School Stores was not only an eating place but also a shop for all manner of things from cricket bats to Swiss watches. That first summer it was at Rowland's that I ate my first strawberry mess. It was a simple enough confection, but wholly delicious: strawberries and cream, sugar and ice-cream all mashed together into a smooth pink mass. Hot food was also served at Rowland's and, when the season for game came round, boys who had had pheasants or partridges sent from home — and in those days they came through the post, unwrapped, unpilfered, with nothing but a label round their necks — would take them there for roasting, garnishing, and delivery to the 'slab', a wide shelf near the kitchen quarters, which was the appointed place for letters and parcels.

Throughout the whole of the High Street from Barnes Pool to the Thames, a distance of a quarter of a mile, there was no commerce which did not owe its principal custom, one way or another, to the school. There were seven tailors, three hosiers and hatters, a bootmaker, two hairdressers all, I think, with premises in London, another stationer, odd shops like grocers and ironmongers, and two teashops, one rather smarter and more expensive than the other, at which we had tea on a Sunday with our parents or other relations or family friends visiting the school who invited us out.

At this distance in time it is impossible to remember in detail those many excursions to the shops. Different people patronized different establishments. Inevitably, one learned a very particular attitude to shopping, at least where clothes were concerned. Very little was bought ready-made. All garments, from tail coats and black overcoats to the strange grey-flannel breeches, buckled at the knee, which were worn for football, or grey trousers for squash and fives, and shorts with padded seats for rowing, were made by hand. Shirts, too, were hand-made, as, for many people, were shoes. What it all amounted to was an introduction to an elegant tradition, a training in becoming consumers of the kind of goods and services to be found in the square mile bounded on the north by Oxford Street and by Pall Mall on the south. When I went to Canada in 1937, there were a number of stipulations about my wardrobe, so the London establishments of my Eton tailor and hosier furnished me with tail coats for day and evening, and stiff-fronted piqué evening shirts and quantities of hard, white collars.

It has been said shrewdly, if unkindly, that Eton is a school for the *fathers* of gentlemen. As I have indicated there are, or were, in addition to first-class instruction in the classics, history, literature, political philosophy, music, science, languages and much else, many influences, personal and atmospheric, teaching an elegant and authoritative approach to life. Many of my comrades were long-descended, quietly established on their land; many bore names and titles so resounding as to seem too heavy for the young shoulders of their bearers; many, on the other hand, were descendants of Victorian and Edwardian entrepreneurs, manufacturers, ironmasters who, once grown rich, had forsaken their former fields of action to enjoy a gentleman's existence behind park gates and had seen to it that their sons and grandsons should never have to soil their hands in industry or commerce, except as owners of mines or directors of shipping lines, breweries and banks. Towards the end of the nineteenth century Walter Bagehot was already pointing out the harm this tendency was doing to British industry, leaching away commercial brains and industrial energy to waste themselves in copying an aristocracy miraculously preserved by the very mines and railways beneath and above their land, for which the new-risen gentry had been responsible. Recently this thesis has begun to be stated again in the press with an accent of pained discovery, as though it were quite new.

The father might be a thruster, a vulgarian, a thug, or even something of a crook, but the soft, damp air of the Thames Valley, the severe and lofty surroundings, the authority of learning, plus his own adaptability and intelligent appreciation of the things which made for success in such a society, would soon make of the son a very fair copy of the accepted norm, so assimilated to it as to be unnoticeable. Obvious striving was considered bad form; indeed, a certain appearance of languor was part of the ethos of the place. For example, I soon learned not to say that I could not be 'fagged' to do something — slang of my prep school — but, instead, that I could not be *bored* to do it; and to call anyone too exclusively bent on study a 'sap' which, coming from 'sapiens', Latin for 'wise', meant the very opposite of the American term.

If I dwell on my first year at Eton, it is because, unusually, I remember it as brightly lit, untroubled, deeply interesting, even successful, one of those rare reaches of experience which come back to mind under the heading of happiness. Not until my stay in Florence nine years later was I to know another period as good. Which is not, of course, to say that there were no good times in between, even at school. Nor do I wish to be like the well-known dial and 'tell only the sunny hours'. It is simply that so much has been written, so much too much, in my opinion, about public schools and their disastrous effects, that I have no wish to add my packet to that pile, and in any event, Eton, or my part of it, hardly at all resembled the schools so fiercely dismembered in any of the well-known books on the subject. Finally, anything I may have suffered as adolescence took hold of me was partly attributable to physical misfortune, but chiefly to faults of my own. Writing elsewhere about Eton, I put this: 'To say that I was not entirely happy there is merely a note about myself, it is no reflection whatever on the school. I should not have been entirely happy in any school... I arrived at school in my thirteenth year, a compact rather sunny child; I had done well in the Common Entrance, and found my new work easy and agreeable. Apart from its size and strangeness, the truly terrifying mass of traditional rules and customs needing to be learned quickly on pain of a beating, and in spite of my feeling extremely small and newly hatched, Eton during my first half was fascinating rather than frightening...After my rather too enthusiastic start at school, the worst effects of adolescence set in. All the screws came loose. From being what I have described, a compact and sunny small boy, I lost all my positive qualities and, most particularly, the power to work.'

The above passage more or less sums up my difficulties, which were at their most acute during my fifteenth and sixteenth years: by the age of seventeen, although still exasperating my mentors and disappointing my wellwishers, I had sufficient experience to have begun to develop a kind of style. And, at almost all times, there was the solace of friendship. At the beginning, as is usual with young creatures thrown together in non-familiar circumstances, there were trials and errors, setting to partners, changes of allegiance, divergence of interests. It was of the nature of the place that friends could only be made of fellow-members of the same house, since friendship with boys in other houses was not encouraged and we were entirely forbidden their rooms: in any case, for reasons of timetables and the hour of 'lock-up' in the evening, external friendships were difficult to achieve on any relaxed basis.

Our parents, no doubt on good advice, had elected to send their three sons to different houses, so Johnnie went to Adie's, I to Lambart's, Alastair to Rowlatt's. Because of the gaps in our ages I had Johnnie at school with me for only one year, and Alastair for three. For all that we ever met, each of us might have been at a different school.

My best-remembered friendships at Lambart's were with Lyulph Stanley, John Gwyer, Christopher Beckett, Freddy Fermor-Hesketh and Maurice Cardiff. During my first half Maurice was, for some reason of health, absent from school. Like Lyulph he was a half ahead of Freddy and myself, and clearly had made his mark, for in his absence he was much spoken about. As often happens with young friendships, that one began with wariness, even turning to active hostility, only to steady down later into something truly reciprocal, creative and, to me, rewarding. Christopher Beckett's father was the Lord Grimthorpe who backed Nevil Shute in the foundation of his aircraft-building company, Airspeed. John Gwyer's was a clever, aloof and saturnine lawyer, at that time King's Proctor, later to be Treasury Solicitor, who lived apart from his wife. Maurice came from a county family with a place in Shropshire, and Freddy from another such in Northamptonshire, the wonderful house of Easton Neston, designed by Hawksmoor. Most of my contemporaries seemed to have difficult fathers, either remote and over-busy, or uncertain tempered, some because of continual pain from war-wounds, and nearly all from the permanent state of fury and frustration common to landowners in the inter-war years. By comparison my own father seemed a different kind of being: cleverer, swifter-moving, more humorous, and infinitely more approachable — when, that is, he was there to approach.

Once or twice in later years I would meet a man, usually a prosperous businessman, who would look at me with a jealous eye and say something like: 'I don't know where I wouldn't have got to by now if I'd had your advantages!' Since truth and reason are powerless against a self-flattering myth, I refrained from giving the answer on the tip of my tongue which would have been something like 'What you call my advantages, although real enough in themselves, were not conducive to the kind of worldly success that you have in mind. Suppose I had had your advantages, left school at fourteen, gone into life at the deep end, learned to bite, scratch, stab and compete with others, using any means, fair or foul, to get and keep my snout in the trough? *You* were never bothered by consideration of scruple or fair play or even letting ladies go first through doors. In your world strife was the key-note, and going one better the only law. With your advantages, and supposing I hadn't gone under at the first trial, I'd probably now be richer than you, at least in terms of cash.'

It is curious to contemplate the nature of our schooling and to realize that we were being given the very last of the old Imperial education. Explicitly, or by implication, we were being taught habits of thought, rules of conduct which would find their best application in service to some conception wider than our own immediate interest. Even at that late date, it was likely that those of us who had not great inheritances to manage would find our way into our country's service, not only the armed forces, but the Foreign Service, the Indian, Sudan, or Malay Civil, the Colonial Service, or some branch of the Government at home. It was possible that some boys would find an early death on the North-West Frontier, or in tribal Africa, and it was understood that the possibility of this would be accepted without question both by the parents and by the young men themselves. And of course, in the event of war we should have been expected to be among the first to go. (George Orwell, an old Etonian whose sense of fairness must greatly irritate his more radical admirers, writes somewhere of the upper classes that, if they sometimes let the country in for wars, they do at least fight in them.)

An illustration of what I have just stated was given by my brother Johnnie who, after leaving Oxford, joined the Colonial Service and, in 1933 went to Uganda as an Assistant District Commissioner. Nobody at home thought it strange that a young man of twenty-two, almost straight from university, should be put to dispense justice over an area of many hundred square miles, with no backing but a dozen African policemen, and at some distance from his immediate white superior; but that was how things were done, and effectively done, in those days. Uganda, in fact, very nearly claimed Johnnie's life, for he fell sick of amoebic dysentery so severely that he had, in the end, to be invalided home.

It would be unjust to my school friends not to give them credit for a (perhaps exasperated) sympathy with my frequent downfalls at work or embroilments with my masters; but they were, in more or less degree, subject to the same pressures, prey to the same world-filling youthful depressions. The one exception in respect of the latter was Freddy Hesketh who, physically strong and square-built, was morally of the same construction; he adopted a tough, common sense view of our lives which was both astringent and, beyond question, necessary.

For my first two years at Eton Mr Lambart's house held a pre-eminent position in both work and games. By the time that the seniors whom I first knew came to the end of their school careers, Lambart's had won just about every athletic contest worth winning. The long tables in the boys' dining-room were freighted with silver cups, some of great size and splendour. Much of that success was owed to Cecil Atkinson-Clark, a very fine all-round athlete, later to be killed in action. The intellectual side was upheld and illuminated by the captain of the house, Con O'Neil, who went on to a distinguished career in diplomacy, and the brilliant, delightful Jasper Ridley who would not survive the war.

It does not always happen that success at school continues into adult life. For some of those dazzling creatures strolling beautiful as butterflies in the pale blue coat of the Eleven, or the white edged with pale blue of the Eight, or striding along in the blue and scarlet colours of the Field — that most enjoyable football game, somewhere between Rugby and Association, which was an Eton speciality — their success in games, their membership of Pop, would represent a peak of achievement, a high point in their lives. Very often they would not be heard of again, whereas certain inky boys, of gallows mien and undistinguished record, would, a moment after leaving, blossom out with Rolls-Bentleys and beautiful girl-companions, for the reason that their parents were rich and indulgent. Money really never talked at school, but afterwards it was not slow in finding its voice.

Things were otherwise with Mr Lambart's senior boys. One or two had their careers dictated for them by history; the others made their way by ability alone. Thus Bowmont became a duke and Elcho an earl because that was their inheritance already set about with its own special duties and sanctions. Con O'Neil entered the Diplomatic Service and, after serving in the war, was twice an Ambassador and, finally, that most powerful figure, Under-Secretary at the Foreign Office. I have long ago forgiven him for beating me on several occasions, since he never, unlike some, seemed to enjoy the exercise. Martin Charteris, after war service, became a courtier, ending as Private Secretary to the Queen and, finally, on retirement, being appointed Provost of Eton, perhaps the first to be chosen for worldly rather than theological attainments. Martin Gilliatt is, at the time of writing, Comptroller of the Household to the Queen Mother. Certainly they were an impressive generation, and one almost impossible to follow with any degree of grace.

Houses at Eton were governed for the house-tutor by a body known as the Library. This was something of a misnomer, most Libraries being simply large studies, furnished with a table and some battered basket chairs and for reading matter a couple of detective stories and a magazine or two. After the golden age of Mr Lambart's house, things quietened down considerably. The excitement departed, leaving a rather dusty calm. By the time that Maurice Cardiff and I reached the Library, the house had ceased to be distinguished for anything in particular, except perhaps a sense of humour. We thought that we might try a different style altogether, make of our time at the head of the house a kind of silver age, relaxed, liberal-minded, unstrenuous, given over to cultivation of the arts. Our chief innovation, which had an entirely predictable result, was to abolish beating. Freed from fear the Lower Boys got thoroughly above themselves, rioting about the place like the mice in *The Tailor of Gloucester*. As good liberals we let it be understood that they might do pretty well what they liked, provided that our own reflective existence was not disturbed. We did not, however, abolish fagging, or the system of calling 'Boy!'. That would have been to subvert a strong tradition, which was not really our aim, whereas beating, we thought, was merely a bad habit.

Without becoming exactly a book-lined room the Library soon took on the looks of our own lairs. Books lay about the place. A wind-up gramophone was in use at all permissible hours, as together or singly we tried out our tastes in music. Sometimes, in spring time, we even bought flowers. Generally, our attitudes were somewhat *fin de siècle*. It has to be remembered that, although Oscar Wilde had died more than thirty years before, his scandal and his tragedy were part of the history of our parents' generation, and his name was still taboo to a lot of older people; yet his plays and other writings had survived him, as had many of his sayings. Accordingly he represented, where we were concerned, things which to admire or appear to emulate would greatly annoy most of our elders; and we were at the age to treat our elders like the back wall of a squash court, something against which to bat ideas, the more scandalous the better, just to test their effect.

Sex, and the consequences of unleashing its powers, were a constant anxiety to our parents' generation. (My own is far more concerned about drugs.) Great pains were taken at school to ensure that sexual congress between boys should be made next to impossible — dangerous as well, for it was one of the things, like stealing, or being caught at the races, which would entail instant expulsion. Our clever elders seemed to miss the point that, for the adventurous young, forbidden fruit has its attraction; but, indeed, they were not quite sane on the subject. For some — and I am thinking of one or two rather alarming survivals from the Victorian age — it may not have been so much a question of 'damning the vice to which they had no mind', as damning the vice to which, if they'd been able to admit it, their mind would have been much inclined. So, in our simple silliness, we made a cult of the nineties in their more equivocal aspects, and adopted fashions and mannerisms guaranteed to disquiet our mentors and, so to speak, keep them on their toes. One distinct and persistent cause of friction between myself and my elders had to do with hair. Looking around me nowadays and observing the heads of young and even middle-aged men sprouting fantastically into bushes, aureoles, manes, pony-tails, pigtails and beards, I can imagine the apoplexy which such sights would have produced, could my elders ever have seen them.

As part of a mildly rebellious attitude to adult conventions my school-friends and I attempted to grow our hair a trifle longer than the 'short back and sides', often slickly oiled, which had become traditional. Not only our masters objected to this, but our parents as well. My own father, no doubt already irritated by evidence of a slide into *fin de siècle* affectations on my part, made quite a severe fuss about my hair worn, then, no longer than I have it at present which is by today's standards short. The 1960s saw hair and its unbridled growth as a symbol of liberation from convention, and

131

doubtless my friends and I had much the same idea. The opposition we encountered surely stemmed from the furious popular reaction against Wilde and his circle and the consequent abomination of anything seemingly loose and unorthodox, even by people who truly revered the arts and those who practised them.

Meanwhile literature was our prime concern. We read a great deal and, far from confining our reading to the past, were consciously modernist in our researches, buying Geoffrey Grigson's periodical *New Verse*, and (with real excitement) the productions of Faber and Faber, the works of Eliot, Auden, Spender and Day Lewis, together with every word which Aldous Huxley had ever written. Reading Jean Cocteau's *Opium*, journal of a disintoxication, probably saved me from ever experimenting with narcotic drugs.

It had been a practice at Eton, for some years, for a group of literarily inclined boys to combine to produce, for the Fourth of June, a printed magazine which, since it would only appear once, was known as an 'ephemeral'. In due course Maurice and I decided to try our hand at such a thing. With our Tutor's somewhat anxious permission (for he knew that the enterprise would seriously interfere with our work) we set about the planning of our ephemeral, which duly appeared on 4 June 1933 under the title of *Masquerade*.

All through the Lent half, and into the summer one, and in the intervening holidays, we had an enjoyable time. For some reason we chose as printers the St Catherine's Press, then belonging to W.H. Smith, and I have the pleasantest recollection of visits, in the holidays, to their works in Southwark, and to receiving as much attention and valuable advice as though I had been founding a national review. The thing was to be paid for by advertisements, and so Maurice and I took ourselves to one or two advertising agencies. I best remember Crawford's, where the proprietor, Sir William Crawford, a 'dynamic' character if ever there was one, gave us a highly inspirational lecture, before suborning a couple of his clients to take space in *Masquerade*. The rest of the advertising came from Eton tradesmen who could not refuse it. Contributions from fellow Etonians were hard to elicit. In the end we wrote most of them ourselves. Meanwhile, my father, grateful perhaps that I seemed to be about to make some mark, even an ephemeral one, on the life of the school, went into action with his usual gusto. In no time at all he had produced contributions from Sir

James Barrie, Noël Coward, Ronald Knox and, of course, himself. John Gwyer had an uncle called Osbert Burdett, an authentic minor littérateur of the nineties and hanger-on in literary London, who supplied a 'fable' to the magazine. A cousin of Maurice's gave a full-page drawing, and my sister provided the cover design.

That mixture of established styles and halting attempts at style was not really a success. The famous names overbalanced the whole thing, effectively smothering its Etonian quality. However, there it was, something planned and brought to birth, a modest bid for distinction in an unusual mode. What strikes me now, looking at what we wrote then, is the lack of maturity in both style and thought, and an uncertain swithering between facetiousness and solemnity. Marks, however, would undoubtedly have been awarded for effort.

At the end of the Great War my father wrote: 'Everywhere in the world was heard the sound of things breaking.' That sound was to go on being heard for twenty years, sometimes as a distant crash or explosion, sometimes as the rumble of some structure collapsing nearer home. What, though, is extraordinary in my recollection, is how much in that time of my growing-up remained unbroken. That this was so was due in large measure to the determination of those who had survived the catastrophe of 1914-1918 to preserve, revive, shore up by every available means, those customs, habits, traditions, possessions, political and economic systems without which their world would have seemed to them total chaos. At the same time a post-war generation, supported by those writers and artists who thought that the last remnants of an older world which had allowed war to happen should be swept away entirely, to make room for rebuilding in quite different terms, were busily engaged in trying to tear down or kick to pieces such relics of the past as their elders had managed to preserve. Patriotism, national pride, the whole conception of Empire, the fixed social rules and prescriptions of different classes, were all to be jeered out of existence. Even though my contemporaries and I were not, in fact, untouched by this expression of the *zeitgeist*, I can say that it would have been possible at Eton to ignore it entirely. Accordingly, the time between my thirteenth and eighteenth years, for all that I was to learn later about the violent and destructive nature of that period, can still seem in memory a Land of Afternoon. No doubt there

133

were boys at the school who were politically sensitive, and therefore concerned, appalled or exhilarated by the manic personality of their time, but they were not to be found at my Tutor's.

For myself I was finding the troubles of puberty, which included a severe and long-lasting attack of spots on my face, and were certainly the cause of hopeless vagueness and inability to connect, in any but an intermittent way, with the instruction I was receiving, quite enough to struggle with. My world was bounded by the school's own boundaries both moral and physical and I had neither heart nor mind for the great issues of the greater world, except as they came to me in the work of poets whom I admired. Even with those, when they strayed from the lyrical or aloofly satiric into what a later age would call 'political commitment', I often felt irritation, their tone reminding me too nearly of prep-school politics, of vague threats of retribution or warnings of doom to come for failure to toe some popular line. Auden was quite evidently a real poet, his contemporaries interesting but, by him, outclassed. Their determined embracing of technological advance caused Virginia Woolf to label them the 'Pylon Boys'. At Oxford, after reading Isherwood's *Lions and Shadows*, my friend Michael Clark declared them 'school-bound', something which he and I very much hoped to prove that we were not.

Meanwhile, seeing Eton College on a fine fourth of June in the early thirties, even a shrewd and politically knowledgeable observer could have been forgiven for concluding that the old world was still firmly in place. The event was a colourful one and lavish, with luncheons offered to boys and their parents in most houses, an afternoon-long *corso* of well-dressed people and their schoolboy relations under the elms and chestnuts, the boys spruced up for the occasion as seldom in ordinary life, and a smart crowd to watch a cricket match on the field called Agar's Plough. Towards the end of the day, as dusk was approaching, there would be the Procession of Boats and, finally, a firework display of great elaboration. The whole affair was conceived in honour of the birthday of the school's patron, George III, and the boys in the boats were dressed as sailors of his time. It was one of the many quirks of Eton that its affectionate remembrances should fix, not on its saintly, sickly Founder, but upon a much less admirable later monarch.

It was during my first half, in 1929, that the word *economy* first came to be heard at Eton. That year Depression had descended like a fire-storm on America; its effects were already on their way

134

eastwards. It was traditional, on the Fourth of June, to allow
Lower Boys a share in the glory which, for the members of Pop,
was a condition of daily life. For that day, and for the Eton and
Harrow match at Lord's, we were allowed to wear fancy
waistcoats, chosen from the gorgeous stuffs displayed by the
town's hosiers, and made to our measure. Mine was an affair of
pale yellow brocade dotted with green, of which I was extremely
proud. I hope that I made the most of it, for it was to be my last.
By autumn the Provost and Fellows had taken note of the bad
financial omens and decreed certain economies. I have no idea
what the other economies were, and I doubt whether they were
very radical, but fancy waistcoats except, of course, for the
members of Pop, were for evermore forbidden.

Except that not all were as brilliantly hot and sunny, that first
Fourth of June, waistcoats apart, set the pattern for the rest. At
that and other functions such as Henley and the Eton and Harrow
match there would be luncheon tents and tea tents and much the
same crowd of parents and sisters all wearing their best clothes,
some dowdy, some extremely smart, some beautiful, many
showing faces familiar from the 'shiny' papers — *Tatler, Sketch*
and *Bystander* — which we pored over at the hairdresser's.

I was at an age to be interested in other people's motor-cars.
Those were still the days when it was usual to have any large car
coach-built to specification, the chassis alone having been supplied
by the manufacturer. The phrase 'owner-driver' was still in
currency to denote those owners who preferred, or were obliged,
to dispense with a chauffeur. The astonishing variety of cars,
many of them foreign, which I had been able to 'collect' in Oxford
in the twenties was thinning out a little. Soon it would be only
rarely that one would see a Talbot-Darracq, an Isotta-Fraschini, an
OM, an Austro-Daimler or a shovel-nosed Renault. In the
production-car business the humbler models, the Trojans, Beans
and Clynos were being elbowed aside by Morrises and Austin
Sevens. My schoolfellows' parents' cars — known to the young as
'family hearses' — were Rolls-Royces, Daimlers, Minervas,
Sunbeams, Austins, mostly with tall and stately bodies, usually
painted black. Once in a while some cosmopolitan would turn up
in a Delage with a body by Figoni, or a Hispano-Suiza *sedanca de
ville* where the chauffeur sat in the open and the passengers in a
brougham-like box at the back. Freddy Hesketh's father was on
the board of the Daimler company, and his family car had a very
special body, tall and square, with an enclosed compartment for

the footman who had his own entrance door at the rear.

Mary Elizabeth Lucy, in her diaries, complained, after a party which she had found insufficiently smart, that 'there were few coronet carriages'★. Heraldry on motor cars is something which has almost completely disappeared from the modern scene. In my schooldays it was quite usual to see coronets or family crests, of unobtrusive size, painted in correct heraldic colours on the passenger doors of limousines, and sometimes on the more splendid sports cars as well. It may be that my parents thought such displays unnecessary. Our large Wolseley motor bore no crest, or did not, at least, until it went to Canada, when the Government House cars all bloomed with the family sunflower surmounted by a coronet, as protocol required.

★ *Mistress of Charlecote: The Memoirs of Mary Elizabeth Lucy.*

IO

'OWERCOMES'

Describing his mother in *Memory Hold-The-Door* John Buchan wrote: 'In the ordinary business of life she was apt to deal in moral and religious platitudes and in the prudential maxims which the Scots call "owercomes" and which flourished especially in her family.' The Scots, like the French in Rebecca West's phrase, sometimes show a fondness for 'filling their mouths with the good bread of platitude', and producing moral sayings or biblical quotations, at a moment's notice, for almost any eventuality.

Each generation has its own 'owercomes', things that have come over from the wisdom, the humour or the prejudice of the past. Thus, as young children, we were treated to ancient jokes, sayings, maxims, scraps of verse which had served our forebears for instruction or amusement a hundred years before. Miss Smeaton was a perfect mine of such things. A sample of her jokes, and one with an extraordinarily antique flavour, was a riddle about the three fruits first mentioned in the Bible. The answer was: 'The Apple, the Pear (pair) and the Rotten Medlar!' To get the flavour of this you had to know that medlars are not eaten until 'bletted', that is to say rotten, and accept that Satan's role was to meddle in the affairs of Adam and Eve. Other jokes came to us by way of our parents, and were usually of a similar naivety or innocence, with a tinge of very mild naughtiness. Most were riddles, such as 'Why did the lobster blush?', the answer to which was 'Because he saw the salad dressing!' There were 'in' jokes too, which required a special knowledge for their enjoyment. One example was: 'Why did Bertie hide?', and the answer to that was: 'Because he saw the lady's leg!' To get the full beauty of this gem you had to know that Lord Hyde, eldest son of the 6th Earl of Clarendon, was known as Bertie, and that the two daughters of the 7th Earl of Darmouth were the Ladies Dorothy and Joan Legge.

Tin, my English grandmother, was also a source of jokes belonging to another age, some of which had worn rather well.

My favourite was another riddle, asking why Orpheus should be thought superior to Wagner — the answer to that one was: 'Orpheus charmed all birds and beasts, but Wagner only made one low hen grin!' Some jokes echoed Edwardian high life. 'Champagne at night, real pain in the morning!' struck Johnnie and me as highly amusing in a grown-up sort of way. We also liked the story of the young man who peppered his father at a shooting-party and was forever afterwards known as 'Bagdad'. The Edwardian habit of eating game at almost every meal, and referring to it in a general way as 'birds' came up in a parody of a moral poem by Isaac Watts:

> Birds in their little nests agree,
> It is their nature to:
> But if you eat too many birds
> They won't agree with you!

Of many limericks I remember this:

> There was a young lady called Maud
> Who was a most terrible fraud:
> She never seemed able to take much at table
> But in the back-kitchen — Oh Lord!

In the tones of voice of my older English relations there were detectable accents and ways of pronunciation belonging to the mid-Victorian heyday. Tin sometimes said 'It ain't' or 'He don't', reflecting a fashion of her youth which was to become a fashion again in the 1920s. My mother, from her childhood, could remember people pronouncing the name Harriet or the small carriage known as a chariot, as 'Har'yet' and 'char'yot'. Once she went for a Christmas visit to her aunt and uncle, the Lovelaces, at Ockham Park near Woking. She arrived to find her uncle Ralph in his library. He looked at her over his spectacles with some distaste: 'Your A'nt has gawn to a Christmas Tree in the village. I wish the *nassty* little child*renn* would go to the Dev*ill*!' The sneering, flat 'a' or 'e' in nasty was very much a mark of Victorian speech. Another recollection of my mother's was hearing her grandmother, Charlotte Ebury, say severely: 'Nessty vulgar woman — wears di'monds in the daytime!' which remark leads to the sad reflection that anyone nowadays who possesses a few diamonds wears them morning and evening and probably in bed, for fear of robbers, or, in some nasty, vulgar circles, wears them as what French tax-gatherers call 'exterior marks of wealth'.

My mother's family and contemporaries had certain pronunciations and inflexions in common. People tended to say 'grey deal' for great deal, and 'good eel' for good deal, and complain that they were having 'difficklety' over something. To my mother ants had the same pronunciation as aunts, and ancestors were ahncestors. Anything romantic was 'romahntic', and the noun was pronounced 'romahnce'. Ships were 'lahnched' and linen was sent to the 'lahndry'. An odd effect of this custom, in the days of the Indian Empire, showed in the spelling of the name Punjaub. Modern spelling would have this, probably, as Panjab, the first 'a' being short and somewhere between 'pan' and 'pun', and the last strongly accented as in 'last'. However, in the days of lahnch and lahndry, the correct phoneme for that second 'a' was thought best written as 'au'.

Every family in our relationship had its own voice, its own peculiar modulations and emphases, and very often a private language of some elaboration. Tin's family, the Stuart-Wortleys, had certain private words, such as 'Cayenne': to scold or abuse; 'Monkey' (from the French *manqué*): failure or disappointment; 'Gub': sad, touching or touched; 'Sticco': unpleasantness. A member of the Russell family once told me this sentence which had been made up to contain some distinctive family pronunciations: 'We had sawsages and cawfee on the bal-coney of the 'otel at Calaiss.' (Byron, in *Beppo*, rhymes balcony with Giorgione). Such things a little resemble the ways of speech of the *gratin*, those inhabitants of the Faubourg Saint-Germain who form the upper crust of Parisian social life.

My mother sometimes regaled me with the peculiar slang of the Edwardian English *gratin* which, since she disliked smart society on the whole, she might have learned from her lovely cousin, Alice Wimborne, who was in the thick of it. Some of this, particularly the tacking on of Italian endings, to make words such as 'horribilino', is recorded in Vita Sackville-West's *The Edwardians*. From my mother I learned 'deevy' for divine; 'disgy' for 'disgusting'; and 'dinpy' for 'dinner-party'; and from Jessica Mitford, who may have had it from her mother, 'teagy' for 'tea-gown', and 'beaty' for 'beautiful', resoundingly brought together in 'deevy, beaty teagy'.

The fashionable world has always loved private jokes, idiotic language, all things which help towards an exclusiveness, a being set apart. It does not usually take very long for a smart fashion to

139

find its way down from stratum to stratum of society, the difference nowadays being that popular fancy no longer follows the looks and ways of the aristocracy but finds its shibboleths, passwords, wisecracks and objects of emulation in the worlds of television and pop music. Even so, I was a little surprised the other day to be addressed by a taxi-driver as 'darling'. That word, once only used sparingly and with deep emotion, began to be bandied about and cheapened by smart people between the wars, who sometimes pronounced it 'dulling' or 'daaarling'. Its adoption by Cockneys was obviously derisive, but it still seemed to have taken rather a long time on its way to my taxi-driver. On the other hand 'my dear' was always, and still remains, a normal mode of address between men friends in the upper classes, as it does in my Oxfordshire village. Someone who was close at hand one day when the American Secretary of State, Dean Acheson, was seeing Anthony Eden off at Idlewild Airport, heard him say to a colleague as soon as his guest had embarked: 'If that guy calls me "my dear" once again I'll knock his hat over his eyes!'

The limerick I have quoted about the young lady called Maud contains two social howlers for which I should have been firmly pulled up. My mother made very little fuss, on the whole, about what were and were not the 'right' ways of expressing oneself, but 'at table' was definitely not allowed; nor would one be permitted to 'take' food. In the 1950s Nancy Mitford, inspired partly, I think, by sheer naughtiness and her well-known fondness for teasing, greatly expanded a lecture by Professor Alan Ross on upper-class ways of speaking and use of language, which he had labelled 'U' and 'non-U'. Many of Nancy's teases were funny and harmless, if sometimes acutely embarrassing to the persons teased: but, once in a while, there was more than a touch of cruelty about them. It seems to me to have been cruel on her part to cause such extreme anxiety amongst persons who had not, as is said, 'had her advantages' by proscribing, in memorably scornful terms, such words as 'mirror' (sc: 'looking-glass'), 'mantelpiece' (sc: 'chimney-piece'), 'notepaper' (sc: 'writing-paper') and so on. She must have made perfectly miserable numbers of harmless bourgeois who, believing that they had arrived socially, and had everything *nice* around them, were suddenly made to feel that all that they said, did or possessed was in some way a social solecism. I say that this was naughty because, although 'looking-glass' is correct for a pier-glass, say, or a hand-glass, it simply won't do for twelve-foot high mirrors above console-tables. And who ever heard the Salle de Glaces at Versailles called The Hall of Looking Glasses? I think of all the people I have known, whose ancestry was impeccable, whose manners exemplary, who lived fashionable lives, who nevertheless unblushingly spoke of mirrors and mantelpieces and notepaper without feeling in any way diminished thereby. I have even known of some who could use fish-knives and forks without turning a hair. To put it all more shortly Nancy Mitford, in promulgating her U- and Non-U regulations with such pith and authority was exhibiting something very much to be observed in the early years after the last war, a positive revolt by some of its members against what were felt to be attacks upon the upper class, and not merely upon its traditions and way of life, but against its very existence. At that time she was also mounting a challenging tease against the solemn left wing which believed itself for ever triumphant.

My mother, as I have said, made few rules about custom and usage, but those that she made were immutable. For example, we were carefully and explicitly trained never to say 'girl', nor yet 'gal', but quite definitely 'gairl'. That this caused problems in reciting poetry is obvious, when it was question of rhyming with 'swirl' or 'whirl' or even 'curl' or 'pearl'. But there it was: by 'gairl' my mother stood firm. Not much else of the sort comes back to mind, except that we spoke always of 'relations', never 'relatives', and, although I've seldom, if ever, used the word, I should have had to say 'gentlemanlike' rather than 'gentlemanly'; and *paying* calls' and *getting* married' and *getting* engaged' were completely barred.

Now that I have mentioned Nancy Mitford, so much lamented, whose work, I am perfectly certain, will be read with pleasure a hundred years from now when more ponderous writers have been quite forgotten, I should like to dwell for a little on my experience of the Mitford family. In the summer of 1932 my father fulfilled a long-held ambition to visit the Faroe Islands. He took Johnnie with him for a fortnight's fishing and bird-watching; they were then due to rejoin the rest of us for a family holiday in Wales. So Elsfield was shut for a while and my mother, Alastair and I settled for the time being into a house in Sheep Street, Burford, which someone had lent us. The month must have been July, because it was holiday time and I remember a succession of fine days sunbathing in the steep-sided garden behind the house. With the family's two most energetic members away in the North Atlantic, Alastair and I had a peaceful time reading, writing, painting,

141

swimming in the Windrush, going for picnics. We must have had Amos Webb and the car with us, for I remember a number of longish excursions but, most particularly, one very short one when we set off to tea with Lady Redesdale, two miles away down the Windrush valley at Swinbrook.

For some reason, Alastair seems to have refused that excursion, for I can only remember that it was my mother and I who presented ourselves at the large, rather bleak new house of Cotswold stone, set against dark woodland, above Swinbrook village. I think that my mother wanted to talk to our hostess about county affairs, most probably those of the Women's Institutes. Neither of us had the least idea, I am sure, into what a world of varied and conflicting enchantments, what a breeding-ground of myth and speculation we were venturing for the simple purpose of having tea.

Lady Redesdale was alone when we arrived. She said that her girls (gairls) were away that afternoon, except for Decca who was somewhere about. 'Decca', I thought, turning the nickname round in my head, thinking of gramophone records, but liking it all the same. We were in a long drawing-room with tall french windows giving on to a view of the valley — very much my kind of room, long and light and lavishly provided with books and flowers. There was a chimney-piece of rough stone. The walls were brilliant white. I sat quietly and covertly looked about me while the ladies talked. Then the door opened and with what seemed a single swift movement Jessica was in the room, closing the door behind her, standing straight, feet together, smiling. She was wearing a print frock and a black, patent leather belt tight to her waist. Her brown hair was short and thick. Her eyes were full of amusement, and also some friendliness, as they took me in. She shook hands, and sat down, feet together, back straight, the very picture of *une jeune fille parfaitement bien élevée*, but with an expression of such intelligence and humour as I had rarely seen in a girl of her age. Jessica, who was tall for her years, and well-formed, seemed older than she was; in fact she was two months short of her fifteenth birthday, and so a year and seven months younger than me. When her mother suggested that she take me to see the gardens and various livestock, she gave me a glance of cheerful complicity.

The conception of a boy-and-girl friendship, in the sense in which I knew it might nowadays seem strange, a sentimental conception impossible in contemporary terms. Yet, in 1932, in the

142

world which Decca and I inhabited, it was not simply one possibility, it was really the only one, and I was to be immeasurably grateful to Decca for the qualities she brought to that friendship. She had come into my life at a moment when school and my difficulties with it had become deeply irksome, seemingly endless, where every move I made was clumsy, and successes were few. As I have suggested earlier I had, at a very young age, dreamed of finding a girl who should be a true companion, someone in whom I could confide, who would support me in my very frequent arguments with my elders and share my tastes. Again and again I had caught glimpses of girls of more or less my own age who, by a certain remoteness from their families and contemporaries, a demeanour which promised sympathy, thought, some seriousness underlying gaiety, gave me a longing for their company, and fed my dreams of escape, as to a kind of private island, to a perfect companionship.

Decca, at that time, would have been thought of as a child by most elders. She was certainly not grown-up, nor would she be considered so until, at eighteen, she 'came out' in London: nevertheless there was nothing childish about her, in any sense implying weakness or silliness or inability to hold her own in the world. That first summer afternoon I swiftly came to know that my first impression of originality had been quite correct: here was a spirit both lively and adventurous, a keen mind fed by a highly varied diet of reading, a sparkling sense of humour, and all allied to a delicious appearance and a flattering interest in myself and in what I had to say; small wonder that I had taken so short a time to become her devoted admirer.

Nancy, the year before I met her, had published her first novel, *Highland Fling*, which had had some success. It is a very funny book, although written, naturally enough, with less of the assurance and sense of shape of such works as *The Pursuit of Love* and *The Blessing* which she was to publish after the war. As it had been for my sister Alice, it was a thousand pities for Nancy that she could not have been sent to school and university: her regret for this shows up in her novels, where Fanny, the cousin and narrator, is given these advantages, and also in her writing life, where she trained herself to research most rigorously for her works on Louis XIV, Voltaire and Frederick the Great.

Nancy would have come out in London only four years after the end of the Great War, at the moment when the post-war fever for change and greed for pleasure were coming to full strength.

She was thus truly of the Twenties and her books give priceless insights into the world then existing of a society not yet completely rattled to pieces by taxation, the scarcity of servants, the cost of maintaining property, as it would be by the end of the next war. Her life would have been much as that described for Julia Flyte in Waugh's *Brideshead Revisited*. She would have found a number of the great Whig or Tory town houses still open to her, for dining or dancing — Bridgwater House, Norfolk House, Londonderry House — not to speak of the mansions where the 'new' money of newspaper proprietors, financiers, and those who had prospered from the war, was making its bid, by lavish entertainment, for her consideration. Society apart, there were artists and writers and musicians, some smart and sociable, others disdaining the social round, but each, in his way, contributing to the heady excitement of a world where every new thing must be good, and everything old a matter for derision.

Where the life of the arts was concerned Nancy grew up at a period of great interest. A year younger than Evelyn Waugh, a year older than Anthony Powell, an exact contemporary of Harold Acton, and a friend of all three, she could scarcely have been better placed, given her predilection for the novel of manners, and her aristocratic instinct for styles of living where worldly concerns were balanced by continual interest in the arts.

I was to visit Swinbrook again on several occasions, and even produced a play there in which the younger girls took part. Decca's letters to me at Eton had the power to brighten my life for days at a time. Meanwhile, on the first afternoon, whilst our mothers, who were near-contemporaries, chatted calmly together, Decca and I, gabbling, interrupting, turning to face one another in delighted recognition of identical views, managed to cover a lot of ground in the time allowed. Back in Burford I told it all over to myself again, happy in a feeling that, somehow, a cloud had been pierced, that there would be light now, to lighten my gloom.

I I

MOVING PICTURES

My father's appointment, in 1935, to be Governor-General of Canada, and his consequent elevation to the peerage, more or less coincided with my parting from the University of Oxford. The Warden and Fellows of New College had concluded that I, although evidently having a most amusing time, was contributing too little to scholarship, and deriving too little from it, to be allowed to go on occupying a place better suited to a more serious person. Accordingly, and in a manner courteous and even regretful, and out of respect, I am sure for my parents, they indicated that I might leave voluntarily, rather than be ignominiously sent down. Thus what to do with me became suddenly an urgent matter for decision, to add to the multitude of others which my parents were having to face.

The end of my Oxford career did not, of course, arrive without warning. It had been coming for some time. My father had already asked me what, if Oxford was no longer in question, I intended to do, and that before his Canadian appointment was a certainty. It had happened that I had gone with him, the year before, to visit the studios where Alfred Hitchcock was making *The Thirty-nine Steps*, the film which was to increase enormously his already considerable reputation, although many, my mother included, would think it a travesty of a much-loved book. I then wrote a short story for the *Isis*, set in a film studio. My father, who perhaps was grateful for any sign I could give of being reasonably effective, liked the story and was impressed by the studio atmosphere which I had tried to re-create. During that visit to Gaumont-British I had been greatly interested, not so much by the acting of a particular scene which we saw repeated half a dozen times, as by the technical equipment of the sound stage where we saw Robert Donat performing. I have written of my fascination by stage lighting and, although the lighting of film sets was wholly different from that in the theatre, lacking colour and often specifically aimed only at 'killing' shadows, the great Klieg lamps, the mass of cables thick as boa-constrictors and massive junction-boxes which made an obstacle course of the floor, the cameras heavy and black as weapons, struck me as having a curious power and personality. Wanting the chance to learn more about them I admitted to my father that I should be glad to try my hand at film-making. Not long afterwards he returned from London one evening, looking pleased, and announced that he had got me a job with the Gaumont-British Motion Picture Corporation, to work with Alfred Hitchcock, and that I was to lunch with Hitchcock in London in a week's time. He also mentioned a salary which sounded almost princely.

When the day came for my luncheon with Hitchcock I decided, with customary lack of the most rudimentary common sense, to travel to London by car rather than by one of the reliable trains of the Great Western Railway. For that excursion I borrowed from an Oxford friend an open Bentley, by no means in its first youth, and set off for London in a mood of mingled nervousness and elation. The day was fine, luckily, but the Bentley did not take kindly to my driving, or else was seriously in need of a service for, at about Beaconsfield, it began to cough and splutter and lose speed. I got it to a garage where a gifted mechanic did things to the engine which put it back on form, but not without losing me a good deal of time. When I finally pulled up at the May Fair Hotel, with black hands and a smudge of oil on one cheek, I was more than an hour late for luncheon.

It would not have been surprising if Mr Hitchcock had left in a huff long before my arrival, perhaps leaving a note cancelling any further commerce between us; but there he was, sitting patiently in front of an empty glass, his large bulk more than fitting a flimsy hotel chair. Once again, I think that I owed his courtesy, and indeed forgiveness, to respect for my father: the patience I was to see at work later on, throughout many trying passages of film-making. Hitchcock had great calm of manner. When at work he never raised his voice, never bullied, cursed, made impossible demands, or showed off as did most other directors. Massive as a dolmen, he would stay planted, reflecting, as he was doing on that occasion at the May Fair — no doubt reflecting on the shocking bad manners of the young. When he spoke it was in a rather high, breathy voice, with a marked accent: not quite Cockney, more, I think, belonging to the part of Essex from which he came.

In the course of luncheon it became apparent that Hitchcock had been a trifle over-generous when discussing salary with my father.

146

No doubt he had since had a word with the Gaumont British administration, and had been reminded of the need for strict economy in those days of depression. In the event, and after explaining the job which he had in mind for me, that of Third Assistant Director on his next film, he told me that I was to join the company's apprenticeship scheme at the notably diminished wages of five shillings a week. This was not the only instance I was to know of John Buchan's extraordinarily exhilarating effect on people, which made it so that, whilst he was with them, they rose grandly to promises and projections upon which, once returned to the colder reality of their own affairs, they felt obliged to retrench.

It was arranged that I should join the film company in the autumn of that year, 1935, when the final script and shooting schedules for Hitchcock's new film would be settled. All that summer I watched with interest, and occasionally took a hand in, the preparations for my parents' departure. My new-found prospects of employment were clearly a matter of great relief to my father. There was no place for me in Canada and he was naturally anxious, in an exacting and fascinating new phase of his career, to be as free as possible from anxieties about what might be happening at home. Alice was married and settled in Gloucestershire; Johnnie was with the Colonial Service in Uganda; Alastair, aged seventeen, was to leave Eton a year ahead of time, to go to Canada with my parents and there continue working for entrance to Oxford. Almost until the last moment my own future had been under several question marks. Now my father could turn his eyes and his whole attention westwards with a comparatively quiet mind.

My feelings about joining the film industry and being launched, more or less on my own, in London, were mixed. Elsfield was to be shut up, perhaps for five years, certainly for an experimental period of one, and so I should no longer have its haven to retire to, as I had often done from Oxford, if the going became too rough. Most of my wishes were indeed concerned with moving forward, acquiring independence, learning new things: but something, some still powerful attachment to early youth, to childhood and what was safe and familiar, gave me shivers of misgiving from time to time. I have often wondered, without sympathy, indeed with exasperation, at a streak of timidity which has sometimes made me hesitate, needlessly, before undertakings with which I was really quite adequately equipped to deal. It was the Cherwell swimming lessons over again. Once in the water I could manage well enough: but the plunge...

There was in my immediate future, however, one vividly bright spot. It had been arranged that I should go, in the early autumn, some weeks after presenting myself at Gaumont-British, to stay as a paying guest with Elizabeth and Alan Cameron.

Elizabeth Dorothea Cole Bowen was born in Dublin in 1899, an only child, last representative of an old landed family in County Cork. In her early twenties she had married Alan Cameron, who had come out of the Great War with a Military Cross and an experience which few would have cared to share, in that he stayed in Europe for two years after the war was officially over, helping, in various ways, to restore order. That he was willing to do this, when most of his comrades could have had no other wish than to get home as quickly as possible, is an indication of a character moulded by duty and responsibility, and of the fact that he (also an only child) was a rather lonely young man who had not, then, much of significance to go back to. Yet he was a cultivated man, of many interests. In his Oxford days he had decorated his rooms with coloured engravings after Holbein, which later hung in the study of his London house. They were all portraits of women, and each bore a quite strong resemblance to his future wife.

When the Camerons first came into our lives they were living in Headington, now a northern suburb of Oxford sprawled out round the original small village. Lying about two miles away, as the crow flies, from Elsfield, it was an easy walk or a mere few minutes in a car. Alan Cameron was appointed Director of Education for Oxfordshire in 1933, having previously done the same job for Northamptonshire. It was in Old Headington, tucked away down a narrow lane, that the Camerons bought what I think was a converted stable, a minute house with a scrap of a garden, surrounded by trees and old walls; a little like a London mews house, full of character and promise.

To that house I would sometimes go for luncheon or tea, or to help with the drinks at a party. My good fortune was incomputable, when one considers how many people in Britain and America would have given almost anything to be invited to join the company which came so eagerly to the Camerons' house, and of which I, at seventeen, was made free. Isaiah Berlin of All Souls, Maurice Bowra of Wadham; Tom Boase, one day to be Master of Magdalen, Lord David Cecil, were amongst Elizabeth's 'regulars'. Conversation, rushing at great speed — both Shaya Berlin and

David Cecil spoke in rushes, punctuated by gasps — went on without let or pause. I had, of course, nothing of my own to contribute to that kind of intellectual badminton, beyond an occasional question which I hoped might seem intelligent, but nothing in my life, lived for the most part amongst liberal-minded, articulate and thoughtful people, can be remembered with quite such a sense of quintessential civility, of learning worn with grace, of life itself approached with wit and energy, a kind of acute, discriminating glee. Reading of that 'College in a clearer air' which Lucius Cary, Lord Falkland, conducted thirty miles away at Great Tew in the seventeenth century, my memory goes at once to those gatherings of a summer evening, in the Camerons' house and garden: to the intensely individual voices, the sheer informed, deliberate goodwill of it all. Even malice, which was by no means absent, was light and glancing, although none the less telling for that. Alan Cameron took up the role of thoughtful provider, lending a benevolent presence, a keen eye and ready hand for his guests' comfort, so that Elizabeth should be free to take her part in all the exchanges; and her I remember excited, high-coloured, sparkling, showing by every look and word and gesture that there, at last, she had found the sphere to which she truly belonged.

One winter day a man and a woman are standing on an iron foot-bridge in Regent's Park, having a rather momentous talk: 'The islands stood in frozen woody brown dusk: it was now between three and four in the afternoon... Bronze cold of January bound the sky and the landscape; the sky was shut to the sun — but the swans, the rims of the ice, the pallid withdrawn Regency terraces had an unnatural burnish, as though cold were light.' That quotation is from the first paragraph of Elizabeth's novel *The Death of the Heart*, which came out in 1938, three years after she and Alan Cameron had taken possession, on a Crown lease, of Number 2 Clarence Terrace, Regent's Park. The bridge in question lies on the other side of the carriageway from the house, visible from windows on the eastern side. In so far as it is ever actually described, rather than conveyed as an atmosphere around, an influence upon the chief characters, the house in that book is the house where I lived with the Camerons during part of my nineteenth and twentieth years.

My parents left for Canada at the end of October 1935. The house in Regent's Park not being quite ready for occupation, I

149

went to perch for a while in bed-sittingrooms, first a small one in Nottingham Terrace, just by Madame Tussaud's, and then in something vaster and colder in a late-classical cliff of a house in Queen's Gate. Daily I took the journey to Shepherd's Bush, to the Gaumont-British studios, and began trying to fit myself into a workaday world every aspect of which was totally strange to me.

Alan Cameron had recently been appointed Head of Schools Broadcasting at the BBC, and his and Elizabeth's move to London had been determined by that appointment. It was an exciting time for both of them; for Alan an important new job, reward for his years of work directing education in two Midland counties; for Elizabeth, now coming into the fullness of her powers as a writer, the exchange of the charming but exiguous house in Headington for something much more splendid, and the prospect of living at the very heart of London's literary world. If Elizabeth regretted leaving Oxford, she could be sure that Oxford, in the form of friends she had made there, would not be slow in finding its way to her door. Not only did Number 2 Clarence Terrace give one the feeling of living in a wing of a large country house, but the great spread of the park with its tall trees, its lakes with their wooded islands, its ample sky unfretted by tall buildings, added to the impression. At any season the light seemed larger, less metropolitan than in other parts of London. Regent's Park well reflected Regency people's fondness for space, for a classical civility combining buildings with an orderly nature, for the ideal of *rus in urbe*.

To Elizabeth Bowen light meant as much as it would to a painter. Again and again it is used to set a scene, enhance atmosphere, underline or counterpoint emotion. Her first exploration of her new house must have been under a rain of light from uncurtained windows: white light reflected from the stucco of the Terrace beyond, a tinted radiance from sky and water and trees. If ever there was a house brimful of light it was Number 2, and, in her furnishing, Elizabeth did little to muffle or exclude it. In her drawing-room two tall sash-windows with narrow glazing bars went from the cornice almost to the floor. One of them, facing north, was filled with a classical perspective; the other, which looked eastwards, had trees, flowers, a glimpse of water, the caryatid-embellished bay window of a terrace-end, the glinting black or coloured tops of cars and taxis slipping by.

The house was tall, with three floors over a deep basement. From the stone-flagged hall a delicate staircase shot upwards in a steep curve, making the most of its space. The drawing-room had a shining hardwood floor and, once ,arranged, never altered or became cluttered. From Bowen's Court, her home in County Cork, built in the eighteenth century, Elizabeth brought furniture and watery Irish glass. She also brought two members of the Barry family, who had served the Bowens for several generations, to be cook and kitchen-maid. For house-parlourmaid she engaged Nancy, who had been with my family for the past two years at Elsfield, a cheerful, pretty girl whose smiling welcome no doubt added to the charm of the place for the arriving guest.

In those days the firm of Haynes, in Spring Street, Paddington, was much in favour for furnishing materials, glazed chintzes especially. Elizabeth hung her drawing-room windows with a stuff of dusky pink patterned with white acanthus, near enough in feeling for the date of the house. From Ireland came a Regency settee and sofa-table, the first a long, light affair on short, straight legs, with a gilded back-rail and arms, upholstered in dark green silk; the second a sumptuous piece in satinwood, kingwood, tulip-wood, with an inlaid, eight-pointed star at its centre. There were book-shelves on both sides of the fireplace, and a giltwood mirror, also correct for the date, over the slim marble chimney-piece. Elizabeth sat always in a corner of the settee to the right of the fire. Beside her on a glass-topped table were two telephones. One of those was a house-telephone, something which I think she had always wanted to have, and which was, in fact, very useful in that tall, steep house. Also on that table would usually be a yellow box of a hundred Gold Flake cigarettes, then an unremarkable sight but, in retrospect, sinister-seeming for, in 1973, Elizabeth would die of lung cancer in her seventy-fourth year.

If I remember the physical features of Clarence Terrace with exactitude it is because I participated in some of its choices and arrangements. My own room on the top floor was large and light and had probably once been a nursery. There I had my bed and table and space for clothes, and a view towards the Zoo and the slopes of Primrose Hill. I also had a bathroom and my own telephone. On the ground floor were Alan Cameron's study, to the right of the front door and, to the left, the dining-room, directly beneath the drawing-room and sharing, from its lower angle, the same view. It was a house made for entertaining and, one way and another, the Camerons entertained a great deal. The somewhat sparse arrangement of the drawing-room, where ample floor space had been left free, lent itself admirably to parties,

151

especially of the stand–up, early evening kind which were usually called sherry–parties, 'cocktail party' as a category having become rather *démodé*.

Of the people who came to drink Alan's excellent sherry and talk and argue and, sometimes, show off amusingly, I remember names and faces but, typically, not very much of the conversation. It is perhaps because I have always talked so much myself that I remember so little in the way of pregnant sayings, significant *obiter dicta*, from the many distinguished people with whom I have been privileged to converse. Most of her visitors would have been roughly of Elizabeth's own age, that is to say in their thirties, although Rose Macaulay and T.S.Eliot who came sometimes to tea, were, in that first year, respectively fifty-four and forty-seven. The conversation was, to me, absorbing, for I did manage to listen for quite a lot of the time, as well as talk: and that I was allowed, even encouraged, to talk at all was a mark of the courtesy and consideration towards the young displayed by that brilliant and successful group of people advancing into middle age with all flags flying. For someone like myself who found (with glorious exceptions) his own contemporaries unrestful because, thrusting, envious and insecure themselves, the cause of insecurity in others, those easy-mannered, humorous elders, already confirmed in some intellectual or artistic distinction, were the ones whose company I would always have preferred to seek. I benefited greatly from their patience, perception and forbearance, qualities not to be found amongst the generality of people my own age.

Elizabeth's parties were a continual excitement. I sometimes helped with the arrangements and the handing-round of food and drink. It has to be said that some of Elizabeth's friends, those who came to the house especially to see her, to appraise that new phenomenon of the London scene, often treated Alan discourteously. For several of the less agreeable among them (nasty visitors!) he could be seen to be rated the merest appendage, no more to be noticed or considered than a hired waiter. His abilities residing in another sphere, and his perfectly good mind being of a practical, common-sense cast, he could take little part in the conversational fireworks which were a speciality with many of his guests. If, however, they were under the impression that Alan was a negligible factor in Elizabeth's life they were entirely wrong. She was not only physically short-sighted but, when working, inclined to extreme vagueness. Without Alan's practical help and forethought, without his skill at dealing with domestic matters,

152

his undertaking of all kinds of organization, Elizabeth could never have enjoyed the serenity which she needed for her writing. I remember once saying crossly to someone: 'If you think Alan negligible I can tell you that there are times when Elizabeth couldn't cross the street without him!'

There was one particular way in which I could make myself useful at parties. The critic John Hayward sometimes came to the house. A sufferer, since childhood, from muscular dystrophy, he came in a wheelchair, and it was a question of selecting a strongish man from among the guests to help get the wheelchair as far, first, as the hall from the conveyance in which he had arrived. Next, with my fellow-guest in front, pulling and lifting, and myself below, lifting and pushing, we would carry him up the steep, narrow and, in the circumstances rather dizzying curve of the staircase. John Hayward had, at the best of times, a severe and searching look: rocking up the stairs, as in a palanquin, he would fix me with a piercing, cold eye, positively daring me to feel sorry for him. It was, in fact, not so much pity that I felt on those occasions as anxiety. It was a great relief to get safely to the landing and know that there would be an hour or two's respite before the process would have to be repeated in reverse.

One of the figures which stand most clearly in my memory is that of David Cecil, tall and thin, with long, fine features, a broad forehead usually crossed by a loose lock of black hair, and an incomparable eagerness of manner, matched by the hurrying, somewhat staccato, but musical tones of his voice. He was also one of a small handful of people to whom I would award the very highest marks for good manners. Of Graham Greene I can only say that he had the faculty of looming, of bending from a considerable height, of carrying with him a kind of personal weather, less clement perhaps than that of the other guests. He was amenable, he was courteous, but in some way he would always appear isolated, irredeemably alone, even in a press of people. Cyril Connolly and Jean, his American wife, made an altogether different effect. Both short and heavily built, they appeared massive, monolithic. If they had been turned to stone they would have looked well on, say, Easter Island.

People came to the house sometimes whom I could greet as old friends. Raymond Mortimer was then literary editor of the *New Statesman* and the chief reason why many people bought that publication, since the political views of Kingsley Martin, its editor, were capricious and liable to frequent falsification by

153

events, whereas Raymond's literary touch never fumbled. Perhaps, having written that, I should not add that he had given me my very first jobs of book-reviewing, for which I was grateful not so much for the money, which was not generous, as for the chance to get my name into print. Several people whose company I had enjoyed at Oxford continued to be part of the Cameron's circle, among them Maurice Bowra who, with a rather severe air of scholarly deliberation, could be wonderfully amusing and memorably malicious. ('I think Wystan *Auden* is the *reincarnation* of Martin *Tupper!*') Being invited to his rooms in Wadham was as exciting as it could be, sometimes, disconcerting. If, by chance, I had to be among the first to leave one of his sparkling sherry-parties and, after the door had closed behind me, was on my way downstairs, I should have had to have been much less self-conscious than I was not to be disquieted by the great crash of laughter coming from the room behind. Another guest, of course, might just have made a very good joke, something which he had been saving up to amuse the future Warden of Wadham, but the suspicion was irresistible that my late host had just pinned me, as a butterfly to cork, with a sharp and highly repeatable phrase. I had heard that done to others often enough for my suspicions to have some substance.

They came and went, Elizabeth's visitors, and, when I could lend attention from my own preoccupations, which were un-necessarily many and, largely, unnecessarily miserable, I found great pleasure in them and was glad for Elizabeth that she had become the focus of so lively and gifted a group.

One new friend who came often to the house was the novelist and poet William Plomer. William, who was born in South Africa, had all his life been close to calamity of one kind and another. When he was a boy a little sister, ill with diphtheria in a remote homestead, died under the knife of a drunken doctor attempting a tracheotomy. In his earliest days in England he had a room over a pub in North London which was kept by a consumptive Spaniard and his young, rather beautiful wife. The Spaniard was a fiercely jealous man. Quite soon, he had decided, without any justification whatever, that his wife had tender feelings for her young lodger, and that she and William were having an affair. One night he cut her throat in William's room, William being out at the time. Telling the story years later William remarked that he had always thought it the job of the police to clear up after such incidents, but no, nothing of the kind. The clearing up was left to him and he had to scrape dried blood off the wallpaper with his nail-scissors. Proving the truth of Freud's dictum about the luck which writers have in being able to transfer evil experiences on to paper, and so rid themselves of excessive traumata, William used his story as the foundation for a novel, *The Case is Altered.*

Even the comedies of William's existence had a sinister side. At one time he lived in Linden Gardens, off Notting Hill Gate, and was severely troubled by a woman upstairs who had — through frustrated passion perhaps — taken a fierce dislike to him. One of her ways of expressing this was to collect all her hair-combings and drop them on to his balcony. William, a fastidious man, found it deeply disagreeable to have his balcony inches deep in swatches of frowsy hair. Much later, during the war, at the time of the flying bombs, he was lunching in the vegetarian restaurant near Leicester Square when a bomb landed rather close. The chief casualty was an unfortunate dray-horse, one half of whose hindquarters flew through the air and landed, an excess of raw meat, amongst the vegetarians. Once again turning misfortune to art, William produced a poem called 'The Flying Bum'.

I cherish in memory the sardonic quality of William Plomer's view of the world. Still more years later, after the war, at the time when Dr Christian Barnard's much-publicized heart-transplants, performed in South Africa, coincided with the first landings on the moon, he published in the *Sunday Times* the following verses:

> If when you gaze at the moon
> About which so many have raved
> Your susceptible heart gives a thump —
> Think that a dull desert craved
> By yet-to-be-far-flung bores
> Can excite a transplantable pump.

William had a beautifully exact capacity for irony, and his stories, told without particular expression, were of a neatness I have seldom known equalled. He had the rare gift of perfect detachment combined with much charm. In literary history he will probably be best remembered for his edition of Kilvert's *Diaries*, but it is as a poet that I think of him most. His 'yet-to-be-far-flung bores' recurs to me often, as does: 'The hypodermic steeple/Ever ready to inject/The opium of the people.'

Parties were all very well but too many of them were inclined to leave 'a burning forehead and parching tongue'. Of all my experiences at Clarence Terrace I believe that I liked best the times when only one person came to tea or drinks or when, rarely, I was alone with Elizabeth. T.S.Eliot was not, I think, a 'party-goer'; he had too many difficulties in his domestic life to be consistently sociable, apart from what seems a likely temperamental disinclination. Once in a while on some Saturday or Sunday, he would come to tea at Clarence Terrace and I, looking at him crouched in a big armchair beside the fire, could only wonder that the mind behind those round spectacles, beneath that neat slick of rather thin hair, could so have shaken the world with *The Waste Land* or conceived *A Song for Simeon* or *Ash Wednesday*. In dress, manner, and general demeanour he could have been taken, at first glance, for a provincial solicitor. His conversation, with its pleasant New England tones, was not, in my recollection, striking, but I could see that he was likeable, immensely well worth knowing if he would allow one to know him. I could also see why people often referred to him as 'poor Tom'.

Apart from occasional evenings, either at home or out together at restaurant or theatre, I saw little of Elizabeth and Alan during the week. Each morning I took the Metropolitan line from Baker Street station, happily only a hundred yards away, to Shepherd's Bush, and there entered a world as clangorous, unplanned, and untidy as the surroundings of Clarence Terrace were orderly and calm. The early train rattled and banged its way through a landscape of waste ground, factories and the backs of houses, sometimes riding high above a hugger-mugger of builders' yards and small green spaces surviving from the rural Middlesex of a hundred years before. Sometimes, with my eyes shut, I smoked Gauloise cigarettes, to try to believe for a moment that the old red Metropolitan Railway was really the Métro, and I in that city which, even then, I thought 'the flow'r of cities all'. Such self-deception, however, held no power against the actuality of Shepherd's Bush or the singular hideousness of the Gaumont-British premises in Lime Grove.

The studios, now occupied by the BBC, had been specially built for their purpose, and consisted of a block of sound-proof 'stages', one above the other, with an outer casing of offices, laboratories, and cutting-rooms. There were also dressing rooms, large for 'extras' and small (in varying degrees) for actors and actresses of all qualities. The symbol of my introduction to industrial practices of which I had never even heard might have been the time-clock on which I had to punch a card at every arrival and departure.

The studios were an innovation for their time, in that they had been designed to obviate the expense and weather-hazard of filming outdoor scenes 'on location'. By the use of sky-cloths and huge photographic blow-ups of woods and mountains or city roof-lines it was thought that the real thing could be convincingly counterfeited indoors. Not long ago, on television, I saw again, for the first time in nearly fifty years, the black-and-white film of Maugham's Ashenden stories, *Secret Agent*, which Hitchcock directed and on which I worked. Of course, even after so long, I knew what to look for, but nevertheless could only wonder that anybody, even in those less sophisticated days, should have been deceived for a minute by such crude effects.

One day Tin telephoned to tell me, in a tone of humorous despair, that my car had been parked outside her house for nearly a week, and the police had come to enquire whether it belonged where it was, or whether it had been abandoned there. Today it is a solemn thought that someone could leave a car in Upper Grosvenor Street, the very heart of Mayfair, for five or six days without arousing official interest; nowadays it would be next to impossible to do so for five or six minutes, most especially at the Grosvenor Square end, a few yards from the American Embassy.

Tin's house, since demolished to make way for the Americans, was another Number 2. She had moved there six years before from the opposite side of the street nearest to Park Lane, when my birthplace, Number 30, was pulled down. What caused me to lose touch with my little car for so long I cannot recall, but no doubt it had something to do with a weekend to which I had gone by train, plus three or so days' and nights' intensive work at Gaumont-British. The car was a Morris Oxford, dark blue with a folding hood. It had seating for two in the front, and for a further two in the dickey, whose lid could be raised to disclose, and form the back of, another seat. The dickey was really only for the brave in any but the finest weather, since there was no protection against rain or cold. My father had given me the car as a sort of parting present. It cost about fifty pounds second-hand and was, I imagine, a thoroughly good buy, having been the subject of long and detailed discussions between Amos Webb and his friends at the Morris Garages in Oxford.

That car had been a source of great pleasure in Oxfordshire, serving to take me quite long distances to places or people I needed to see. In it Maurice Cardiff and I had conveyed Mr Stead, the poet, to the Windrush Valley, near Burford, for a rather elaborate riverside picnic. I am sure that we had something more substantial to eat than the mound of Elsfield raspberries and the *petits fours* which are all that I can remember; the flavour of the conversation matched the food, being delicate and a trifle rarefied. William Force Stead, an interesting poet, was, like his friend T.S.Eliot, an American and an Anglican. He was also a clergyman. He spoke, that day, of poetry and metaphysics in his soft transatlantic accent to his respectful and assiduous hosts. We had gone to fetch him from his square red house in Clifton Hampden, hard by the Thames, where the garden, I remember, was entirely given up to lilies. A story was told that Stead one day had discovered, to his surprise and shock, that his friend Tom Eliot had never been baptized, and had taken decisive action, locking the two of them into a Cotswold church and there putting matters right. He was a gentle, rather melancholy man, scholarly, sensitive, beautifully mannered. The picnic must have gone well for I remember it as an entirely successful occasion, significant in some ways, rounded out and blessed by an unusually fine summer day.

It was curious how, for all excursions or parties of pleasure, my family's natural inclination was to head westwards to the Cotswold villages and small towns: to a Burford practically unknown to tourists, where there were fine buildings from every period since the Middle Ages, a splendid church, and the Windrush looping between its pollard willows like a river in an illuminated book. When Elsfield had to be sold my mother moved to Burford, to an ancient house in the High Street, where she died in her ninety-fifth year. When, on being widowed, my sister had to leave her home at Fossebridge, she too settled in Burford. The poem with which I won the Harvey English Verse Prize at Eton in 1934 had for title 'The Windrush at Minster Lovell'. Burford, now, for most of the year is a shifting pack of cars and coaches and, since I first knew the town, the number of its shops must have multiplied twentyfold. Dogs no longer sleep undisturbed in the middle of the street. Yet the place is still a powerful magnet and the valley where William Force Stead entertained Maurice and me with lofty speculation whilst we plied him with raspberries and cream, has scarcely changed at all.

Sometimes, in London, I used the car to get to work; sometimes I took it with me when I went out in the evening. On the whole, however, it was less useful than might be supposed, since in those days travel about London by bus or tube or, sometimes, taxi, was rapid, easy and cheap. The Morris became in the end more of a responsibility than a convenience, one more problem to be considered when my hands were already full of them, and so we had to part. Its chief value, in those early London days, was as a getaway car; that is to say the means by which I could escape into the country which I found myself missing severely. I think that, without my knowing it, my health was beginning to suffer, had indeed begun to do so quite soon after I went to work at the film studios. Those massively soundproofed areas were badly ventilated: what we breathed was an air superheated, used up, thick with chemical fumes from paint, and dust from a hundred sources. Since working hours were unspecified, elastic, it was often not possible to get away until quite late in the evening. (Sometimes we worked all night.) Then, badly needing a change of atmosphere, in both senses of the word, I would hurry to a rendezvous with friends in a restaurant or café, there to plunge back into waves of talk which had first begun to roll, perhaps, at Oxford and which would roll on for as long as any place could be found in which to stay awake, eat, drink, and keep on talking. One result of all that, for me, was a perpetual shortage of sleep.

From earliest childhood London had been part of my life. Our departure for Oxfordshire in 1919 was simply to take a step away. My father had bought the Elsfield property because it was near Oxford, which had fast trains to and from London, as well as the University he loved and with the business of which he was much concerned.

My first recollection of seeing London as a visitor were of one or two visits I made by myself between the ages of seven and nine, to stay with Tin; and of these my memory holds an impression of great security, of London's low, continuous roar and rumble held back by thick curtains, deadened by deep carpets; of a treasury of curious and beautiful things; of my grandmother's stately presence, her charming voice, her discreet, affectionate interest in myself.

London then was a safer place for pedestrians than it is now. Although we sometimes made a sober small procession — Tin, Alice Butterfield, the pekinese and I — to cross Park Lane and enter Hyde Park by the Grosvenor Gate (now gone) I remember no great sense of urgency in crossing streets, or threat from teeming traffic. The streets of Mayfair were traversed, in the

159

main, by large, quiet cars driven by cautious, elderly, chauffeurs. Other traffic, apart from the electric vans of Harrods and Fortnum & Mason, was usually horse-drawn, milkmen's and bakers' carts and such, and there were large boxes attached to bicycles for various deliveries. Shops, it should be noted, still delivered goods and were glad to do so. Trade was bad, wages of drivers and delivery-boys were low, and purchasers had to have every encouragement. If, however, a cake was wanted from the bakery in North Audley Street, I was allowed to make the journey by myself, so unhazardous were the streets. Longer excursions were made in the company of Alice Butterfield and once or twice I was taken by Tin to the theatre to see a children's play (but, for some reason, never a pantomime) and once to Maskelyne and Cook's marvellous conjuring show at the St George's Hall.

Those London visits were the purest pleasure. It was a fine thing to be away from my family for a little while, and to be treated as an interesting individual. Not many concessions were made to my childish state. It was a very long time since Tin had had anything much to do with young children; accordingly I was allowed to stay up to dinner, at which no thought was given to suitable food. One such occasion ended badly. My grandmother had been sent a haunch of venison and so, for dinner, we ate spinach soup which was mostly cream and roast venison with port-wine sauce. That was too much for my stomach. I spent most of the night being extremely sick.

To compare London as it is now with the London of the twenties and thirties is hard to do intelligibly. It is not only the obvious changes in skyline, in transport, in clothes, and, above all the vast increase of tourists and of new elements in the population, but the atmosphere is wholly different, as are the sound and the light. London then was coloured in a darker tone. Smoke-abatement and the electrification of the railways have had admirable results, but no one now will see the beauty of that particular smoky light, which gave a pearly tinge to even the finest summer day and which, in a freezing winter would darken dramatically as the air swirled and coagulated into the dangerous, the truly infernal London fog. Those fogs are not to be regretted. They often choked people to death and came near to doing the same for the city itself. Nevertheless it was a wonder to see a great metropolis brought nearly to a standstill by a natural phenomenon. Now I think of it, though, this seems to be happening again with an unnatural one, a congestion of traffic unimaginable fifty years ago.

Later on, for any event in London to which we went as units of the family, we usually stayed with Tin. There was, in many London houses of the day, a marked contrast between the downstairs rooms and the bedrooms above. In drawing-room, dining-room, morning-room, fires burned and lights were arranged so that it was possible to see to eat or read. Upstairs things were different. An electric fire with one or two dimly glowing bars was likely to be all one had for dressing by on a cold winter evening. Brushing hair or tying bow-ties was made difficult by two weak electric lights in frosted glass shades which hung, on a pulley arrangement, directly over the looking-glass, casting unhelpful shadows. Bathrooms were usually tiled or painted a clinical white, and thought adequately lit by another weak bulb hanging overhead. Somewhere in the town there must have been people whose bathrooms were wonders of marble and concealed lighting, whose bedrooms were warm and bathed in rosy light; it was not so in the houses of my relations. One had to be ill in bed, or a much revered visitor, to have a coal fire in one's bedroom, although all bedrooms possessed grates. Nancy Mitford writes somewhere of bedroom fires being replaced by central heating, and remarks: 'The days of luxury were over. The days of comfort had begun.' Luxury it was to lie warm in bed while someone made a quiet, competent bustle with paper, sticks and coal, and then to see the red and yellow flames streaking upwards and hear the sharp crack and low mutter of a fire beginning to take hold.

Comfort, however, in the sense of draughtless all-round warmth, scientifically placed lighting, prettily designed bath-rooms, was a conception yet to come. Meanwhile, being young, one was not much discommoded; and there is the point of such reminiscence as this. What is being recalled is something seen with the eyes of youth, encountered with youth's own particular vigour and resilience. At an age when one could cheerfully sleep on floors or even window-sills, could make long, complicated journeys in pursuit of small pleasures or the needs of love, one thought no worse than with mild amusement of one's elders' unhandy domestic arrangements. The London of which I write is largely the city I came to know well between my eighteenth and twenty-third years, and nearly all the aspects of it that I remember most clearly are gone, buried or effaced as though they had never been.

In *Memory Hold-The-Door* my father wrote of London at the end of the Victorian Age. 'Fleet Street and the City had still a Dickens flavour, and Holywell Street had not yet been destroyed. In the daytime...I penetrated into queer alleys and offices which in appearance were unchanged since Mr Pickwick's day. On foggy evenings I would dine beside a tavern fire on the kind of fare which Mr Weller affected. Behind all the dirt and gloom there was a wonderful cosiness, and every street corner was peopled by ghosts from literature and history.'

By the time of my schooldays much had changed. Gaslight had largely given way to electricity, petrol fumes had replaced a pervasive smell of horse manure. Nash's lovely Regent Street had been made pompous, weighty, although it still kept its fluent curve. Industry and commerce had erected palaces in their own honour — Bush House in Aldwych, Thames House on the river, some banks as stonily fortified as Florentine palazzi — but my father's wonderful cosiness was still to be found, here and there, especially in the City.

My first non-familial visit to London was to stay with a friend from the Dragon School, Richard Inge. I must have been eleven or twelve, and that was only the second time I had ever stayed alone with strangers. Richard's father was the Very Reverend W.R.Inge, Dean of St Paul's, and he lived with his family in Wren's noble Deanery, a hundred yards or so from the Cathedral, down a narrow street.

My friend, coming as he did from many generations of clerics, seemed to have been destined from birth for the church. His first names might have proclaimed this for, after Richard, he had Wycliffe and Spooner, the last in honour of his mother's family, she being the daughter of Warden Spooner, famous as the originator of 'spoonerisms'. (I think, in fact, that he only ever made one, in public at any rate, announcing a well-known hymn as 'Kinquering Congs their Titles Take', but that others, a large body, were made up later by various wits.)

The Dean, whom I liked, even revered, from the first moment, wore the full decanal rig of silk hat with strings, frock-coat, knee breeches and gaiters. He had a fine, thin, thoughtful face, and great courtesy of manner even with a small boy. Journalists had dubbed him 'the gloomy Dean', because of certain pronouncements he made which ran sharply counter to the hedonism and rather shaky optimism of the post-war years, and, thanks to the general odiousness of schoolboys, my own included, poor

Richard suffered a good deal of teasing on that account.

Richard's mother was vivacious, small and pretty and given to wearing rather unusual clothes, such as cloaks and tricorne hats, which gave her an eighteenth-century look. She no more than came up to her tall husband's shoulder, indeed she looked up to him in all possible ways. There is a story of a moment at a Royal garden party when the Dean, confronted by King George V, was looking down on the latter with mild benevolence but without uncovering. A small, anguished voice came up to him: 'Ralph, Ralph, the hat, *the hat!*'

The Deanery was a very large house, difficult to warm, and the Dean's stipend, like that of most clergymen, was probably inadequate for all his duties, social and ecclesiastic. Somehow Mrs Inge managed not only to make a home for her family but also to entertain charmingly in the vast drawing-room and dining-room thought proper for a Dean of St Paul's in ampler days. I remember best the great hall, the pleasant bedrooms upstairs, and a little blue-and-white octagonal breakfast-room where the window-panes were set in octagonal mouldings.

Richard showed me his London, which was chiefly the City itself. Earlier, at Lynam's, I had been given a prize for making a speech — I who now so hate making speeches — in the form of a book called *London Alleys, Byways and Courts*. That book had fascinated me and, since German bombs in the first war had done little harm to the City of London, I was able to look for, and find, the originals of its illustrations. Thus Richard and I went exploring. We began with such famous names as Paternoster Row and Amen Court, before going deeper into narrow, winding passages leading to minute courtyards with, here and there, a worn stone sculpture or the bowl of a fountain long run dry. We spent much time in the cathedral where Richard was greeted indulgently by its functionaries and we were allowed to run about at will. One day we climbed, up and up and ever higher, past the Whispering Gallery and the Golden Gallery with its dizzying near-perpendicular view of the marble pavement below, and on, up a stair almost too narrow even for children, into the golden ball at the top of the dome, and then just succeeded in getting our heads into the finial cross. It cannot have been long after that I quite lost the ability to look down from heights. That expedition could never, now, be repeated.

The City, in those days, presented a spectacle of almost unrelieved

163

black, where men were concerned, and there were many top-hats to be seen. There were women about, as well, secretaries who had not long ceased to be called 'lady typewriters', and their dress was discreet in colour and style. They were in a minority since much of the work in the more old-fashioned offices was still done by male clerks. One day Richard and I discovered an old eating-house patronized, I imagine, by the younger, poorer clerks, where a 'shilling ordinary' was offered; and so for a shilling apiece we had a good meal of grilled herrings and bread-and-butter, and some sort of pudding. That place had certainly not changed since the days of Charles Dickens. There was even a tall lectern at which, in past days, someone would have stood to read aloud to the assembled lunchers.

Richard, who was kind, intelligent and a loyal friend, would have made a good clergyman, but the Church of England was never to have his services. When war broke out he abandoned all ideas of ordination, joined the Royal Air Force to train as a pilot, and was killed in a flying accident.

'Harrod will have it, I expect,' my grandmother would say, if I was wondering where some particular thing might be bought, 'Harrod or Selfridge'. To her these names were names of shop-keepers rather than of shops. She could remember Harrod himself coming to the door of his emporium to welcome the carriage-trade; and Gordon Selfridge, although a knight, was still a kind of popular hero wholly identified with his monumental Oxford Street shop. Shops were, and perhaps still are, part of the magic of London life. In those inter-war years the multiplicity of big stores was a matter of pride to Londoners, even though the majority of them had little chance to do more than look in at the windows. One frequent sight on fine summer days, or at Christmas time, was a small family trailing behind a battered pram pushed by an equally battered mother, come up a long way from the East End, perhaps, or from south of the river to see the shops or the Christmas lights, and seeming cheerfully, uncovetously to be enjoying themselves.

I have the impression, nowadays, that the Londoners' deep-rooted pride in their city and all its manifestations, their love of shows and parades, of Royal processions and fashionable weddings is less strong than it was. Somehow the life of the city has been fragmented, the sense of identity with its celebrations dissipated. London is known to be a city of sights for foreigners, but I think that true Londoners, what is left of them, may well look on the tourists, thought to be so valuable a source of revenue, as usurpers.

Boundaries once were easy to determine. London could still be seen as a collection of villages only quite recently joined together. South Kensington, on the whole was dowdy, Earl's Court dusty and dull, and both of them home to sad, drably-clothed people eking out inadequate pensions in a hundred small hotels. Fulham seemed a great distance off. Places like Hampstead and Highgate, Twickenham and Strand-on-the-Green were, for the charm of their houses and gardens, much sought after by persons of taste. Even so an old lady of my acquaintance used to infuriate her correspondents by writing to them at 'Hampstead, near London'.

After the First War large London houses, especially in Bayswater and Kensington, must have become impossible of occupation by a single family, and so they had been cut up into flats, small and large, or even into single rooms. The thirties saw the development of 'bedsitter land' and speculators put up what were called 'one-roomed flatlets' which possessed a kitchen and, perhaps, an unshared bath. A sort of upper underworld had come into being, not actually criminal in character although often shady, made up of young and not-so-young people still possessing a small income, or some undemanding kind of job, who were able to live a more or less idle, if financially restricted, life. They formed groups, usually around someone significantly better-off, who was willing to fund their pleasures for the sake of their company. Such people made part of the population of certain quarters of London, once rigidly respectable, which, for reasons of war and economic recession had come down in the world. Nowhere has this society of the dispossessed been better described than in Patrick Hamilton's desolating novel *Hangover Square*. For them the coming war would, very probably, prove a godsend.

I have mentioned clothes as being one set of things where change in our time has been immeasurable. There were other differences as well. Tube trains, buses, trams, in hot weather or particularly on wet days, quite simply stank, and that for good reasons. Most of the small houses or tall tenements in the older parts of London had no bathrooms, nor even much running water. Cleaning bills were not to be thought of. Soap was a luxury. Clothing was often bought second- or third-hand and had already acquired a strong personality at the time of purchase. It made my mother very angry when some people opposed the idea

165

of providing bathrooms for what were still thought of as 'the poor' on the grounds that they would only keep coal in them (I suppose that that must once have happened, somewhere, to give base to a cruel legend). 'Can you imagine,' she would say, 'when every boy and girl wants to look like a film star, that they would allow a bath to be used for anything but bathing?'

For anyone enamoured of contrasts the London of my day provided a fine field for research. Something was in the air — possibly put there by shrewd propagandists of the left — which had a certain influence on young people of my upbringing. Some of us were insufficiently grateful for the security and comfort of our lives, so hardly achieved and maintained by our elders. We began to question the values by which they lived, and came to believe, or imagine that we believed, that the life of the submerged, the criminal, those at odds with society, had a greater validity than our own. Even though we were not *rentiers* someone, somehow, had managed to infect us with a touch of '*rentier* guilt'. Real life, we felt, was not to be found in country houses or at the dances and dinner-parties to which we were so kindly and innocently bidden. Logically pursued those impulses would lead to identification with some serious political movement, but not in my case. My attitude was romantic and logic had little to do with it.

Compton Mackenzie's *Sinister Street*, which I still think a remarkable book, had a strong influence on me. *Sinister Street* continues to be read, but I should not expect it to have the same sort of effect on male adolescents less sheltered, more 'streetwise' than I was at that date.

The book concerns a young man, Michael Fane, who grows up in West Kensington with a vague, and vaguely unhappy mother and the usual small complement of domestic servants. Although his circumstances are restricted there is mystery and some grandeur in his background, for he is in fact illegitimate, the natural son of a peer. The whole story of Michael's upbringing is done with close attention to detail and, when it comes to his time at Oxford, there is perhaps the best description of university life before the First World War that has ever been achieved.

After Oxford Michael returns to London, falls romantically and most unsuitably in love, persuades his girl to live with him, instals her in the extraordinary Ararat House, and then, through her immediate infidelity, suffers a shattering disillusion. Thereafter he departs on a lonely exploration of the more desolate, deprived,

166

and eventually criminal aspects of London life. He takes lodgings near Seven Sisters Road, that infinite stretch of dreariness in north-east London which, in his time, must have been drabber, noisier, smellier and more melancholy even than it is today, and thus, perhaps, appearing to him more 'real' than the hard-held respectability of West Kensington. Michael's flight from his family and his pleasant, cultivated, post-university world, must have held some strong appeal for me. Having no exquisite, questionable girl to set up *parmi ses meubles*, nor indeed the means to do so, I set out instead to follow Michael's footsteps into a London quite different from the one I had already known. In my wanderings through many dilapidated, uncared-for, and yet oddly attractive areas of the town I had little touch with the criminal but much with an unmitigatable sadness, with random violence in streets and pubs, with every evidence of misery and disease, and yet gained some appreciation of the resigned, unsentimental, ironical and often good-natured character of people half-submerged in a metropolitan world over which they had little or no control. They certainly made the most of such pleasures or scraps of good fortune as came their way, and they greeted trouble with the same sturdy, jeering defiance as they would give to German bombers in a few years' time.

I explored London in all directions, relishing the decay of once orderly bourgeois haunts such as Aberdeen Park, Clapham and Muswell Hill; not, like the young John Betjeman, in search of chapels and churches, but rather the emanations of other times, of other aspirations, as illustrated in buildings, gardens, parks and the domestic amenities of an earlier day. In Islington and Highbury there were still dairies largely run, I believe, by Welsh people, old-fashioned 'chymists' with their great bottles of coloured water, funeral parlours done out in black and gold, Dining Rooms where cubicles stood in ranks on a sawdust floor. One of the latter, in Shepherd's Bush, often provided me with breakfast — juicy, fat kippers, 'doorsteps' of bread with margarine, and tall, unbreakable-looking cups of strong tea. It may be that the impulse which, in childhood, had taken me bird's-nesting and botanizing, together with a growing interest in architecture of all kinds, had modulated from woods and hedgerows to another manifestation of nature, human this time, as expressed in forests of brick and high hedges of stone. My sociological researches were not scientific, nor were they inspired by any fixed ideas of progress or amelioration. Most probably I was simply preparing

167

for the novels which I was never really to give myself the chance to write.

One day, nosing about in a new direction, west of Edgware Road, I came upon Ararat House. There it stood — there could be no question about its identity — by a corner of the Regent's Canal basin at the southern end of Warwick Avenue. It was a large house, late classical of a stark and eccentric kind, out of scale with the neat terraces round about, almost a folly. Its lower windows boarded over, its stucco scaling, its paint peeling, it stood alone, grandiose, uncommunicative, quietly falling apart in its weed-grown garden by the green waters of the canal. Houses were already a passion with me and I could easily let slip all scruple in my determination to get inside one which took my fancy, provided, of course, that it should be uninhabited. Burglary, in that particular house, was not difficult. Somewhere at the back of it I found a window to prise open and made my way inside without serious difficulty, wondering as I did so how such an elephantine edifice had come to be so utterly neglected. Perhaps, in those days vandals, like the majority of London's population, were undernourished, for no harm had been done to the place but what was due to a long process of decay. Dust and fallen plaster lay thick on floor and stairway; gilded pelmets still showed rags of curtain material blackened with age and damp. The whole house smelled very like the grooms' rooms at home. If, as I am certain, Compton Mackenzie took that building for his model of Ararat House he must have known it in a healthier phase before the First War, but even then it would seem to have been divided into flats. Alongside the canal, at the foot of the garden, was a row of brick studios which I should come to know well when Feliks Topolski settled there for a while and entertained me wonderfully.

That part of Maida Vale, absurdly known as Little Venice, is now extremely fashionable and expensive. At the time of my first acquaintance the area, although pretty and full of well-designed, medium-sized early Victorian stucco houses, was little sought after. It probably seemed too far away, in terms of fashion rather than of distance, even for those who might have appreciated its gentle urbanity, because it was still possible for such people to live in mews cottages in Mayfair or Belgravia, or in flats or small houses in the more attractive parts of Kensington and Bayswater, and so be nearer to what could still be thought of as the centre of things.

I did not, of course, spend the whole of my spare time on the perambulations I have described and, after my return from Canada in 1937 I had other worlds to explore. Today, on my rare and rather unrewarding visits to London from the country, I can only see its present face as insubstantial, transparent, superimposed upon the much greater solidity of the city I knew before the war.

After the last war many London landlords still dealt in leases framed a hundred years ago. By one lease in Kensington I was enjoined neither to keep a disorderly house nor to skin cats on the premises. The London of my early days was a hive of odd trades and manufactures. The 'rubber shop' is no more, killed, at least temporarily, for its wares seem to be coming back into favour, by the priapic revolution of the past few years and the prevalence of the contraceptive pill. The rubber shop presented a discreet, recessive front to the world, its windows full of small boxes, serious-looking books, and appliances of red rubber and vulcanite whose use was obvious, together with others, sinister-seeming, whose purpose, by a polite mind, was unguessable. Sometimes a sign over the shop said 'Damaroids' and referred to a compound designed to restore failing sexual powers: more often there was no sign at all. All this came to mind the other day when, at a chemist's, my eye met a large tray of what are now called condoms, prettily packaged and temptingly displayed. No one, nowadays, need sidle furtively into the kind of shop that I have described. All is open, frank and bright as day. Before the war a heavy seriousness surrounded a commerce which could not, then, have been nearly so brisk as it is at present. Indeed, the largest shop of its kind, which occupied a site in St Giles's Circus, must, in the late thirties have suffered some recession, for it split itself into three, letting off the centre portion to a Moo Cow Milk Bar.

To ramble on about changes observed over a longish lifetime can be boring, but there is one that should be mentioned, the price of entertainment. For anyone living in a great city the chance of hearing and seeing concerts, plays and films must be an essential part of a reasonable urban life, and yet all these things have become enormously expensive. Looking back, it seems that scarcely a week passed during my time in London that I did not go to cinema or theatre, to an exhibition or a concert. I could certainly not afford to do so now. London could still show many traditional amusements, for example music-halls; the Metropolitan in Edgware Road, the Bedford in Camden Town, and, least affected by time of all of them, Collins's Music Hall at the far end of Upper Street, Islington, still offered bills of time-honoured music-hall fare. There were many bars, and drinks were often carried into the auditorium. At Collins's the price of a box for four people, pretty nearly on stage, was ten shillings.

Perhaps a wish to detect continuity in things may be a weakness. Perhaps one should 'greet the unseen with a cheer', while sturdily ignoring the past? I have two recollections which connect with the London my father knew. A kind lady, mother of a great friend, thought that I led a deplorably rackety life and very likely missed being properly fed. She instructed the staff at her house in Cadogan Square to give me a decent meal, should I turn up when she was not there. My father, as a young bachelor came, in his early London days, to the notice of a very august old lady who lived in St James's Square. She told him that, being somewhat infirm, she would not be able to entertain him herself but that, any time he might require them, there would always be 'a bottle and a bird' available to him at her house. And I have one recollection which, but for the absence of gaslight, must go clear back to the London days of which he wrote, and that is of having supper between matinée and evening performance in a theatrical dressing-room; steak and black velvet from a pub near by, a light November fog in the street, and, outside the window, a one-legged man playing on a cornet a sentimental tune.

12

OXFORD, BRIEFLY

If I have represented myself as lonely and friendless at the time of first living in London I have offered a false picture. It is true that, with the removal of half my nearest family to Canada, with my elder brother in Africa and my sister in the country, I felt myself unusually exposed. With the total severance from Elsfield I was, I suppose, rootless, and to the new soil in which I expected to root myself I did not take altogether kindly. Nevertheless, apart from my host and hostess, there were many who were interested in my progress, and enough friends of my own age to ensure parties of pleasure and those sessions of talk which our natures seemed to need.

My mother, accurately divining my probable state of mind, and fearful as any mother what footlooseness in the great metropolis might incur for her son in the way of trouble, had written to a number of friends and relations asking them to keep an eye on me. Thus I went often to Tin, my grandmother, and sometimes to great-aunts Margaret Talbot and Sophie Gray. I saw something of my Peyton-Jones cousins and their mother, who were often at Upper Grosvenor Street. There were weekends in the country and occasional invitations to dinner-parties, or balls, or those 'small dances' which were given by a committee of mothers for their daughters' coming-out in various private houses of Kensington or Belgravia. My excursions into conventional polite society were, however, infrequent. I refused invitations, as often as not, out of a preference for what was still thought a bohemian way of living, for long, sat-over meals in small Soho restaurants (a five-course dinner for three shillings and sixpence), for drawings and poems scribbled on paper tablecloths amongst wine and gravy stains, and sometimes kept as mementoes of especially fruitful evenings. Of friends from Eton, I saw something of Maurice Cardiff, although he was much away on travels, in Italy or France or exploring as far away as Prague. From Oxford two close friends joined me in London in the vacations, both of them called Michael. (That

Christian name must have taken a strong hold after the success of Compton Mackenzie's *Sinister Street*, published at the beginning of the First World War, the hero of which is called Michael Fane.)

Michael Clark came to Oxford from Rugby School — 'a cultural desert beside a railway station', in his own words — and greatly enlivened my brief stay at the University. His upbringing had been somewhat cosmopolitan and his knowledge of food and drink and great European hotels wholly surpassed my own. His main interests were journalism and politics. He did much to awaken me to the immediate political anxieties of my time to which, as I have shown, I had formerly paid little attention. He brought to our conversations an alert, critical and sometimes (to my ear) iconoclastic flavour, expressed with his own brand of slightly despairing humour. For most of the established politicians of the day he had little reverence, and this was new to me, who had so often heard them spoken of at home with admiration and respect. Michael's radical temperament may have come to him through his mother's family. His great-grandfather, I believe, had been a cobbler in Manchester and, like so many of that trade, a powerful political thinker, influential in his city. One of his relations was that Miss Slade, daughter of an Admiral, who had set up as Gandhi's amanuensis and travelling companion to the profound shock of the British community in India. (When the Mahatma visited Eton during my time there, his visit became the theme of one of Hester Alington's best stories: how Miss Slade had searched the playing field, their trees and shrubs, for a particular twig needed to brush her master's teeth, and how she had cut up pineapple for his breakfast on the lucent glaze of the mahogany dining-table in the Headmaster's house, to its lasting detriment.)

I was far from indifferent to food and indeed, after leaving the nursery, had greatly enjoyed the productions of Mrs Charlett, or of Tin's highly accomplished Mrs Bird, or at the tables of country neighbours in Oxfordshire. But there were explorations to be made, and what had been initiated at school by Lyulph Stanley, which is to say an interest in the unusual and exotic, was furthered by Michael at dinners at the George. In Oxford, that city of splendid tea-shops, the George was then the only sophisticated restaurant and there, in its faded green and white décor, beneath the incongruous fringed electric punkahs which stirred smoke and cooking smells around without contributing much to ventilation, we put the kitchen to various culinary tests. Sometimes, in my room at New College, I would give a luncheon party, and that would entail much serious conversation with the college chef, and much useful advice from Michael Clark. It is odd now, bizarre almost, to consider that young ladies from Somerville, say, or St Hugh's, when they came as guests to those luncheons, had to come in pairs, chaperoning one another, and wore their very best clothes complete with hats and gloves. Thus they lent a note of grace and freshness to masculine rooms frowsty with smells of alcohol and tobacco. In late spring the great cherry trees beneath the window added their own exuberant prettiness to those innocent festivities. The chef, who came from Alsace, excelled himself in the provision of rare dishes; red Burgundy — Corton 1924 — came from the college cellars at half-a-crown a bottle.

Michael Clark had a delightful appearance. His face, still youthfully round, wore always an expression of amusement, ironic sometimes, occasionally cheeky. His fair hair was inclined to stand up in spikes and he was largely indifferent to niceties of dress. What comes back to me most tellingly is his particular sparkle, an unblunted eagerness and enthusiasm, a turn of phrase which enhanced with humour even his most serious conversation. As with many who die young, to remember him is to see him clear-cut, detached from his background, lit by an unchanging aura of youthful energy and zest. Sayings of his come back to me frequently. At the time of our first meeting my father was pursuing, with Stanley Baldwin and Leo Amery, some wide and ambitious schemes concerning the British Empire. He was worried, as many were, that what he still thought a noble conception was losing clarity, that its mercantile aspect had usurped the idealistic, and that the younger generation mostly felt for it indifference, ridicule, or even contempt. His long-held devotion to T.E.Lawrence, his belief in the latter's possession of almost magical powers of leadership together with the authority of a living legend which could still catch the hearts of many who were impatient and adventurous, had led him to discuss with Baldwin the possibility of founding a movement which should revive, revise and refresh the idea of Empire amongst the nation's young. My father believed profoundly in leadership. He would have had no objection to being 'led' by someone whom he admired. Had he not once proclaimed that he would follow Lawrence over the edge of the world? It went without saying, therefore, that Lawrence would be asked to become the chief figure in the movement thus proposed. What my only half-attentive ear may have caught from my father's discourse it may have misinterpreted. Clearly there was thought and consideration behind the scheme he outlined: serious, far-seeing, imaginative people might take it seriously, even if they had, in the end, as I think that Lawrence had, to oppose it. However that might be, I took my version to Michael Clark, to see how he would respond. Typically he gave it full consideration. Since what I quoted came from my father, his good manners led him to treat it with respect. He brooded for a while and then gave me one of his broad grins. 'I think,' he said, 'that what the Empire needs is not a Leader but a Keeper!'

That conversation was to come back to me, with pathos, a short time later when there occurred what many thought a national tragedy, Lawrence's death following a motor-cycle accident. The accident happened on Monday 13 May 1935, as he was riding back to his home in Dorset, Clouds Hill. I cannot give an exact date, but I think that it was late in the previous week, perhaps Friday the 10th, that Lawrence made one of his surprise visits to Elsfield. My father was away on that day, but my mother and I were at home, with Alastair slightly ill in bed upstairs. That was to be my second sight of the man whom my parents so greatly revered, the first having happened when I was aged about ten and more inclined to remember the singularity of his special Brough Superior motor-cycle than the singular personality of the visitor. On this occasion, however, I took much closer note of the man who had every right to the journalist's description 'a living legend'.

T.E.Lawrence has been so often described, in every tone of admiration or denigration, that I can add nothing towards a 'final' judgement. I can only tell of that morning's encounter as one of memorable charm and easiness which has left a recollection, stronger than most, of something at once pleasurable and deeply sad. Distinction, perhaps, is in the eye of the beholder. The man who to Gertrude Bell was 'a little imp' was to my father the leader he would 'follow over the edge of the world'. I see him standing by the tall window in the library, facing me as we talked and giving me every strand of his attention. He was not a tall man, indeed decidedly short: I think that the top of his head came half way up my own and I am only of medium height. Yet, like my father who was also short, he possessed the ability to dominate his surroundings by a combination of powerful controlled energy, poise and eager interest in what was being said. Then there were his fair good looks and, of course, his extraordinary eyes, eyes blue as the sky, brilliant, oddly innocent and yet penetrating. Having blue eyes myself, and knowing the effect they make on Arabs, who will never meet them directly, believing them the property of demons, of *afreets*, I can imagine the effect Lawrence's would have had in his desert days.

Although Lawrence must have been disappointed not to find my father at home, since they always had so much to say to each other, he stayed for several hours and even took some time to visit Alastair on his sick-bed. What struck my mother and myself from the outset was the impression he gave of being gleefully off on an adventure, albeit one of a strictly private kind. He was full of an enthusiasm which was almost boyish, an excitement which clearly possessed him completely and gave him a youthful, a holiday air. What he was doing, in fact, was setting out to start on a new way of living.

We sat in the library, in the mild light of that late-spring day, and listened to the plans which Lawrence was about to put into effect. He told us of the bothy in a thicket of rhododendron which from then on was to be his home, his place of retreat, where he hoped to think and read and write in utter peace, free from disturbance by any but his most cherished friends. Clearly his experience of trying, and failing, to sink himself and his burdensome legend in the anonymity of the Royal Air Force had not taught him that such anonymity could never be his. Too many intruders, from story-hunting editors to high-minded admirers determined to make him *play a part*, would always be about to ensure that the true peace of mind he desired would never be achieved.

What he had to tell us was touching in the extreme. He planned a daily round of the utmost simplicity, in which his physical needs would be pared to the bone. A petrol-driven pump would fetch him water from a nearby stream. In his larder there were to be three or four bell-glasses to cover cheese, butter, bread and (I think) bacon, and these would supply his culinary needs. I think that, amongst the comestibles, he also mentioned jam. Now the reason why these modest, almost childish arrangements struck me with such force that I have pondered them ever since, was that they chimed — bell-glasses and pump apart — almost exactly with a long-dreamt ambition of my own childhood. I too had had ideas of escaping the influence of others, their wishes for me, their ambitions and sanctions, and setting up a dwelling of some sort, probably in the depths of Noke Wood, simply provisioned and hard to find, where I could read and botanize and feel free of a scrutiny which, at times, I had found so irksome. That was of course only a dream; translated to reality it would never have worked. I should probably have been frightened to death on my first night alone. Nevertheless its recollection made me feel a deep sympathy with what Lawrence was proposing to do.

When that unforgettable visit was over, Lawrence mounted his fearsome machine and was off with a roar up the village street, leaving behind, for memory to lay hold of, the dying growl of a powerful motor and a whiff of castor oil.

The second Michael, Michael Asquith, was different in many ways from the first, but no less attractive as a person. Like myself he had been brought up in close proximity to high affairs, to the scrutiny of the clever and successful of his day. He was grandson of Herbert Asquith, the Liberal Prime Minister who became Earl of Oxford. His father, also Herbert, was that statesman's younger son. His mother, born Cynthia Charteris, was granddaughter to the eleventh Earl of Wemyss, and daughter of that Lord Elcho, killed in battle in the Great War, who was one of the lost stars of a brilliant constellation which included Michael's uncle Raymond. Lady Cynthia was celebrated for her beauty, wit and intelligence. Michael and his brother Simon were thus in the same situation as myself, in that many eyes were on them, and much was expected of them. The Herbert Asquiths were not well-off, at least by the standards of their world. Cynthia wrote stories, edited children's books, and held a permanent position as a kind of amanuensis, adviser and social guide to Sir James Barrie, the playwright.

Michael Asquith's appearance was striking. He was tall and strong, with a clear-cut profile, and a shock of auburn hair in unruly waves, a colouring inherited from his mother. He walked very fast, bent slightly forward, his head thrust out as though it were trying to reach a destination before the rest of him. He shared with the other Michael an unquenchable eagerness: even when the air was still he could look like someone facing into a strong wind. Although he had been at Winchester he was the least typical Wykehamist I have ever known.

In 1934 Michael Asquith became editor of *Isis*, one of the two Oxford weekly magazines —the other being *Cherwell* — which were edited by undergraduates. Not long afterwards he appointed me his deputy. Thus for a couple of days each week, we toiled in a dark office in the bricky Gothic headquarters of the Holywell

Press, enjoying ourselves greatly, to the further neglect of our already neglected studies. We were far from being crusading editors; indeed we set our faces against the increasing solemnity of university life, the social and political anxieties which were so much a product of the times, subscribed to by the kind of serious person for whom, one day, I should be required to give up my place.

Thanks to the two Michaels, and friends from my two schools rediscovered after a long interval, and a host of new acquaintances all hard at work trying out attitudes, constructing for themselves a desirable *persona* to present to the adult world, some earnest and hard-working, others as scattered and frivolous as myself, my short experience of university life was one of fairly continuous amusement. In many ways it was a mistake to send me to Oxford. A university should offer a wholly new experience, new down to the last detail of setting and architecture, new in all its rules and traditions and eccentricities. Oxford, however, was my home town, the site of my first four years of formal education at the Dragon School, the place where I went to children's parties, to have my hair cut, to visit the dentist, to do my Christmas shopping. From many passages of exploration in my early schooldays, from visits to dons and undergraduates in their colleges — tea in his rooms with Evelyn Baring when I was about eight; magnificent strawberries, huge meringues, tall, grave young men in dazzling white flannels — watching the races in Eights Week from a college barge, I had a familiarity with the place which, while in no way breeding contempt, denied me the necessary feeling of awe, of privilege and good fortune at being at Oxford at all. I have the impression that awe and sense of privilege and submission to ancient ways are not much in evidence nowadays. The present-day undergraduate often seems to regard the University with irritation, finding neither romance in its traditions nor sense in its rules. His or her life appears fraught with struggle; frivolity takes a harsher tone. One day in the sixties, walking down Broad Street with my sister, I felt her clutch my arm. She pointed across the street to a tall grey wall where someone had spray-painted two words in foot-high letters. 'Goodness!' she exclaimed, 'I've waited a long time to see someone write up Bugger Balliol!' My friends and I had not, I think, any animosity towards tradition, nor resentment of regulations. Where the latter appeared inconvenient we simply ignored them, sometimes (but not always) incurring punishment thereby.

The two Michaels duly sat out their time at Oxford. During their vacations we met in London and took up again the endless threads of talk first spun at the university. Conversation was resumed in a variety of places, chiefly Soho restaurants or pubs because they were cheap. Sometimes we went to the Café Royal, then unreconstructed, where the wide open spaces below the balcony had marble-topped tables and benches covered in red plush, and it was possible to sit for hours, slowly absorbing excellent Pilsener beer which came in foot-high glasses, and eating an occasional sandwich for a small enough price. In summer we explored remote London parks, or walked on Hampstead Heath. Sometimes Michael Asquith and I would go for long night walks, crossing the river, hearing our steps coming back to us from the gaunt walls of Dockland warehouses, seeing rats scamper over cobbles, meeting nothing else alive but starved and savage-looking cats, walking on and on, down into Deptford, even, perhaps as far as Greenwich, before picking our way back through half a dozen distinct urban atmospheres to the green leaves and water and early birdsong of Regent's Park. In those days, people who had steady jobs worked hard at them and needed their sleep; many also needed to economize electricity and gas. So the long streets of small houses showed neither light nor life, and our footsteps, to anyone awake, may have sounded strange, disquieting, too rapid for policemen, not urgent enough for absconding thieves.

One day, after reading a story of mine, Michael Clark said severely, 'You really should relate your characters more to their economic background' — a saying perfectly in key with contemporary literary thought. About the generality of economic backgrounds I knew little; our own were our homes and what our parents gave us in the way of an allowance. There was no official source to which we could apply if we ran short; we should be obliged to take refuge at home — a situation wonderfully described in Waugh's *Brideshead Revisited* — or, if extremely enterprising, to take to the sea and work a passage to some foreign port. In those days parents had real power over their children, for financial reasons if for nothing else. My father's generous allowance began when I went to Oxford and continued until his death five years later. I cannot admire the spirit in which I accepted that bounty whilst continuing to please myself in ways not always pleasing to him, yet I must record my gratitude that he never, at any time, used the threat of cutting off or reducing my allowance to persuade me to embrace or abandon any particular course. Other fathers thought differently. Once, at my club, I overheard a conversation between two elderly men discussing the 'unsatisfactory' son of a friend. 'I've told him,' said one, 'if the boy goes on in the way he's going, the only thing to do will be to *cut off supplies*.' I should add that casual labour, even if one were in any way equipped for it, would have been extremely hard to find. At a time of serious and unalleviated unemployment, work on, say, a building site would not have been available to polite young men temporarily strapped for cash.

Quite often I feel like kicking myself for what now seems a dismal lack of adventurousness, a tendency to seek solace from the familiar and to cocoon myself in what was known, predictable and safe, rather than push out to wider kinds of exploration; for, whatever the economic and conventional stringencies may have been, there were many who advanced to meet the wider world with courage and good humour, sometimes from an urgent need to know more of it and its peoples, to ring every possible change on experience while still young, sometimes from generous idealism, a passionate desire to be part of the time's turbulences, as with those who set off, courting death, to lend a hand in the Spanish Civil War. To read the enchanting autobiography of Patrick Leigh-Fermor, for example, is to see how much might be made of travelling in Europe on a small handful of money and a large one of genial audacity, with eyes and mind open to all phenomena and an educated, keen, poetic intelligence ready and eager to absorb, record, collate and fruitfully conclude upon them.

My elder brother, who had inherited his father's taste for challenges, and for pitting his forces against hostile elements, and having little stomach for a life of aesthetic amusement and inconclusive speculation, passed his Oxford vacations in a variety of strenuous ways. One summer he signed on as deck-hand on a North Sea trawler; on another he went as ornithologist with the Oxford expedition to St Kilda, then as remote as Thule, where he suffered extreme discomfort while gathering material for his very first publication, *Some Notes on the St Kilda Wren*. My younger brother's great friend, Alastair Campbell, went as crewman in a ship sailing to South America while still a schoolboy at Eton. Adventurous conduct of the sort was not uncommon at that time. Most of us, however, whilst giving a full meed of admiration and respect for such enterprise, were content simply to be spectators.

179

I3

A NOTE ON STYLE

When he wrote *Crome Yellow* Aldous Huxley, describing the house of Crome, borrowed the great yew hedges from Garsington Manor, and the tall towers housing privies from Beckley Park, both of them houses within easy visiting range of Elsfield. He also composed portraits, as unflattering as they were ungrateful, of his patrons and frequent hosts, Philip and Ottoline Morrell. The way of the patron is often hard. For all the food, drink, shelter and influential help she bestowed on them, Lady Ottoline was not kindly treated by the lions she fed and watered at Garsington. There is a story of a summer evening when two or three writers, of whom D.H.Lawrence, that inveterate hand-biter, was one, were drinking their after-dinner brandy in deck-chairs beneath their hostess's bedroom window. She had gone early to bed, and it would be charitable to hope that her exact whereabouts were unknown to her guests, for they proceeded to a detailed, cruel unpicking of her looks and character to which, through windows open on a hot evening, she was obliged to listen.

Ottoline Morrell's appearance has been fixed for ever in Augustus John's portrait. Her individual style has been the subject of much reminiscence, her significance in the literary and artistic history of the time between the wars variously assessed. The Morrells came to Garsington not long after my family arrived at Elsfield, and left it in 1924 when I was eight years old. Thus, although I was never taken to see them, I knew their names, for those and anecdotes about them came up often in conversation at home.

Lady Ottoline was sister to the 6th Duke of Portland. She had married Philip Morrell, of the brewing family, landowners in Oxfordshire and benefactors of Oxford city, which marriage somewhat resembled (at least to the eye of a spectator) the union of a peacock and a domestic fowl. Philip Morrell is said to have been decidedly conventional, quiet to the point of silence, invariably well turned-out, a perfect foil, in fact, to his wife's extravagances. As a child I heard tales of haymaking in the fields round Garsington Manor, when its châtelaine, dressed in a style derived from the French eighteenth century, and hatted like Queen Marie Antoinette, helped with the hay and then rode home on the top of a loaded wagon, perched like some exotic bird in a wide nest of satin skirts. The villagers certainly laughed at her, but all the same may have appreciated an unconventionality, an aristocratic insouciance rare amongst the sober squirearchy to which they were used.

Philip Morrell was MP for South Oxfordshire in the early 1900s and for Burnley a few years later. During an election campaign for one or other of those constituencies, his wife took to the platform in his support. Democracy was much in the air and Lady Ottoline made a great deal of her sympathy with the common people. Philip, meanwhile, sat by, beautifully dressed, probably wearing the pale grey bowler to which Huxley compared Mr Wimbush's face, moodily nuzzling the silver knob of a cane and no doubt praying that his lady would soon give over. 'I love the people!' proclaimed Lady Ottoline. 'I revere the people!', and (turning with a wide gesture towards her husband), 'I married from the people!'

Ottoline Morrell had a particular turn of phrase, idiosyncratic, surprising, which was remembered when much of greater moment was forgotten. One day she visited a young painter whom she admired — I think it was Mark Gertler — who inhabited a single attic room which was studio, kitchen and bedroom, and which contained, in one corner, a water-closet complete with plug and chain. The attic was reached by a ladder through a trapdoor and the first the painter saw of his visitor would have been a wide scarfed or feathered hat rising grandly through the floor. After a long inspection of the pictures, and no doubt the giving of much encouragement and promises of immediate, practical help, Lady Ottoline prepared to leave. As she descended the ladder, at the moment when nothing was to be seen of her but her strange face under the great hat, she said goodbye. 'So nice to have seen you in your attic, your little *sanitary* attic!'

One summer afternoon in 1936 I went with Elizabeth Bowen to tea with Lady Ottoline. I do not know how I came to be invited; whether my hostess, knowing my parents, had expressed a kindly interest, or whether Elizabeth herself had asked to be allowed to bring me. We went by tube from Baker Street to Euston Square, and walked the whole length of Gower Street with its ranks of uncommunicative, flat-fronted eighteenth-century houses which Ruskin, rather unfairly, called 'the *ne plus ultra* of ugliness in street architecture', until we came to the brown-brick front, the tall door with its fanlight, of Number 10. The inside of the house struck me as familiar, since it matched exactly its neighbour, Number 8, home of Aunt Violet. (Mrs James Carruthers CH, born Violet Markham, Liberal politician and tireless worker for important causes, was one of our honorary aunts, being in fact Alastair's godmother as well as one of my parents' dearest friends.) I recognized the shape of hall and staircase and of the long, lofty drawing-room with windows looking on to green lawn and black-green shrubs and up to the towering bulk of London University's Senate House, a monstrous structure seemingly influenced by Soviet official architecture and known to many as the Bloomsbury Kremlin.

I believe that, for once, I spoke very little, being far too fascinated by my surroundings and by the interchange taking place between the two women, each of whom, in her way, was clearly a phenomenon, quite unrepeatable. How Lady Ottoline was dressed I cannot describe, except that what she wore was richly dark and flowing. Her face, where wit and imaginative intelligence triumphed over an absence of conventional good looks, was absorbing to watch, which I did as often as I could this side of rudeness. Her hair struck me then, and strikes me still, as being of a colour never seen before or since, most resembling a whorled mound of chestnut purée lightly striped with cream, as in a confection called a Mont Blanc. If Aldous Huxley (*op. cit.*) meant to parody Ottoline Morrell as Mrs Wimbush, he was wrong to ascribe to her purple hair. The colour was far subtler than that and, in its way, wholly successful.

Those were the days when every London lady with a large house to manage possessed lists of 'little men', artisans and craftsmen working for themselves, and very cheaply: what Parisians call '*bonnes adresses*'. They might be plumbers or clockmakers, upholsterers or dressmakers ('little women'), painters or cabinet-makers. Ottoline Morrell had, as protégé, one of the last, who had lined one long wall of her drawing-room with bookcases, the style of which, owing something to Adam, was right for the date of the house, whilst being, in its simplicity, quite congruous with the powerful modern paintings hanging on the other walls. When we arrived our hostess was seated in a high winged chair beside the fireplace. The room was full of a scent at once sweet and sharp and decidedly heady coming from a recessed table beside her chair which, I could see, was full of small bottles. Lady Ottoline, it seemed, had been experimenting, compounding something from the essences those bottles contained. It was not possible therefore, to take one's seat, open one's mouth on some polite bromide, without being already half-enchanted by evidence of a sure taste, a wilful, bold originality in all around.

Having vowed to try to speak only when spoken to, I used my periods of silence to cast covert glances at features of the room or, as often as I dared, at the two heads confronting one another, bent forward in the urgency of talk, of a rapport immediately established, two faces alight with spirit, beautiful in their animation.

If Ottoline Morrell's face was strange, impossible to refer to any type, the same might have been said of Elizabeth. She can never have been conventionally pretty; her features were too strongly moulded, her forehead too noble for any kind of chocolate-box; yet, in the time of another Elizabeth she would have been admired, and might, in the previous reign, have sat to Holbein, as her husband had so romantically prefigured. She had certainly never lacked devoted admirers in her own time. The fine, luminously intelligent eyes, the mobility of expression, combined with rather short sight to give the effect of the most powerful and acute concentration when she was speaking, her slight stammer adding to the often surprising quality of her remarks. Those, made with an idiosyncratic use of language, bore her own stamp of humour, the style of her wholly personal point of view, full of critical wisdom, sometimes memorably funny. One of her most famous remarks, concerning a cult of intense realism in literature, was: 'Life with the lid off? It's so much more interesting with the lid on.' On another occasion I asked her how she supposed it was that a well-known and particularly ugly literary man seemed always to be attended by a troop of pretty girls. She said: 'I think he lays his horrible g-great head in their l-laps and makes them feel sorry for him!'

The word 'style' is much in the air these days and dozens of glossy magazines give instruction on means of achieving it, sometimes combining it with 'life' to make the irritating compound 'life-style'. It may be that increasing standardization breeds a wistful wish, if not a positive temperamental need, to be a little different from other people, and to be so seen; to be admired for eating, entertaining, decorating, spending money in an original way. Originality must nevertheless, be hard to sustain, since the publications mentioned depend upon their readers following suit and buying the paint, fabrics, tiles, clothes, kitchens which their advertisers are hoping to sell; whereupon the original 'originals' must change their way of doing things in order, once again, to be seen to be out in front. This all seems fatiguing and, ultimately, frustrating. I suppose, when I think of style, and of certain people who possessed a distinct variety of it, that I am harking back to a time when it was the possible property only of a very few people and they, for the most part, rich.

Enid Bagnold was a friend of my parents' whom I began to notice and to admire when I was about seventeen, for her approach to living as much as for what she wrote. She had married Sir Roderick Jones (my father's Chairman at Reuter's). The Joneses had a house in Hyde Park Gardens, then a quiet enclave of Kensington Gore — large houses with large gardens, ideal for entertaining — and another in Sussex, at Rottingdean. Enid entertained a great deal and went, as they say, everywhere, and in the London Season of those days there was a great deal of 'everywhere' to which to go. It was a special misfortune, therefore, that she should one day be afflicted with what was then called a 'poverty rash', something due to a deficiency in the blood, not serious but extremely disfiguring. Most fashionable women would have fallen into despair over this, gone into nursing homes or buried themselves in the country, seeing no one, until the thing went away, but not Lady Jones. She had made for her a veil of some dark material through which she could see well enough but which was impenetrable by the eyes of others. This she wore round the brim of a hat and, thus safeguarded, continued her social round with equanimity. That this action was stylish, I would suggest, was because it contained an element of quite high courage as well as a refusal to be downed by fate or to relinquish pleasures for a temporary disability. All personal style contains, perhaps, a quantum of 'showing off', of ostentation, of the imposition of a personal whim. However it was, that action of Enid's struck me as both daring and singular, in short *chic*.

My eldest great-aunt, Mary Lovelace, who lived at Ockham Park, near Woking in Surrey, possessed a very definite style. No one, I think, would have dreamed of calling her eccentric, for her actions and pronouncements followed a personal logic of a consistent, if uncompromising, kind. Close family apart, and a few favoured friends (amongst whom, incidentally, were Henry James and my father) she did not care to have guests in her house. This prejudice was given trenchant expression when she declared: 'They cook in their bedrooms and go to bed in their boots!' The second part of that proposition may be regarded as a baroque flourish, but the first must have referred to the then general practice amongst women of travelling with spririt lamps and the means of making tea, together with devices for heating curling-tongs.

My mother, following her habit of encouraging people to invite me to various occasions and thereafter, perhaps, write to her reassuringly about me, must have begged Aunt Mamie to ask me down to Ockham. And so, one summer day, I arrived at Horsley station to be met — in 1936! — by a beautifully turned-out open landau, with liveried coachman and footman in cockaded top-hats. My great-aunt, when pressed to adopt the motor-car as a means of transport, had roundly stated that she had no wish 'to rattle about the countryside like the kernel in a nut'. To prove that her consistency was no hobgoblin of a little mind she then underwent a sudden conversion. At my next visit, and to my great regret, the beautiful equipage had gone, to be replaced by a gleaming American 'convertible', all dark blue upholstery and blue hood, which would not have been sneezed at by a Hollywood starlet. Clearly it was the car's convertibility which had persuaded Aunt Mamie to this change. Horses and coachman were near retirement, and the new car need be no more of a nutshell than an open carriage.

Another 'life-style' or, more appropriately, *train de vie* which intrigued me was that of the Harley Granville-Barkers. Harley was not well thought of amongst my theatrical friends, all of whom belonged to the serious or 'legitimate' theatre, for his had been a great name in theatrical production, his reputation that of a brilliant innovator, a leader. I had only to mention him to hear mutterings along the lines of 'just for a handful of silver he left us...', for there were some who never forgave him for leaving the London theatre, marrying a rich wife, and disappearing to France. His career had indeed been dazzling. He had a handsome presence and a fine voice, and with these, in 1892, he had set out as an actor. He early became a friend of George Bernard Shaw, and it was with Shaw's plays that he established a unique reputation as a producer at the Court Theatre between 1904 and 1907. He then went on to Shakespeare. The *Dictionary of National Biography* says of him that 'his productions of *The Winter's Tale* and *Twelfth Night* (1912) and *A Midsummer Night's Dream* (1914) set a completely new standard and proved profoundly influential'. With that last production, however, and in spite of a brief return to the London theatre in the thirties, his theatrical career came largely to an end. I do not know what the 1914 war did to him, but it may be thought to have altered radically his direction in life. In 1918 he married Helen Huntington, an heiress of the great American railway fortune, and settled with her in Paris.

Unlike most actors and some producers Harley Granville-Barker was a true intellectual. In the stately and profoundly comfortable life which Helen provided for him in Paris he worked on his admirable *Prefaces to Shakespeare* between 1923 and 1946. Of his own seven plays *The Madras House*, *The Voysey Inheritance* and *Waste* are the most remembered, the last being, in my view, the best play ever written about British party politics.

The Granville-Barkers lived in a tall nineteenth-century stone house in the Place des Etats-Unis, in restrained but considerable style. I was kindly entertained there on several occasions and would say that I have never seen great wealth more tellingly employed. Not only furniture and pictures and the services of a master chef were there to enjoy, but the conversation of my hosts was never less than stimulating. Their interests and the people they knew were various and surprising. It is, however, of their visits to London that I keep the most crystalline memory. Every so often they would come over for a few weeks, to see friends and publishers and to go to the theatre. Their method of housing themselves at those times impressed me greatly, for they had a permanent suite at the Ritz from which had been banished all the pleasant but slightly trumpery furniture, of a style known to me as 'hotel Louis Seize', and their own furniture, carpets and pictures substituted for it. Thus the transition from the Sixteenth Arrondissement to Piccadilly could be made with the least possible aesthetic jar or spiritual bruising by the unfamiliar.

14

A NEAR-RUN THING

In 1933, when I was seventeen years old, my mother took me to Paris. Yet another honorary aunt, Alice Wimborne, my mother's first cousin on her Grosvenor side, had a house in Passy to which she went occasionally for the Parisian season. Having a high opinion (shared by myself) of French doctors, she had urged my mother to consult one of those whom she especially admired. What the consultation was to be about I never learned, but both my mother and aunt belonged to a generation which enjoyed medical exploration: new doctors, new treatments were for ever being tried. My mother, who lived to be ninety-five, was never, I think, in serious ill-health; she always seemed well enough to me. Nevertheless, for whatever physical ailment, real or imagined, hers may have been, the Parisian doctor and his treatment were thought certain to provide a cure. So we set off, in fine summer weather, on an excursion which was to be not only a pleasure in itself, for so much beguiling strangeness and newness, but the introduction to a city, a people, a pattern of living which wholly satisfied some buried wish, offering me prospects to which a part of my nature responded with joy and a quickening sense of release.

Few seventeen-year-olds, nowadays, travel abroad with their mothers. As it happened I could not at that age have had a better travelling companion. My father, wishing to see some solid good come from what he may privately have thought an unnecessary venture, decreed that I must take charge of all the details of travel, deal with tickets and porters and taxis, and act in every way as a responsible courier. None of that caused me any anxiety. From the moment of leaving Victoria Station I read and re-read the neat books of tickets provided by Thomas Cook, got us both on to the steamer at Dover and off again at Calais capably enough. I was delighted by the crowd of nimble, blue-bloused, garlic-smelling porters who suddenly appeared, darting amongst the passengers before, it seemed, the boat had properly docked. Forethought, responsibility, care of another — qualities for which I was scarcely famous — came easily to me in that foreign land, so high and all-embracing were my spirits. Like a small boat moored to a sea-wall at ebb tide something in me had been straining for a long time to escape my moorings. What the goal of that escape might be I never fully realized, but it at once became clear to me that it must be, must always have been France, first and foremost, and, thereafter, as much of Europe as I could reach.

After a couple of visits to Aunt Alice's doctor my mother was evidently much reassured about her health. She became wonderfully cheerful, open to all suggestions, tireless in the pursuit of small pleasures, so indefatigable in fact that I, still a victim of adolescent feebleness, sometimes flagged disgracefully. Our pleasures may have been small in money terms — long sessions in pavement cafés drinking an orange drink called Pam-Pam, seeing films at cinemas in the Champs-Elysées, visiting churches, museums, the Palace of Versailles, sampling every kind of shop from perfumers in the rue de Rivoli to M. Rouault's *bondieuserie* in the Place St Sulpice where my mother was much taken by some plaster statuettes of saints — but they all served to open my eyes to an architectural satisfaction, a tempo of living, an appealing kind of positiveness which would ensure that, for ever after, Paris would be for me a home of the heart. I could not now count the number of visits which I have since made to Paris, whether for pleasure or, in recent years, on business. Of all the cities I have known that is the one in which I have never been unhappy nor, except very occasionally, bored; but of course it has been only as a visitor, an explorer and observer, that I have known the place. My longest stay there has been no more than two months. Custom, therefore, has never had the chance to stale a variety which I believe to be infinite.

Every detail of that first visit is clear to me, from the strange-sounding advertisements (Byrrh, Suze, Savon Cadum) and the slogan repeated at the entrance to each Métro station 'Dubo...Dubon...Dubonnet', to the two-note yapping of the taxi horns, the look of the intently hurrying crowds, and food: ices at Rumpelmeyer's, wild strawberries smothered in thick yellow cream at luncheon in the Bois de Boulogne.

No writer has caught the colour, the movement, the very sound and smell of 1930s Paris, the Paris of ordinary people, so well as Robert Sabatier in *Les Alumettes Suédoises*. That title refers to an international scandal caused by Kreuger, the Swedish Match King, whose financial crash ruined a multitude of people all over Europe. Sabatier's book is the simple history of a boy growing up in modest circumstances somewhere on the slope of Montmarte. What is so remarkable about it is the author's apparently total recall of the period in a great number of its aspects, from radio programmes to advertisements, makes of cars and bicycles, sporting events, food, the games of children, the small treats and limited aspirations of an honest *petite bourgeoisie* struggling to live decently in bad economic times, all counterpointed by glimpses of a morbid political condition and the follies and failures which were tending inevitably towards war.

My next visit to Paris came three years later, in the early summer of 1936. I had managed to acquire a lump sum of money, about forty pounds, at the same time that I was awarded a week's holiday by the film company. That money, lent to me in cash, was too great a bonus to be shared with my bank. I decided on a visit to Paris with Maurice Cardiff.

We flew from Heston in an aircraft belonging to a private company, Hillman's Airways. It was a small cabin machine which held about eight passengers. The whole proceeding was simple and businesslike. We were not pampered, the entire provision for passenger comfort being a packet of chewing-gum and a paper bag in which to be sick. Our luggage must have been substantial, since we had both taken with us clothes for almost any social eventuality.

Our aircraft probably never flew higher than a couple of thousand feet, so our progress was punctuated by bumps and lurches as we met various up- and down-draughts over valleys or woodland. I cannot recall the duration of the flight (which now takes about half an hour) but it must have been between three and four hours. We landed at Le Bourget, to the north-east of Paris, which was then, like Heston, a grass field. There, in one corner, stood a line of military aircraft, fighters, probably Moranes, drawn up with their noses in the air, drab in their grey livery but purposeful, menacing. Thoughts of war, become by then a leaden underlay of consciousness for almost everyone, surfaced for a moment through my excitement, soon to be chased away by the succeeding rush of impressions as a bus whisked us with enormous brio down miles of broad cobbled streets lined with warehouses, shops, dwellings in an extraordinary jumble of

styles, where no two frontages resembled one another, all seeming
to illustrate the rooted individualism of Parisians; an impression
shortly to be corrected when we moved into the city's central
districts, straightened out, straightened up and rigorously formal-
ized by the iron hand of Baron Haussmann.

Our hotel, the same in which I had stayed with my mother,
stood in a quiet, short street off the rue de Rivoli. Its address,
Hotel Louis le Grand, rue Rouget de Lisle, was in itself an exercise
in pronunciation which had to be performed with care. Its interior
was spacious, old-fashioned, a trifle shabby. To reach our rooms
we went up in a lift like a decapitated sedan chair, the doors of
which came no higher than our chests. Once settled in our
quarters, Maurice and I sat down to make a plan of action,
determined to extract the maximum value, both in pleasure and
instruction, from our week's stay.

Together we consulted a list made in London of people to see,
and some notes of introduction which went with them. Most of
the latter had been given to me by Franzi Goodman, whose
Parisian acquaintance was large and varied and who, early in a
successful career as a photographer, had worked for a while with
Man Ray. Franzi's parents had had to leave Germany, for
compelling reasons, a few years before, and had somehow come
under my grandmother's tutelage; and so I owe to Tin a
much-valued friendship which lasted for more than fifty years.

The tempo of social life in Paris, unlike that of its politics, was
not at that time especially hectic. The English, where considered
at all, were on the whole quite popular. One introduction taken up
led to others, and soon we were darting hither and thither, to
luncheons, cocktails and visits to see something or other which
must be seen in somebody's house or apartment; and all that
combined with forays to museums and galleries and random,
exhilarating, foot-free explorations of obscure corners of the
town.

The habit of 'dressing down' for almost every occasion had not
yet taken root. However dangerously unconventional our families
might think us, our school training was still strong, and so we
went visiting properly dressed in suits — summer suits of pale
grey flannel, I rather think — with brown felt hats and chamois
gloves (carried, not worn) and that article which was to become,
two years later, the object of much cruel satire concerning
Englishmen, the slim, tightly rolled umbrella.

It was a week of perfect summer weather. Pink chestnuts

glowed along the lower part of the Champs-Elysées, playground of the young Marcel Proust, and in the warm, blue evenings the fountains at the Rond Point sent up dissolving cones of water coloured pink by the lights set round their bowls.

Paris was all green leaf, water, sunshine, wide clear light and endless perspectives of quiet grey stone. The crowds streaming past the cafés were, as they still are, a spectacle of unfailing interest. They were workaday crowds, on the whole. The world of elegance, then as now, was not much to be seen. The temper of the Parisians, set on edge by financial and political scandals, angry with government, fearful of the future, and borne on by the difficulties of daily living, was not sympathetic to conspicuous displays of wealth. *Les élégants* prudently kept to themselves, were little seen on the streets, moved unostentatiously in sober vehicles between splendid interiors, grand restaurants and lavish entertainments in each other's homes. Nevertheless the crowds looked neither drab nor dispirited; preoccupied certainly, and tenaciously intent on the business of living, they still showed an alertness, a quick responsiveness, apparent in vivid explosions of greeting when friends came together, their ranks decorated, coloured by the bright dresses of the working girls.

It was a Paris of fewer cars, and infinitely fewer tourists. The English, the other Europeans, the Americans who travelled abroad in those days were, on the whole, experienced at the game, at ease with favourite places, able for the most part to melt into the scene without appearing noticeably foreign. There were no coaches, no package tours (or none to be recognized as such), no crowds of bewildered foreign schoolchildren, and so I remember pre-war Paris as spacious, easy to negotiate, qualities which, as with all great cities nowadays, it has rather sadly lost. Not that the place was quiet: far from it. Over the growl and grind of blunt-nosed buses, I can still hear the taxi-horns, long since silenced by decree, with their high-pitched 'pah-p'm', and the shrill voices of newsboys calling 'Paris-Midi dernier! Paris-Mid-ee-ee!'

So it wore on, that hot summer of 1936, with long, weary stretches between small islands of pleasure. At Gaumont-British all excitement, novelty, variety had gone by the board. After the completion, at the end of the winter, of the Hitchcock film, I had been shipped off to the sister studios of Gainsborough Pictures, a collection of draughty, barn-like buildings somewhere in Islington, to work with another director. His film was a plodding historical piece, *Lady Jane Grey*, only memorable for the looks and personality of a very young actress, Nova Pilbeam. I joined the production team half-way through its schedule, and soon found myself on a tented field somewhere near Isleworth trying, in driving rain, to organize some extras on horseback into a stately cavalcade. Of that assignment my chief recollection is of the wardrobe's Tudor finery collapsing in the wet, and the utter misery on the faces of those extras who had claimed that they could ride, matched only by that of the poor, beaten-looking nags with which they had been provided.

After that there were no more productions to employ my uncertain skills. Wondering what to do with me, someone must have said 'literature', for I was drafted to the script department, to help plough through the mounds of screenplays sent in by literary agents or by hopeful authors acting on their own. I shared a small room with a dark, elegant young man whom I suspected of literary ambitions, but with whom I found it hard to reach agreement on any point. Our room was low down in the building, next to the boilers. Its single small window looked out on to and partly through the scabbed and sweating brick of the low viaduct which carried the Metropolitan Railway. The heat was fierce. With the sash-window fully open some flabby air, exhausted and smelling of rotten fruit, came in but brought no real relief because with it came also, very frequently, the clang, click and hammer of the Metropolitan coaches as they swung past above our heads; nor was theirs the only noise. Most of the brick arches of that long viaduct had been thriftily let out to small businesses of one kind or another, and a rackety street market had its place on the other side, hence the smell of stale greengrocery. Immediately opposite the window one arch contained a gramophone shop, where records were played at full volume nearly all day long, but in no sense as a recital because there were only two. One was 'Red Sails in the Sunset'; the words of the other I could never make out. Perhaps, after a few weeks, another pair of songs might be chosen to attract customers, but I should not hear them for, at some time towards the end of July, I began to be rather ill.

I do not know whether that summer of 1936 was unusually fine, yet I remember it as continually hot and dry. London grew steadily dustier. Parching winds blew scraps of paper, grit and straw to eye-level at street corners. Shepherd's Bush, no beauty spot at the best of times, took on an extra tinge of dreariness in the glaring light; the scarlet of the buses hurt the eyes; flies blackened the nameless meat in the cut-price butchers' shops. Coolness was hard to find, even at night, and the trees in Regent's Park began to look jaded, their green turned dark, brown-edged, their freshness forgotten. Light from the lakes struck back at the eye with a hard unsympathetic glitter. I suppose that it must sometimes have rained, but I remember no slaking of the dust, no cooling of hot pavement and melting asphalt. Sometimes, at weekends, I escaped to Stratford-upon-Avon, where my sister was playing small parts at the theatre, and those visits brought a most welcome release to one who had begun to feel altogether 'too long in city pent'.

That summer the Camerons went away to Ireland, to Bowen's Court, which Elizabeth loved and which, anyway, required her attention. The servants went too, and so I had the house in Clarence Terrace all to myself. That state of affairs which, at another time, might have given me pleasure, served only to underline a loneliness with which I had not succeeded in coming to terms. I went out whenever I could with such friends as were stuck, like myself, in London, accepted occasional invitations, visited my grandmother, but with a diminishing zest which must have owed much to my deteriorating physical condition.

On top of all other distresses — my unpromising, unrewarding 'job', my feeling of being at sea in a world of ambitions and interests which I could not share — my heart was sore with the coming to an end of a love affair, begun the summer before, which had sustained my need for romantic affection, for the focus of another being as solitary in her own way as I was, to fill that incompleteness which had been with me since childhood. That the affair could have no practical issue I knew well enough: both of us were too young for any conclusion acceptable at that time and, as I was beginning miserably to feel, my devotion was less and less reciprocated, the responding signal was growing weak. The poor girl could not be blamed. She was in thrall to a powerful family; decisions about her young life were not hers to make. When I heard that she was to be sent abroad, to be 'finished' in some European country, I knew that finishing would not stop at that.

The immediate effect of this jolt to my sentimentalism was that I began to live still more hectically, seeking 'madder music, stronger wine' in the fashion of an absurd, a really out-of-date romanticism which still governed my moods. I stayed up later, lost more sleep, drank more than I should, scattered in talk a few possibly worthwhile ideas which would better have been put soberly on to paper. All such activities must have accelerated my physical decline which, as August came on, began to declare itself in alarming ways.

It all began with a sore throat, of a kind that I had never known before. Sore throats in childhood, attendant on measles or other traditional ailments, the kind of rasping discomfort and difficulty in swallowing which went with really bad colds, all those were part of my own, of everybody's experience. This, though, was something different, a raging fiery soreness, present at all times, which made eating and drinking a torture, sleep next to impossible; a thing malign, obsessive which held station in the forefront of my consciousness night and day.

There came then a time when I virtually took myself out of circulation. Telling the studios that I was too ill to come in, I shut myself into my high room hoping that, if I rested, starved, saw nobody, the wretched ailment would go away. Irrational I was, but not so lost to normal forms as not to see a doctor, who diagnosed quinsy, gave me a gargle and sent me on my way. The throat did not improve, but rather seemed to grow worse. I think that I must have been feverish, for time itself seemed to expand and contract as it does in fever. I lost count of the days, and, sleeping badly or not at all during the night, found it desperately hard to move in the mornings. One day the pain, quite literally driving me silly, sent me to a chemist for some ether with which I tried to anaesthetize myself.

Anyone might ask: why, in this plight, did I not appeal to friends or relations? and the answer would be that London in August, in those days, and for the people concerned, was a city of the dead. My grandmother was in the country where, according to custom, she had taken a house for the summer, to give her servants a holiday. My sister was acting at Stratford. All my friends were scattered, either at home or abroad, on various vacationary ploys, their parents away on holiday. My own doctor was on holiday as well.

In the end it was to Michael Asquith that I owed my rescue from a situation which I had quite lost the power to control. For a year or more, and *pari passu* with my own doomed affair, Michael had been in love with Diana Battye, who was destined to come much into my life and that of my family and whom he would one day marry. Diana, or Didy as she was known to a wide circle, was a girl of great beauty and sweetness of character, who had the

194

power to excite the most passionate devotion in all whom she met. She particularly appealed to my father, who perhaps found in her the living embodiment of his most interesting heroine, Corrie Arabin in *The Dancing Floor*, for Didy had Greek blood, and her large eyes, of a perfect bird's-egg blue, looked out from a face tinted and featured as though she carried with her some magic of the Aegean.

For a couple of days my complaint gave me what doctors call a remission, and then attacked again with redoubled ferocity. A new element appeared: I began to choke; that is to say my breathing apparatus went almost completely out of action, so that I fought for breath, gasped and floundered as though drowning in mud. Such spasms of the larynx, as I was later to hear them called, were not, I suppose, of long duration, but they seemed eternal and were decidedly frightening. At the second one, which occurred one evening at about eleven o'clock, I rushed from the house half-dressed, found a taxi and managed to croak 'Doctor!' to an astonished but sympathetic driver. We drove a little way round the Park until we saw the small red light over a door which was still sometimes used to indicate a doctor's house. The taxi-driver rang the bell, waited and rang again. No one came to the door. After some minutes a window was thrown up, a female head in a hairnet was thrust out, and a voice called down, 'Go away, *please*, the doctor's not well.'

Still trying to dredge up breath, and making a hideous noise doing so, by means of signs I got the taxi-driver to fish out an old envelope and a scrap of pencil. I wrote down the name and address of my doctor's partner in Ladbroke Square, and begged him to telephone for me. I leaned against a telephone-box, roaring like a tubed horse, while the driver, that good man, got through to the doctor. His message must have been impressive: 'There's a gent 'ere choking something 'orrible!' In a minute we were on our way, and, as nearly always happens, by the time that I reached Ladbroke Square the spasm had abated. The doctor, who came to the door in his dressing gown, was both forgiving and sympathetic, but beyond diagnosing 'quinsy', and recommending a couple of days in bed, he had nothing much to say.

Michael Asquith, when in London, lived with his parents in the next terrace to mine, Nash's Sussex Place with its classical frontage and strange octagonal domes. It was my good luck that he and Didy were both in London at that time, she staying with her uncle, the great collector Eumorfopoulos, and that they came

195

on an impulse to see me and so discovered the state I was in. They decided to take me at once to the country, to a place where I could be looked after, be among friends; and so, late one evening I left Clarence Terrace, not guessing that I should never live there again, and was driven to stay with Didy's mother in Berkshire.

If Mrs Battye had misgivings about receiving into her house an obviously very sick young man she gave no sign of them, but treated me with great practical kindness, making me go to bed and providing me with drawing materials and many books. Almost at once, however, I had another attack and, soon after, another again. A doctor was called, who responded seriously to the alarm of the household. It was decided that I should be taken to a nursing home in Windsor. There various remedies were tried, such as a steam tent, but to no avail. The attacks came closer and closer together; with the struggle for breath I was weakening rapidly. A surgeon was consulted and the decision was made, since my throat by then was nearly completely closed, to perform a tracheotomy. I count it a milestone in the, for me, inordinately long road to maturity that I, who had always had a nervous horror of operations, should have had to agree to that one and have been glad to do so.

The operation was performed with a local anaesthetic, since my respiratory system was in such disarray. I felt no pain, only pressure, very heavy at times. I could hear an odd scratching and tearing sound and when, using some force, the surgeon cut through my windpipe there was a hiss of escaping air. Eventually I was returned to bed with a tube in my throat. I was given a good dose of morphia, which had the delightful effect of making everything, including any pain, seem remote and inconsequential.

Consulted by the doctors, and put into a state of high alarm, Tin came to visit me, bringing with her Alice Butterfield and Simon, her pekinese, all but the latter dressed in deepest black. They were followed soon after by Alice, with Brian, my brother-in-law. They found me cheerful enough, glad to be even half out of that particular wood, already much recovered but almost without a voice, because the air I was getting came through the tube and so rendered more or less useless my vocal cords. The operation itself had been, I should say, quite brilliantly performed, for I have never since had any serious trouble at that place. It is curious to think that, had the now universal antibiotics come into use by August 1936, none of the above-mentioned miseries need ever have occurred, for the origin of it all was said to be streptococcus, a microbe easily disposed of by such things as sulphanilamide.

Thus comes to an end one whole phase of my existence, and it makes a fairly futile story. It shames me to think, although I could not even have seen, let alone admitted it at the time, that what I was performing, at least partly, over my first London year was an infantile drama of resentment and rejection for the disruption of my life, the separation from my family, the loss of my home and of an obsessive love. Realizing that almost any young man of strong character would easily have risen above all that, would have opened his eyes to the future, grasped his opportunities, remained without rocking on his own feet, I can only see myself as a perfect nuisance, and an expensive nuisance at that.

Nobody told me that I was a nuisance. Nobody reproached me. On all sides I was treated with the utmost kindness: the most elaborate care was given to my health. It was thought that streptococcus had found a hold through tonsils which had not been sufficiently thoroughly removed. That first operation, when I was three, was undoubtedly the source of my fear of surgery, having left me with a horrible memory of suffocation under chloroform. I suppose that those were early days for the technique of that particular operation. Something had remained behind which had, so to speak, gone bad. So it was decided that I must have a second tonsil operation. When that was accomplished in a London nursing-home I set off to convalesce in Dorset, with a trained nurse for company. It seemed, then, that I had once more arranged for myself a 'time out of life', a moratorium, a situation in which, for a while, no decisions need be taken. My mother was coming home on leave. Elsfield would be opened up once more. At the end of December I should go to Canada to complete my convalescence, before having another try at accommodating myself to the world. What could it have been, I wonder, far back in what must seem an idyllic childhood, that had made such a hole in my psyche that I must for ever feel incomplete, believe myself inadequate, mishandle splendid chances, and repeat the perform- ance over and over again, advancing and retreating as in some idiotic dance?

15

A BITE OF THE BIG APPLE

Spring comes suddenly in Canada and lasts but a short while. Before it has properly declared itself, before the long winter can really be put behind, the season has turned to high summer; or so I remember it. It was a day in April which found me embarking, by invitation, for a proving flight in the Canadian air service's latest acquisition, a Douglas twenty-one-seater. This machine, the largest I had yet seen, I was to see again hundreds of times not, as on that day, polished and shining like a silver fish, but in desert or jungle camouflage; for the twenty-one-seater of which my hosts were so proud was none other than the DC3, later to be named Dakota, the most trusty workhorse amongst all the Allied aircraft of the Second World War.

A few weeks later I was on my way as a paying passenger in that same aircraft bound for New York. I had not done much flying, but I should never forget my first flight. Five years before, on my way home from OTC camp at Tidworth, I had stayed a night with a friend in his mother's Surrey cottage. We had spent an afternoon watching an air display at Brooklands, and I had paid five shillings for a ten-minute flip in a Tiger Moth which I had greatly enjoyed. Now here I was, crossing the Canadian border in something much larger, faster and noisier than a Tiger Moth or the small machines in which I had crossed the Channel. Over the Adirondacks we were served with coffee by the single stewardess; served, too, with some pride, since hot coffee in the air was an innovation, the thin end of a wedge which would open bizarre possibilities of 'in-flight catering' later on.

New York's airport in those days was Newark, New Jersey, on the south side of the Hudson river. Approaching from the north-west I had had my first glimpse of the amazing city, its geometry half rubbed out by sunny mist, its towers insubstantial-seeming, in every sense fantastic. One day I should see the city again, from a lower angle, coming up the river in Atlantic liners, and each time it would break on the eye with the shock of the incredible, sharing with Venice a 'quite special unlikelihood, the one standing its noble buildings on wooden toothpicks in a wide lagoon, the other squeezing them upwards from a narrow shelf of rock. Even before I landed I was in the grip of the excitement, the almost feverish anticipation which New York, for a foreigner, must always produce.

After whisking at what seemed enormous speed through the Holland Tunnel in an elegant black bus I found my way to the Hotel Chatham and sat down to get my breath. The Comptroller of the Household, Eric Mackenzie, had supplied me with a useful wad of dollar bills. My parents had provided introductions. Friends at the American Legation in Ottawa had given me some useful advice. One counsel was repeated several times, most seriously. If I went out alone in the evening, and most particularly if I wore evening dress, I must carry five dollars in my breast pocket, for there was always the possibility that someone lurking in a doorway might poke a gun in my ribs and demand money. On no account was I to argue, or refuse to pay up, but simply hand over the five dollars.

I do not think that the word 'mugging' was then current, but it is interesting to note that the streets of New York, even those most apparently respectable, were not to be thought free of crime fifty years ago. On the other hand five dollars seemed a modest enough quittance and, at least, there was no real danger, as there is now, of one's assailant being so lost to reality through drugs as to kill or maim merely for the contents of a wallet. I doubt whether any sensible person, nowadays, would walk the streets of New York alone at night, and especially not in a dinner-jacket.

The Hotel Chatham was a substantial square building, not tall enough for a skyscraper. It had a peaceful, rather old-fashioned air, and its restaurant offered interesting and unfamiliar food. Already, on board ship and at Ottawa, I had come to appreciate 'hot biscuits' for breakfast, biscuits which were really plump scones and not the crunchy things I was used to at home which, in America, are known as cookies or crackers. I had not long been in New York before I had sampled oyster soup, shad roe with black butter, and a dish in itself worth crossing the Atlantic for, soft-shell crabs. At one dinner-party I was given my first taste of wild rice.

My days were busy; indeed it was almost impossible to imagine an empty day in that city, so powerful was the pressure to get on to the next thing, so irresistible the strong current of curiosity, enthusiasm, experiment, go-getting and pleasure-seeking which swept one along.

There were the galleries, of which the Frick Collection, although not vast like the Metropolitan, and perhaps because of that, gave me the most pleasure. There was the Morgan Library where, thanks to an introduction to its redoubtable librarian, Bella da Costa Green, I was taken into the strong room and allowed to hold in my hand the manuscript of Keats's 'Nightingale'.

There were the clubs with their marvellous echoes of Wharton or Scott Fitzgerald. The American Minister at Ottawa, Norman Armour, had warned his family of my visit, and I was invited to the Brook Club by his father and brother, to find an atmosphere almost indistinguishable from that of a London establishment of the same sort, yet subtly different, perhaps because of a sense of very great, albeit discreetly paraded, wealth. The Brook's name was said to refer to Tennyson's poem, the suggestion being that, like his brook, it would go on for ever. I had a card, also, for the Racquet Club. The weather throughout my stay was very hot and so one afternoon, tired and thirsty, I dropped in there for a long cold drink. The sense of wealth in that place was anything but discreet. Where the Brook was sober, quiet-coloured, full of dignified middle-aged men beautifully dressed, the Racquet Club was the very height of sporting luxury, with every appurtenance of squash- and racquet-court and swimming-pool sparklingly up-to-date, and such members as were about youngish and extremely smart. When the bill came for my drink I realized that one visit was probably going to have to suffice, if my wad of dollars was not to dwindle uncomfortably fast.

For some time past the idea had been in the air at Ottawa that I should not return to England but look instead for some employment in North America, either in Canada itself or in the United States. My trip to New York, therefore, had a serious purpose. Broadcasting or newspaper work had been thought of, and so I had a number of interviews arranged with those ideas in mind. However, as so often happened in my young days, I was altogether too well introduced. My parents' acquaintance was all in the uppermost reaches of various professions and although, for their sake, I was made welcome in a number of splendid offices, I made no mark at those slightly lower levels where jobs were actually handed out. Even at that age I was aware that the position of a young man about whom some president or director has told a subordinate to 'do something' is always a delicate one. Nor can I pretend that I put myself forward with real energy and conviction. Deep down, I had no wish to spend my life on that side of the Atlantic. Europe had far too strong a hold on me and, even after so short a time, was beginning to call imperiously. Finally, America was still in the grip of the Depression and any jobs that were going were not likely to go to a twenty-one-year-old Briton of very limited experience.

In that brilliant weather of early summer the heat seemed to settle and intensify in the canyons between tall buildings. It was made more stifling by humidity from the almost-surrounding sea. Whenever I could, I dodged back to the Chatham for a shower and some moments of coolness in the soothing dusk created by the sunblinds outside my window. Out in the street I walked with eyes half-closed against the minute particles of grit which filled the air. It seemed to me that the vast stone and concrete and marble monoliths must be infinitesimally disintegrating, shedding atoms of their surface, as human skin is said to fill the air with clouds, fortunately invisible, of spent cutaneous matter.

Of the aspects of the city of New York which took my fancy and which I should remember and look for again on later visits, there were the coloured awnings spanning the broad sidewalks of the richer neighbourhoods, bearing the names of restaurants, florists, modistes, or the street numbers of apartment blocks. There were the great stores, proudly glittering, arranged with a delicate yet audacious and ironical skill, on Fifth and Madison Avenues. On less fashionable streets, such as Fourth and Seventh Avenues, there were true junk-shops full to overflowing with fascinating, often pathetic odds and ends, many of which must once have been part of some immigrants' meagre baggage. There were restaurants, French, Italian, German offering a hint, grown faint but still perceptible, of that European atmosphere which I was beginning to crave.

There were people, with their limitless kindness, their sincere and pointed interest in my affairs, their serious, if slightly bewildered anxiety to be of help; for what was it, after all, that I really wanted? I met and was entertained by individuals so clear-cut, living lives of such originality, richness and variety as completely to belie certain ignorant first impressions, gained from streets and subways, of a vast unsmiling mass furiously striving, milling to and fro, hell-bent after purposes whose nature I could not determine, but all engaged in what seemed some desperately urgent pursuit.

For the past few years I had been a regular reader of the *New Yorker* then, under Ross's editorship, at its absolute best. My view of the city, therefore, had been largely conditioned by the worldly wisdom, urbanity, and wide-ranging critical interests of that magazine; its jokes and drawings were among my greatest joys. I also relished the advertisements, which had a flavour of unabashed hedonism, founded for the most part on what the advertising agencies of Madison Avenue called 'snob appeal'. Things advertised might be obtained 'at the better shops'; there were compelling advertisements for the scents of Prince Matchabelli ('Prince and perfumer') and coronets and other symbols of nobility were discreetly strewn about. Although the advertising was obviously the main source of the magazine's revenue since the circulation could never be enormous, the editorial side, fiercely jealous of its independence, refused to have anything at all to do with it. A story is told that, one day, someone from the advertising side strayed on to the editorial floor. The staff there sent for the police and had him arrested.

From my reading, then, I was already familiar with New York names famous at the time: Alexander Woollcott, Dorothy Parker, James Thurber, S.J.Perelman, and all those who attended what sounded such odd and entertaining parties at the Algonquin Hotel.

Recently, in London at the newly opened Curzon Cinema, I had seen a film called *The Scoundrel*, written and produced by Ben Hecht and Charles Macarthur, with Noël Coward in the leading role. For literary New Yorkers that film was very much a *roman à clef*, since the Scoundrel, played by Coward, was based on a certain New York publisher whose commercial ruthlessness and sexual banditry were legendary. What made the whole thing especially piquant was the fact that a number of well-known literary figures were concerned with the production, and Alec Woollcott himself took the part of a stout, pompous and razor-tongued critic, which he did uncommonly well, the part having obviously been written for him.

Woollcott was among the people who gave me their time and their hospitality on that first visit. I saw him in his own apartment, and in other houses, restaurants and meeting-places. He was short and broad and very stout, yet for all his massive bulk he managed to move about the city with great speed and energy, to dine out continually, and to be present at every private view, first night or other artistic manifestation of any significance. He also wrote. He was an admirable essayist and his critical journalism, some of which appeared in the *New Yorker*, was notable for its pungency. He was one of the very best raconteurs that I have ever heard.

When we broached the subject of my employment Woollcott looked at me quizzically. 'When I was a boy,' he said, his voice which always sounded like a slow subsidence in a scrapyard making more of a metallic rumble than ever, 'when I was a boy, you were supposed to go to the bottom of the nearest tree and climb steadily until you got to the top!' That was true enough, I am sure; but then he had been a boy in what was beginning to seem a golden age, the turn of the century, our own Antebellum. For me there was not only not an unlimited choice of trees, with branches relatively unencumbered, but, far more important, I had only the feeblest inclination for any tree but the literary one, surely the most problematic and one of the hardest to climb.

Certain New Yorkers encountered at that time had the power, as some pictures have, to establish a perfectly clear and brilliant image never to be lost in recollection. My parents had long been friends of Ruth Draper, whose highly original performances I had seen more than once during her regular visits to the London theatre. What she did on the stage is hard to classify, but I suppose that, at another period, she would have been called a *diseuse*, someone who gave a solo performance of sketches, humorous or dramatic, with nothing but her own looks and voice and a couple of properties for the purpose. In the wrong hands such an exhibition could have been embarrassing: worse, a dreadful failure. In Ruth's it had more than a touch of magic. It was often said of her that she could people a whole stage with her imaginary interlocutors. After a very short while one positively began to feel, not simply that she was not alone but that, at any moment, the characters she conversed with would become visible. She wrote her sketches herself. Some were funny, some were sad, all were meticulously finished. It was an extremely clever performance, and something a good deal more than that: moving, revealing, psychologically acute and, as I said, highly entertaining.

Ruth Draper came of a distinguished family and was very much in the New York society which was sometimes called the Four Hundred. Going backstage to visit her between matinée and evening performance, in some such small, intimate theatre as the Criterion at Piccadilly Circus, I would find her drinking tea, entirely composed, unfatigued, as much a lady of the best

American society as she would have been in her apartment in New York's East Seventies.

Much of the significance of that New York excursion had to do with the theatre. There was no, in those pre-war days, professional theatre in Canada. Ottawa, Montreal and Toronto each possessed theatres which were used by touring companies, but of theatrical enterprises permanently established, like that of today at Stratford, Ontario, there were none. Accordingly a vigorous and well-endowed 'little-theatre' movement had come into being in several Canadian towns, where amateur companies performed on stages so well equipped as to have made their British counterparts sick with envy. Just as happened at home a national Drama Festival was held once a year, at which the various companies competed for a prize under the eye of a professional producer of note specially imported from Europe to judge their efforts. The competition was held in Ottawa, and the visiting judge was invited to stay at Government House. That spring of 1937 the celebrity thus invited was a Frenchman, Michel St Denis. That was not my first meeting with St Denis nor was it to be my last. In my days at Gaumont-British, and although I can hardly believe that he remembered me, so humble had been my function there, I had often had to call him from his dressing-room when he was needed for shooting a scene supposedly set beside the Lake of Geneva (blown-up photographs again). In that scene Michel played an elderly Swiss *fiacre*-driver, with whiskers and a red nose. His inimitably juicy voice was intensified for the occasion, to produce an effect of booziness. His was only a small part but, true to the theatrical method, derived from Stanislavsky, which he had espoused, Michel gave it as much thought and meticulous attention, almost, as if he had been playing King Lear. The passengers in his *fiacre* were Madeleine Carroll and the delightful American, Robert Young — quite the nicest, easiest, most modest Hollywood star I was ever to meet. One odd thing that I remember about that scene which, now, might be almost impossible to believe, had to do with a beery-sounding eructation produced by the *fiacre*-driver in accordance with the script. At that time, in America, there existed an institution known as the Hays Office which, self-promoted but, for some incomprehensible reason, enormously powerful, had set itself up as guardian of public decency where cinema films were concerned. The United States is a breeding-ground of moral pressure-groups, but the sanctions declared by the Hays Office, one would have thought, might have seemed excessive at the time of the Civil War. There it was, however. Even the usually irrepressible American movie moguls felt obliged to adapt their stories and their dialogue to the wishes of the Hays Office and, since my employers were keen to sell their film in the United States, those had to be considered. When Michel belched, long and gassily, the script required Robert Young to make a remark about *wind*. Somebody mentioned the Hays Office. There was an immediate conference. The producer was nervous. He thought that the American censors might not stand for that word. Incredibly as it must seem nowadays, when every imaginable licence is taken in film dialogue as a matter of course, it was decided to change the word to *indigestion*.

It was with great pleasure that I welcomed Michel to Government House. He was French; he was from London; he had news of all that was going on in the arts, but most of all in the theatre. When he was not engaged in the business of judging dramatic productions I took him about and introduced him to Ottawa society. That society was small and much inter-related: a new face was always welcome, one which had gained some European celebrity doubly so. Our guest had the experience, which amused him enormously, of becoming a social lion.

Michel St Denis was stocky and fair, with a broad open countenance unmarked by any special feature but a pair of very shrewd eyes which missed nothing and no one; a true actor's face, its components capable of being assembled at will to suit a turn of thought, a reaction or an emotion. He was the nephew of a celebrated French theatrical producer, Jacques Copeau, with whom he had worked at the Théatre du Vieux Colombier in Paris, a focal point of advanced dramatic work in the years between the wars. At the time of his visit to Ottawa he was, I suppose, in his thirties.

In the course of our various excurions, and our walks in the park, where the grass, chlorotic at first from months of deep frost and snow, had quickly recovered its green, just as the trees' brown fans had burst, overnight it seemed, into bud and leaf, Michel told me his plans. He had settled in London and there founded a theatre studio which would serve as a laboratory for his ideas about acting and theatrical production, as well as a school for training young actors, actresses and theatre technicians. He must have found effective financial backing, for the project seemed already to be in full swing. On the north-east side of Islington Green, at the beginning of Upper Street, a disused Methodist chapel had been turned into a small theatre, with a number of studios for scene-painting, costume-making and so on. This was the London Theatre Studio. The whole idea as expounded by Michel sounded exciting, something fresh, original, greatly promising in a world grown shabby and menacing with the effects of economic depression and the dark threat of war.

For some reason which I cannot now recall, but probably to do with a new possibility of employment, I was allowed a second visit to New York, a fortnight after the first. I was in rather bad odour for having then spent the whole of Colonel Mackenzie's provision of dollar bills, and so it was arranged that I should go to stay with friends of my parents, on a markedly reduced allowance.

The friends in question were Alice Duer Miller, poet and novelist, and her husband Henry who was, I think, a lawyer on Wall Street. The Millers had a house in the East Fifties. I, although I admitted my fault, was rather disgruntled about the arrangement, fearing for my freedom of action, governed as it would be by the obligations of a guest. When Michel heard of my proposed visit he insisted that there was someone in New York, a young English actress, whom I positively must see. Already with a high and still growing reputation at home, she was at that time playing in a production on Broadway. He wrote me a note of introduction and his last words before his own departure for England were an injunction to make use of his letter.

So, for the second time, and by the same means, I set off for the fabled city which, already, held for me some slight ease of familiarity, and a promise of further pleasure and excitement such as I had enjoyed tasting a fortnight before. I naturally had no idea that the visit would turn out momentous in a way which nobody could easily have foreseen.

On the eve of my trip, thinking that I must take some token to my unknown hostess in New York, I asked Mr Challis, who looked after the glasshouses attached to the main block of Rideau Hall, to make up a box of flowers for Mrs Miller. His range of glass began as a large conservatory, full of palms and creepers and corners contrived for sitting-out at state balls, and continued as heated greenhouses where flowers and flowering trees and plants in pots were grown for decoration. Many a carnation or gardenia for my buttonhole had I had from Challis. On that occasion he excelled himself. Next morning I was presented with a long box, large enough to be adequate as a gift but not too large to carry comfortably, and with that I set off for New York, once again feeling that pleasurable pain in my diaphragm which accompanies anticipation of adventure or of an important event.

The Millers' house was at the far end of East 52nd Street, directly on the East River. From its back windows could be seen an endlessly interesting parade of river craft, rapidly dashing or steadily forging to and fro, almost as busily as the cars in the streets, turning up white water in long feathers, or making a silky swell full of gleams and small explosions of light under the lambent summer sky.

You need to be rather rich to live in a whole house, even a fairly small one, in such a situation in New York. The circumstances of my stay were extremely comfortable. I was welcomed by a young English butler and taken to my hostess who displayed at once that wonderful mixture of patrician dignity and perfect up–to–dateness which is the perquisite of certain American ladies. She welcomed me kindly. Her clever eyes looked me over with a touch of slightly amused speculation; how should I be placed, how fitted into her scheme of things? She gave me to understand that I would be free, subject to my attending one or two entertainments specially arranged, to come and go as I pleased. A few gentle but authoritative nudges were given me towards certain plays, exhibitions, concerts at that time to be seen or heard in the city. That night we dined together informally, off trays, in the drawing-room. An especially succulent variety of asparagus was on my plate, thick, juicy and green all through, swimming in melted butter. A huge Persian cat leaped to the arm of my chair, reached down and skilfully removed a piece of asparagus with which it proceeded to butter a Persian rug. 'Asparagus-eating cats!' I thought to myself. 'What might one not expect to meet in this extraordinary town?'

As a writer, Alice Duer Miller had a loyal public which was to increase vastly during the first years of the Second World War, after the publication of her long poem 'The White Cliffs'. That work was truly a labour of love, very evidently written from the heart, and definitely intended to encourage sympathy for Britain in her struggle with Germany. It was, in a sense, a generous thank you letter for the pleasures she had had from England and English people throughout a fairly long life. The English society she remembered and celebrated in her poem was very much the counterpart of her own in America, a world of beautiful houses and country estates, of handsome people and noble horses; it was nevertheless a presentation very much to her readers' taste, and the

207

celebration, never mawkish, of certain virtues of courage, fidelity and kindness which she had tested amongst the British went straight to many warm American hearts.

On that occasion, however, whilst I was guarding my asparagus from further raids by the Persian, there was neither talk nor thought of war. My hostess spoke instead of writers and editors and publishers, of plays and playwrights and literary agents, much as a successful writer might have spoken at home. Alice Miller's social circle, containing not merely friends of like background — the old, quiet core of New York society still, even so late as 1937, maintaining enough of its spirit and mores to remind one of an earlier age — but actors and painters and even film-stars. Harpo Marx, for example, was a familiar of the house and, in my view, a rather dull one. Lacking a curly blond wig and a squashed top-hat he seemed insignificant, and was inclined to be serious to the point of boredom. Always dumb in the Marx Brothers films, in real life he was talkative enough. At that time, in American intellectual circles and in those spheres of music, cinema and theatre contingent to them, left-wing politics, even open professions of communism, were much in fashion. Senator McCarthy might have been born but he had not yet been thought of. Harpo Marx was said by some to be a communist, but no one of his acquaintance would have dreamed of holding that against him; a far worse charge might have been that he was something of a bore.

Mr Challis's flowers looked well in Mrs Miller's pine-panelled drawing-room. I realized that I was lucky to have got them there at all, and for this reason: the very friendly staff at the American Legation in Ottawa had provided me with a handsome document on pink paper, with a great scarlet seal, 'requesting and requiring'; in short, a diplomatic *laissez passer*. In those days I was far too ignorant to realize the full value of that piece of paper, but it was to prove its worth remarkably in the matter of flowers. On arrival at Newark airport I queued for customs in the usual way. When I produced my box of flowers a dramatic scene developed. American customs officers are not famous for the elegance of their manners. When mine learned what was in the box he tore it open furiously, giving me at the same time a powerfully phrased speech on the iniquity, and indeed the total illegality of bringing flowers, or plants of any kind, into the United States. Nonplussed, and with some diffidence, I unfolded the pink paper. Its effect was electric. The officer took one astonished look, bundled up my parcel, shoved it under my arm, threw back the passport and told me to be on my way *fast*.

There is no situation more favourable to a rapidly accelerating intimacy than that of two foreigners in a foreign city. Having left Michel's letter with the stage-doorman of a pleasant, small theatre just off Broadway, I took my seat for the evening performance of a play by an American dramatist then much admired, but now, I think, largely forgotten. The play, which was historical in intention, was not very interesting, but the acting of Michel's young friend held it to the highest pitch of which its rather pedestrian nature was capable. I was thus able to admire a performance whose passion and poetry did the fullest justice to the playwright's characterization. So long as she was on stage I found myself enthralled.

Theatrical dressing-rooms, life backstage, had had little part in my experience since the amateur productions of my Oxfordshire past. What I was entering in New York was the real theatre, with all its traditional mystique, its particular authority. The thought of 'going behind the scenes', and there finding so gifted a compatriot, was exciting. As the play proceeded I became more and more interested in the looks and personality of the girl on the stage. When, at the end of the performance, carrying a small bunch of flowers, I found my way up dusty stairs and through harshly lit brick-lined corridors to her dressing-room the sensation in the pit of my stomach was pronounced. So began a close and, for me, immensely rewarding relationship which would last, with one interruption, for two years, completely absorb my emotional existence and govern my daily life to the almost entire exclusion of everything and everybody else.

A few weeks later, alone in the Citadel at Quebec, I would write a short story, touched with the supernatural, which would embody some of the sensations and impressions of that intensely lived brief time in New York. About the city I felt a certain ambivalence for, finding it on the one hand powerfully exciting, exhilarating, fruitful of many thoughts and ideas, on the other I had to admit to having been sometimes a little frightened, bothered by so great an exuberance of energy, chilled by a foreignness much stranger than any I had known before. Something of this would go into my story which was to be, in fact, my first published effort in that line. A few months later it would be accepted by the editor of the *London Mercury*, a publication long since defunct, but then one of several possible outlets for poems and stories which, although rich and varied by present-day standards, were themselves only a shadow of the great literary bazaar known to my father's generation.

It need hardly be said that what grew so fast between another and myself in the emotional forcing-house of New York, not merely took my mind off the search for work, but hardened beyond equivocation my wish to go back to England. Her American contract would end at midsummer. When we parted it was with the promise of the earliest possible meeting in London.

Meanwhile the Coronation of King George VI and Queen Elizabeth had come and gone amidst a fine display of mixed American feelings about Great Britain and its monarchy. The daily press had been full of letters along the lines of: 'Why all this fuss about the King of England? In America every man is a King!' and much sound republican sentiment of the sort. Two weeks before, during my first visit, I had had to answer many questions about the event. By the time of my second visit colour films of the Coronation had arrived and one day, at a small news-cinema, I went to see it. Strange indeed it must all have seemed to the average New Yorker, the man in the street. One such sat next to me in the cinema. He was middle-aged, comfortably drunk and, in a muted way, vociferous. Every so often he expressed his contempt for historic ceremony, for monarchy and, very likely, for the whole tribe of Limeys, by exclaiming: 'Lotta savages! Lotta Zulus!' Some ancestral tug, perhaps, or merely the pleasure of seeing something so unequivocally English, made me see the film more than once. In a letter to my sister I wrote: 'How *was* the Coronation? Several times I have seen films of it, and the moment which never fails to get a laugh is when the Archbishop takes the crown and turns it round, with a v.worried expression. Marc Connely★ says he was thinking: "It's not the one I ordered!" ' Without having done anything either to help or hinder the great occasion I was awarded a Coronation Medal, as were my mother, my brothers, and the entire Government House staff.

I should see New York several times again, in the 1950s, travelling there on business, arriving by sea in one or other of the Cunarder Queens or after a laboured flight in an airliner adapted from a wartime bomber design. The exhilaration would still be there, the warmth of welcome, the procession of new faces, the

★ Author of *Green Pastures*.

gossip, the 'going on somewhere', the almost complete impossibility of getting any sleep. Much, however, would have changed in the intervening years, in the city's looks especially, since no city in the world is more continually subject to restless, ruthless alteration, to demolition and construction which never cease, so that the wonder is that it keeps any recognizable features at all.

Fourteen years after my first amazed, amused encounter I thought that a kind of innocence had departed. The place was dirtier and more dangerous; the people I knew, although they had won a great war and grown prosperous in ways unimaginable in 1937, seemed less spontaneous, less determined to demand from life a kind of perpetual raree-show.

Fourteen years later New York would mean for me long conferences in offices, usually in hot, humid early autumn weather, when shirt-sleeves were in order, the water-cooler was kept busy, and I, too warmly dressed, envied my colleagues their thin seersucker suits. Later still there would be luncheons in bank parlours, with iced water or buttermilk to drink. ('We never drink alcohol at lunch, Bill.' No, of course not, but how about those blindingly strong Martinis beforehand?)

What I had first felt about New York would not be recapturable. Innocence, my own included, had gone from the scene for good. For example, it could no longer have been anything but foolhardy to venture alone, at night, into Harlem, as once, on my first visit I had done. Feeling rather daring, but much intrigued by the legends of that neighbourhood, I remembered all the warnings I had been given, put some dollars into the top pocket of my jacket and also — having somewhere heard this recommended — tucked a larger sum into one of my shoes. In the event, although I was quite expecting small-scale robbery, nothing untoward happened to me on that noisy, hot, neon-lit evening. Rather, I was either unpointedly ignored or welcomed with amused curiosity in the various bars and music-places which I visited. Half-fledged blond young Englishmen were a novelty in that environment, and one which the inhabitants were disposed to treat with mild zoological curiosity or hearty good nature.

For many reasons, then, I am glad that 'my' New York came to me when it did, so that I carry at the back of my mind a detailed, bright-coloured vision, both of place and people, an impression of clear-cut style, sharp wit and vivid energy, of a particular view of life still possible in those last days before the United States were forced to take on the role which for so long, in all but commercial terms, they had consciously avoided, that of a world power inescapably embroiled in international affairs. To appreciate the spirit of well-heeled New York in the late 1930s — and I must plead that I knew, then, no other side — it would be best to consult back numbers of the *New Yorker*, which breathe a positive urbanity, a gently sardonic humour, and a touch of that open-eyed acceptance of human life as a splendid circus which so beguiled me during my short stays in the city. American kindness is legendary; nor do those other North Americans, the Canadians, fall short in that respect. I was scarcely used to being, as I was in both countries, so swiftly, so completely inducted into the lives of those whom I met. If they were engaged to do something, go somewhere, entertain, they simply took me along with them, so that I remember, still with a kind of awed respect, going shopping at Bonwit Teller with Ruth Draper, who wanted gloves; and my admiration growing with every minute as she, with powerful charm masking steely determination, won to her side a sulky salesgirl, so that, in the end, nearly the entire stock of gloves was out on the counter and no one more determined than the salesgirl that Miss Draper should have exactly what she was seeking.

Again, at some odd hour like eleven in the morning, I was taken to a large room in an hotel where a very rich and culturally ambitious lady wished to show a film, made at her own expense, of the life of Pavlova. After we had sat embarrassed through many yards of film which could only be called flat-footage, the voice of Alexander Woollcott was upraised. The rich lady, who clearly had so hoped for kudos by adding her expensive tribute to the history of twentieth-century art forms, asked him what he thought of her film. Loud and clear over so many years comes the catastrophic rumble of Alec's voice: 'I think, if you allowed this film to be shown, you would be doing the greatest possible disservice to Pavlova's memory!' Woollcott, of course, was right. In a way he was being cruel to be kind, for only disappointment could lie in store for the, by then, poor lady, who looked crestfallen to the point of tears, if she persisted with her project. His authority as a critic was great and, in that world, unquestioned. The film was never, I think, seen again.

Towards the end of June I took passage from Quebec in the *Duchess of York*, bound for England. Elsewhere I have written: 'My time in Canada had been spent mostly in Ottawa and Quebec, with visits to Montreal and weekends skiing or sleighing in the Laurentian Hills. My view of the country had been, on the whole, one-sided, taken sometimes from a processional car with motor-cycle outriders, or at charity balls, or state dinners, or squelching up yards of red carpet at a Levee...in pumps a trifle too large, so that I feared to lose one of them before I ever reached the point where I had to bow to my parents. On that warm summer evening at Quebec, when I said goodbye to my father, I was not to know that I should only ever have three months of his company again.'

My Canadian experience had been one of exemplary privilege, even to my being provided with free passes on all the railway systems, such as the Tamiskaming & Northern Ontario Railroad, which existed alongside the two giants, Canadian Pacific and Canadian National. As a final tribute to the status I was relinquishing I was sent out to the *Duchess of York*, which was already under way, in a tender, than which no method of joining a ship could be more conspicuous. Neither did my travelling arrangements entail a drop in living standards. My cabin was on the boat-deck, a desirable position at all times, except when, as on that voyage, the ship ran into summer fog. Then the foghorn, almost above my head, made my quarters into a cave of brutal resonance, as if in the close proximity of a Minotaur.

The *Duchess* ships, sometimes known as 'drunken Duchesses' for their tendency to unbridled movement in almost any weather, were the maids-of-all-work of the Canadian Pacific line. Their senior sisters, the *Empresses*, were larger and altogether more grand. I liked the smaller ships for a certain dowdiness, a homely cosiness, in spite of their tendency to rear and plunge and wallow in even a moderate sea. The saloons were human in scale, the ship's company and the stewards friendly, the other passengers, either travelling on business or returning home, peaceful and unpretentious. The five-day voyage would be pleasantly spent reading, or walking the deck, or joining the evening games of housey-housey, thinking back the while on my Canadian experiences; thinking forward, with hope and some anxiety, to what England might have in store for me.

The north Atlantic is not a kindly sea but, for those few June days, and apart from some hours of fog, it showed its best face. I was no longer convalescent. Even though my Canadian adventures had been far less strenuous than Johnnie's fishing and shooting excursions, or Alastair's days on a ranch, they had served to make me quite fit once more, and so to be obliged to face a future about which something more seriously practical had to be done than simply, so to speak, proceeding from room to room, like a patron at a private view, in a state of calm anticipation as to what pictures might be presented next.

I was twenty-one years old, by which age many young men in the past had already embarked on momentous careers, or were already noteworthy for some contribution to the arts or politics or war. At that age John Buchan had produced an edition of Bacon's essays, his first novel, and a volume of essays of his own. At the same age several of my schoolfellows were already settling into careers which, one day, would bring them honour, or shaping the attitudes to action which would distinguish them in the coming war, or prepare them for an early death. Other contemporaries, from other schools, were making a mark, often of a revolutionary kind, attacking 'the system', violently rejecting values of parents and social class, making a stir in the world which would bring them obloquy or admiration but, in either case, much public notice.

More than most I might have been called an idiot, in the sense of the Greek from which that word is derived. My dictionary has 'Gr: *idiotes*: a private person, 'layman', ignorant person' — a pretty exact description since, in all my dealings I was pursuing private pleasures, private researches, the hoped-for correction of private deficiencies. Where much of what was a matter for professional agitation and anxiety in politics or social affairs was concerned, I was decidedly a layman: and, except in the sphere of my own particular interests, no one could have been more ignorant.

To these considerations I gave little attention as my *Duchess* trod purposefully on towards Liverpool and a future, for me, conventional enough in outline but brightly enticing in its details. I am afraid that I thought less of a worldly career than of a new and exclusive preoccupation, the exploration of another personality, the building of a private (that word again) structure of shared experience and, unformulated because I had, on the whole, too little self-knowledge to recognize it, the desire to come to some substantive and ultimately useful understanding of myself.

I have often wondered how things would have been with me if I had been born of different parents in a social state remote from the ambitions, successes and rewards, the nexus of dynamic and demanding relationships belonging to active life in the public sphere. Thoughts about success and self-fulfilment, and the gratifying of others' expectations, must have bothered me from

214

the beginning for, at an early age, I found the Parable of the Talents extremely disquieting. Beyond continual exhortations from my Scottish grandmother concerning the need to succeed in life and cease, at the first possible moment, to be a burden to my parents, and my mother's quite natural inherited belief that we were all of the sort predestined to *run* things, to take command, to be eminent upon some scene, I had the spectacle of my father going daily from strength to strength. I hadn't the least reason to suppose that what he did was designed to make me feel futile; all he was engaged in was the expression of his own nature, his own inescapable 'thing'. Should I ever be able to do likewise? There is a terrible saying of Chamfort which Cyril Connolly quotes in *The Unquiet Grave*. 'C'est un grand malheur de perdre, par notre caractère, les droits que nos talents nous donnent sur la société.'

I have touched on a, to me, inexplicable sense of a lack of love, and hence of a driving need to seek it in all its forms. In addition to some Bible-reading at home which had brought the Parable of the Talents so early to my notice, we went to church every Sunday, and there were suggestions, in hymns and prayers and lessons, that love, its getting or giving or keeping, was no simple matter. As soon as I could read well enough to take part in hymn-singing I was horror-struck by the verse: 'By many deeds of shame/We learn that love grows cold.' That really made me shiver, made me think anxiously of Elsie who, more than anyone else in the world, I loved. The thought of her love for me growing cold was very nearly unbearable. That the boot, in later life, might too often be on the other foot I could not of course foresee.

16

SUN, SNOW AND CEREMONY

We had embarked for Canada, my mother and I, with Annie Cox and my cousin Carola Peyton-Jones, on Christmas Eve 1936. Our ship, the *Duchess of Bedford* reached Halifax after five days and six nights of ferocious winter gales, so that trying to avoid injury became a preoccupation so absorbing that there was no time for anyone to be sick. A fortnight later I celebrated my twenty-first birthday. My parents, reckoning this an occasion to be marked, allowed me to give a dinner party for a dozen young members of Ottawa society. The dinner took place in the great French Renaissance pile of the Château Laurier Hotel, and turned out, not surprisingly, to be a slightly sticky occasion. Since I then knew no one in Ottawa of my own age, or near it, the guests had had to be chosen for me. Only Carola was a dear familiar; for the rest twelve unknown quantities celebrated the coming-of-age of another.

Except for a brief excursion to Montreal from New York, many years later, I should not see Canada again; yet my five and a half months there had been memorable for new sights, new impressions, preconceptions corrected, discoveries of many kinds. I had arrived in the dead of winter, when the whole world was snow and the ground deep-frozen. New techniques of driving had to be learned for roads coated in ice or slippery with close-packed snow. The low-slung, long-bodied American cars were better for this than the rather top-heavy English limousines. Amos Webb had difficulty with the Wolseley (the family car which had come with us to Canada) and I do not think that he adapted happily to the new conditions; nor do I suppose that he was happy, after so many years of being sole and indispensable chauffeur, at having to take second place after Southgate, whom we had inherited from our predecessors, the Bessboroughs, and who drove the Governor-General's car.

Particular recollections would stay with me always. I should not forget going to stay in a chalet in the Laurentians for a weekend's skiing, and arriving from Montreal in the dark at St Agathe, and there being met by a horse-drawn sleigh which swung and clanged and rumbled along between piled-up banks of hard snow yellow-lit by its oil lamps, under a black canopy of pine and spruce, and coming, at the end of a drive so enchanting that I could have wished it ever-lasting, to a log-cabin, brightly lit, centrally heated, spacious, a' wholly admirable example of civilization tactfully, unblatantly introduced to the wild.

Another moment of pure magic, which might have meant less to one more widely travelled than I, came one afternoon when, with my parents, I was having tea at a Seigneurie, the seventeenth-century manor house of the Lieutenant-Governor of Quebec. The house stood high on the side of a bluff. I was gazing down the steeps of the garden to the immensity of the St Lawrence river gleaming mackerel-blue and silver below, when I became aware of what I took to be a large and spectacularly coloured bee, hovering in the bell of a flower by my chair. A closer look nearly took my breath away, for this was no insect but a humming-bird, one of the smallest of its kind, performing a bee's function, poking its long beak into the honeyed heart of the flower. I have nothing original to say about the miracles of Nature, but surely this must be one of the most impressive, that a bird no bigger than the half of my thumb could find its way the thousand and more miles from somewhere like Florida, to spend summer sampling the honey in a Canadian garden.

There would be amusing and often impressive memories of Vice-regal life. Ceremonial has never irked me, indeed I have usually enjoyed it, and the ceremonial surrounding my father's official state seemed to me handsome, significant and right. The Comptroller of the Household, Colonel Mackenzie, a very tall, much war-wounded Guards officer, was a born courtier, devoted to all the minutiae of his office and eagle-eyed for mistakes in ceremony or deportment. The Canadians, whilst enjoying their ceremonial duties and determined to get them right, nevertheless rode rather more lightly to things than did the stern Comptroller. Amongst the ADCs was one Canadian officer, Lieutenant-Colonel Willis O'Connor, who had served a succession of Governors-General in that capacity. One cold morning I was standing, with others of the household, on the steps of Rideau Hall, watching the departure of my parents for some great event. The event must have been most important, the Opening of Parliament perhaps, for the open state landau was being used, and there was a guard of honour found by one of the Canadian cavalry

217

regiments. A sharp, teasing wind was blowing and both carriage and cavalry horses were restive. There was a certain amount of bumping and boring, rearing and sidling. At one point half the escort was turned the wrong way and decidedly at odds with the other half. With so much confusion the procession could not start. Behind me I heard a low chuckle from Willis, who leaned forward to murmur in my ear, 'That's what I should call a Vice-regal box-up!'

My last weeks in Canada were spent at Quebec, in the Citadel, a stone fortress set high above the town. This made a comfortable house, far smaller than Rideau Hall. It had long corridors of vaulted stone and, outside, a parade ground enclosed by ramparts where the famous French Canadian regiment, the Vingt Deux-ième de Québec, were used to exercise. Their barracks were also in the Citadel, and they provided the guard at the entrance to the snaking, high-walled, narrow roadway which led up from the town to the fort.

Early in June my parents went away for a couple of weeks to visit President Roosevelt, leaving me alone in the Citadel, with no one besides but the servants, and that was one of the pleasantest fortnights that I have ever spent. As soon as my parents and their suite had departed, a delegation from the domestic staff came to make me a proposal. Since I was alone, with no state to keep up, and they had evidently, if unexpressedly, many interesting plans for themselves, would I, if they gave me breakfast, and looked after my bedroom, make myself scarce as much as possible? Greatly amused, I said that I would; I should probably have little difficulty in finding entertainment in the town and, anyway, I had an invitation from Doctor Marius Barbeau, a distinguished ethnologist and specialist in the province's social history, to stay with his family in a farmhouse on the Île d'Orléans, the long island which lies in the St Lawrence downstream from Quebec.

At one corner of the Citadel someone had built a kind of sun-room, glazed on three sides, the wide windows of which enclosed a superb panorama of the great river and the woods and hills beyond. There at times I would sit, reading or writing or simply gazing at the view, and letting imagination run on what might be awaiting me at home. On one evening I was the guest of the officers of the Vingt Deuxième in their mess, an occasion which I certainly enjoyed, but detailed recollection of which was for ever occluded by a really outsize hangover the following morning.

The old city repaid exploration in many ways. Much of Quebec's town plan, and many of its buildings, were of respectable antiquity. American tourists came in large numbers, finding in its atmosphere a fair substitute for a trip to Europe. Not only the language, said by some to be seventeenth-century French unmodified, although with many latter-day accretions — I once, in a street, heard one man say crossly to another, 'Ne me botherez pas!' — but the courts and narrow lanes, the dramatic emplace-ment on a scarp above the St Lawrence, the mixture of the majestic and the quaint, were all unique in their foreign feeling. Certain survivals from the town's French past were especially intriguing. Somehow or other a royal perquisite of Louis XVI had persisted into modern times. By it, the Governor-General had the right, indeed the duty, in view of an unrescinded dispensation, to visit the Ursuline Convent once a year. I went with my parents and a couple of ADCs, plus the Comptroller, to visit the convent on the appointed day. We saw the bare room with its scrubbed floor and the wooden bench whereon General Wolfe lay in the last hours of his life. My mother was delighted to hear one of the younger nuns exclaim on seeing the ADCs: 'Quelle belle suite!'

With all those scenes and impressions a part of my mind was busy, as the ship proceeded under a summer sky and over a long, lazy, unupsetting swell. My cabin-steward had shaken his head at the start, predicting trouble on the voyage because, he said, there were a couple of clergymen among the passengers. 'Black crows!' he grumbled. 'They always bring bad luck!' They brought no bad luck on that occasion. All went on smoothly enough. The ship's company moved equably about their business: the captain dined at his table. An almost cataleptic peacefulness descended on the passengers who read, slept in deck-chairs, ate copiously and often, played unstrenuous games, and gave sleepy smiles in all directions when encountered. As the coast of Ireland drew near I began to wake up from the sea-induced semi-trance, that state of beatitude never to be known by air travellers, and shake myself into a frame of mind to consider my future seriously.

Liverpool, looming darkly across a waste of dirty water traversed by grimly untidy shipping, set the tone for homecoming to the realities of a Europe beset by every trouble, political and economic, known to the history of mankind. This was still the busiest seaport in Europe, but its aspect was not one of healthy prosperity, rather a kind of desperation. The atmosphere, too, was unpropitious. Could the sky have shrunk to come into proportion with our small island? I had become so used to a vast firmament, leaden-grey with snow in winter or a fine, pale blue over wastes of white; glassily lit in floods by spring sunshine; a dome of intense blue in summer, and at all times of the most ample and airy spaciousness. As we approached the coast of England the sky had seemed to darken, to contract, to come closer. The light was muted, beautifully so in a way, but no longer of a wide and mistless clarity. When at length I found myself on shore, another view presented itself. If the air had taken on a sombre tone, that was matched by the look of the people in the streets. After the clear, bright colours still in my mind's eye — skiiers in many-coloured anoraks or parkas against great plains of snow, the summer clothes of holiday-makers in Quebec city — the Liverpool crowd seemed quite tragically drab. Faces were thin and pale, foreheads creased, shoulders bent with anxiety. These were the front-liners in a conflict where the enemy was faceless and the same battles were fought and refought every day of the year. Settling into a first-class corner seat — the last luxury of my privileged journey — in a train which seemed very sleek and purposeful after the lumbering Canadian railway coaches, I looked out at black warehouses, the grimy brick of trackside dwellings, fields and hedgerows turned dull green by falling soot. My recovery from illness had been swift. I had had a magnificent few months of idleness. Soon I must put myself to work; but first there was something which must be confirmed. A single exchange of letters across the Atlantic between two who were still, almost, strangers and not yet settled to communication on paper, left everything in the air. Would what had begun in the hot, exciting light of New York survive in the subtler, lower-toned, more familiar (and familial) atmosphere of London? Excitement, hope, doubt, anxiety — all were in a flux as the hours of the journey unrolled. Euston Station loomed up, as it were in reverse. The place which I had quitted on Christmas Eve amid the salutes and handshakes of stationmasters, shipping company officials, representatives of the Government, received me back into its smoky halls as, simply, one more anonymous passenger. I took a taxi to a small hotel near Marble Arch, and at once picked up the telephone.

The Irish writer, George Moore, was a great one for elaborately hinted scenes of passion in his works, and even more so, it seems, in his conversation. An unkind and disbelieving contemporary said of him: 'Some men kiss and tell; some men kiss and do not tell; George Moore told, but never kissed.' Where love-affairs are concerned, therefore, it is perhaps best to adopt a non-Moorean stance and leave the essential details to the reader's imagination. Since such affairs are the shared, but probably differently interpreted, experience of two people, each has the 'rights' only in his or her portion. Since the whole story would never be told by one person alone, its particular ethos, what made it for a while magical, absorbing, exclusive to one man and one woman, should remain their private property to be neither explored nor explained.

My final crisis of 1936, which could easily be made to seem a kind of attempted suicide, had drawn a line under the first twenty years of my life. After my return from Canada the London I had formerly known would be radically changed for me by the changes in my situation. New people, new places, styles of living hitherto unknown would fill my days. Even the hours I should keep would be governed by close association with a theatrical world which had its own timetables; family and friends would, on the whole, see less of me, and former haunts and fields of exploration stay unvisited.

Gloucester Walk, a short street, lies on the slopes of Campden Hill, just where Kensington Church Street, after a couple of sharp corners, straightens out on its way up to Notting Hill Gate. There, at Number 21 on the south side, I found myself a bedsitting-room, and there I unpacked a few belongings out of the luggage I had brought from Canada. I imagine that my long-suffering grandmother had to let me house the bulk of it at Number 2, which already made a repository for the gear, and often the persons, of Aunt Marnie and her two daughters.

My room, with a quite satisfactory breakfast, cost twenty-one shillings a week. The gas stove was of an unusual pattern, in that it had a ring concealed in its top which I found useful for boiling eggs and sometimes, when winter came on, for mulling claret bought at a nearby wine-shop for a couple of shillings. In other respects my quarters rather resembled my room at school, particularly in the nondescript nature of curtains, carpet and wallpaper, but since I, on the whole, only used the place for sleeping I found it suitable enough. Meanwhile I renewed the acquaintance with Michel St Denis which I had made in Ottawa, and went to work at his Theatre Studio in Islington.

221

Much of Campden Hill was once the old village of Kensington. In my grandmother's childhood three or four large houses stood apart in their own spacious grounds; there were clusters of cottages here and there, among market gardens, and the old houses in Holland Street, once the home of maids of honour and members of the household at Kensington Palace near by, were lived in by comfortably-off writers, museum officials, civil servants and other cultivated persons. The large red blocks of flats, and the streets of late-classical, stuccoed houses had not yet been built. In spite of all changes the district, in my time, still had a countrified feeling: it might have been a rather distinguished small town somewhere in England's south-west. It was eminently human in its atmosphere, full of narrow alleys, hidden gardens, and quiet enclaves of small cottages. In Gloucester Walk, Gloucester Lodge, early Georgian, substantial, with iron gates between stone piers, still stood aloof. At the very top of the hill, beyond Chesterton's 'great, grey water tower' which no longer 'smites the stars on Campden Hill', but which was then a notable landmark, stood eighteenth-century Aubrey House in its gardens, home of Sargent's delicious Cicely Alexander grown old. In the long, narrow streets at the Nottingham Hill Gate end there were studios, 'purpose-built' with huge north windows, housing successful painters and sculptors. Church Street itself was an excellent hunting-ground for attractive junk. Westwards lay Holland Park with Holland House, in all its Tudor pride, for most of the time shuttered and unused.

I doubt whether Tin had travelled so far westwards in a very long time, not often, in fact, since her visits with my grandfather to the Burne-Joneses at Fulham. She seldom moved out of Mayfair and, if she did, it would be more likely to be in an easterly direction, on one of her excursions with Aunt Sophie Gray, driven by the latter's chauffeur, to Franks in Camomile Street, EC3, where interesting bargains in Chinese porcelain were still to be had. (I have been told that George Eumorfopoulos, donor of the famous collection now in the British Museum, laid the foundations for it when, as an impecunious young man in the City, he haunted Franks' emporium. The treasures he sought, and found, were still in those days supplied with careless profligacy by the Chinese as a sort of ballast to the more workaday exports which were the main interest of Oriental importers such as Franks.)

Tin, thinking of Kensington as one large, amorphous and unfashionable entity when she thought of it at all, never quite located Camden Hill, confusing it, I think, with Camden Town. She probably thought that I had settled in some sad waste of decaying brick, peeling paint, dingy lace curtains, having no picture of the essentially quaint and even coquettish and, for that period, prosperous aspects of my surroundings.

To the south of me lay Kensington High Street with its department stores — Barker's, Derry and Toms, Ponting's — stretching away westwards in lines of shops, and full of tall, red buses. To the north Notting Hill lay at the frontier of debatable territory, shading through the shabby but still credible respectability of Ladbroke Square (once a race-course) to the steep slope down into Notting Dale where respectability (and steady incomes) came to an end and anything might happen. I was told at the time, I hope truthfully, that certain streets of small houses on the southside of Notting Hill Gate, now wonderfully done up with colour-wash and carriage lamps and *House and Garden* front doors, were home to a colony of respectable burglars, good citizens all, who favoured a tone of almost suffocating dullness and propriety in their surroundings.

17

ESCAPE TO FLORENCE

Travel abroad, in 1938, was still for most people a considerable adventure, certainly so for most young people. Some elders who could afford it went, as a matter of course, to winter in the south of France or Italy, perhaps even Egypt or Morocco. In summer a favourable exchange and the lure of the Salzburg festival took an increasing number to Austria. Writers and painters did their best to get to Paris, and dons and schoolmasters profited by their extended vacations to go on healthy excursions, walking and climbing, or, the more equivocal ones, to plunge into those less healthy delights in Brussels, Vienna or even Prague, which were an attainable shadow of what had been suppressed in Berlin.

Economically, Great Britain was deep in the Depression. There was little money about, and foreign travel, cheap as it was, could scarcely be thought of by people earning three or four pounds a week. In any case, for all but high-grade commercial travellers, spies, diplomatists and journalists specializing in foreign affairs, regular travel abroad was a remote, perhaps an un-English thing. It was definitely to be thought of as an adventure. If any member of one's circle went abroad, his friends would troop to see him off and enviously watch the blank back-end of the boat-train dwindle away down the line from Victoria Station, before returning to a daily round suddenly become flavourless and dull.

A cold morning in February saw me at the centre of such a farewell party, setting out for Florence, travelling third class. The price of the return ticket was seven pounds ten shillings. I had with me two expanding suitcases, known as Revelations, stuffed to their fullest expansion with nearly my entire wardrobe. Not knowing what sort of social life I might find in Florence, I had decided to take evening dress and suits fit either for an afternoon party or an elegant country walk. What I had on for travelling was as comfortable and untidy as could be wished, and over it, for warmth in that icy fag-end of winter, I wore a so-called camelhair coat which had been with me since Oxford.

A month before that day I had achieved my twenty-second birthday, and not long after that had had to face the breakdown of that relationship, begun in New York, which had so completely filled my world that, without it I felt, for the time being, completely at sea. Full of self-pity I had taken my trouble to my childhood friend Susan Feilding (now Hibbert); and Susan, as usual, had provided an immediate answer.

Her family, for several generations, had been cosmopolitan in the least vulgar sense of that word. Theirs was not the cosmopolitanism of the Sporting Club and the Hotel Negresco, of golf at Le Touquet or racing at Pau, but rather of the arts, of painting and architecture, of music and writing, and a wide circle of practioners of those things. Her father, Percy Feilding, had married Clotilde Brewster. Both were architects and connoisseurs of old houses. Mrs Feilding was the daughter of a man to whom my mother sometimes referred, with an oddly wistful respect, as a true *weltkind*, one who was as much at home in Rome or Paris or London as in his native Massachusetts. Henry Brewster, in addition to being a child of the world, was a scholar and a philosopher of some originality. He had married a German lady, Baroness von Stockhausen, and finally settled in Florence in what had once been the monastery of San Francesco da Paola, on the lower slopes of Bellosguardo. He had been a friend of Henry James, of Violet Paget who wrote under the name of 'Vernon Lee', and of many writers, of many nationalities, belonging to his time. His granddaughter Susan, accordingly, had New England and German mixed with her English blood. Her mother had worked, as a young woman, in the office of Sir Reginald Blomfield, and it was there that she met her husband. Mrs Feilding was said to have been a highly talented architect. One of her projected works was a splendid country house in Russia, with copper domes, for some branch of the Benckendorff family. The fact that she was only in her twenties when entrusted with that commission shows how open the world of that date could be for the gifted (and well-introduced) young.

Susan pondered my problem for only a short time before producing a solution. She advised me to get away from London, make a break, go abroad: pay no attention to the views of my family or anyone else and, quite simply, do a salutary bunk. She wrote at once to Henry Brewster's daughter-in-law, her aunt, now châtelaine of San Francesco, and — the Italian postal service

225

being rather better in those days than it is now — very soon received a reply. I should be most welcome, Mrs Brewster wrote: there was an apartment available at San Francesco, and all I had to do was to give her household a rough idea of when I should arrive. A date was fixed; I somehow scraped up enough money for my ticket and a small quantity of French and Italian currency, gave up my bedsitter, stowed such of my belongings as I was not taking with me at Susan's, and prepared for escape.

At twenty-two, if one is not Werther, however acute may be a pain at the heart the eyes cannot renounce their greedy pleasure in the world and its sights. However much one part of me might hate to leave what I was leaving, another, and that perhaps the dominant part, could not help being excited by the prospect of travel abroad, by that first visit to Italy which had been so profound an experience for certain writers whom I admired. I told myself that I should put the past behind me, bind myself to a daily schedule of writing, and bring back, after a month or two of Italy, a respectable body of work. In the end I did very little of the kind.

Before leaving England I told Tin of my plans. She listened with her usual amused sympathy, and then gave me her blessing. Whatever she may have thought that my parents might think of my suddenly taking myself off into the blue, instead of settling to something sensible in London, she showed no inclination to put a spoke in the wheel. Like most grandmothers Tin felt, I believe, that she understood her daughter's children, or one of them at least, better than did her daughter. I left Upper Grosvenor Street with my ears full of kind wishes, some sparkling recollections of nineteenth-century Italy, and my hands of a Victorian guide to Florence and a copy of Leopardi's poems inscribed to my grandmother by John Addington Symonds.

There were few travellers at that season. I had the third-class section of the cross-Channel steamer pretty much to myself. We drew away from Dover harbour in a shifting greyness: low grey cloud, scarves of grey mist hiding or revealing grey piers and buildings, a heaving grey sea combed white in places by the harsh February wind.

Susan had been wise in her prescription. Movement was the thing. With every turn of a train wheel, every plunge or roll of the boat, I felt a lightening of the heart which no insistent queasiness could affect. Optimism began to reassert itself. Perhaps, just possibly, given time and absence, things at home might change, improve; doors which had seemed so sadly, so irrevocably shut might prove to have been left ajar. In any event, as I lay stretched out on a hard bench, my spirits began to expand towards cheerfulness. Soon I should be in France, country of so many of my dreams, nourisher of so much in living, in literature and art, that most deeply appealed to me. Beyond France there would be Italy; another weather, a different tongue, yet possessing so much that was familiar from earliest childhood, from pictures in books and pictures on walls, and novels and travellers' tales. Ahead lay Florence, already clear to me in the celestial light of early paintings: a great dome, a campanile, the turret of the Palazzo Vecchio rising like a minaret, the bridges over the Arno, the churches and their astounding treasures. Names rolled, rounded and lustrous as drops of syrup, off my mental tongue, as I rehearsed them in my head. Santa Maria Maggiore, Santo Spirito, Lungarno Accaiuoli, Palazzo Medici. Using my forty-year-old guide-book I had already planned excursions, noted distances and the geographical relationships of things I wanted to see. On the map of the city I had traced the route which some vehicle would have to take to convey me over the Ponte alla Carraia and southwards to the slopes of Bellosguardo, to Piazza San Francesco da Paola number 3.

The railway station at Florence was then, and remains still, one of the monuments of Mussolini's Fascist state, at that time a source of pride to the faithful, of jokes to the unconverted. It is largely built of the pleasing, creamy Travertine marble, and its architecture is uncompromisingly square. To my amusement, thinking of its equivalent at Paddington, I was soon to learn that the station restaurant rated highly as a place for Florentine dining out. I dined there often myself, not wholly able to share my hosts' rapture at its spanking modernity. Many Italians, I believe, feel oppressed by their gorgeous past, bowed down by so colossal a weight of history, so sumptuous a heritage of art. A Venetian nobleman, owner of a crumbling but, to our eyes, intensely romantic palazzo, would dearly like to pull it down, sell the watery site for a yacht marina, and use the proceeds to burn up the motorway in a Ferrari, inscrutable behind dark glasses and fascinatingly, incontrovertibly, up-to-date.

I stood for a moment at the station entrance, flanked by my luggage. Somehow, plodding southwards with the train, I had expected the weather to grow warmer. It had done no such thing.

227

The temperature was much the same as that of yesterday's London morning; but there was one important difference: the air was dry. The lights of a great piazza shone clearly. The black and white bulk of Santa Maria Novella, away to my right, stood sharp-eyed, just faintly outlined by an effulgence from the city beyond. I breathed deeply that foreign air, sniffed foreign smells unfamiliar at home, horse-dung and woodsmoke and the fine dust of antiquity. I had been told to look for a *carrozza* and there, in a line of box-like bodies painted green, and horses standing dejectedly, heads down, or feeding from nosebags, was a string of them looking wonderfully antique, like miniature broughams, bringing back some pleasant recollection from my earliest childhood, when there were still carriages to be seen in the London streets.

From its seat on the box of the first cab a shrouded figure bent down towards me a dark, moustached face under a squashed felt hat. I uttered my first words in Italian: 'Tre piazza San Francesco da Paola, signore!' and, remembering too late, murmured, 'per favore!' as the door closed. A porter, my first since leaving England, had flown the Revelations to the roof of the cab with enviable ease. From the calm with which he had accepted my proffered note I guessed that I had overtipped him sensationally. With a rumble of wheels and a jingling of harness, and the sort of commands to the horse which would have sounded much the same in any language, we set off. I sank back into the worn leather seat, rolling a little with the motion, and smelled the leather-polish and horse sweat which were the smells of the harness-room at home. Unable to sit back for long, too excited to pretend that riding in a carriage, even of the humblest sort, was a common-place of my life, I lowered the window and leaned forward, joyfully open to every impression I could get from the luminous evening and the so often imagined town. Soon we were crossing the Arno, a glassy blackness starred with lights, and trundling on up the length of the via dei Seragli to the looming arch of the Porta Romana. Tall houses stood crisply out against the low sky which was faintly touched by the city's glow. All was mysterious, full of shadowy stretches and sudden flares of light, all there to be explored and, to some extent, known; humming with promise, and containing a future not yet possible to guess. Rolling along, at something between a walk and a trot, sometimes smoothly, sometimes joltingly over areas of rough stone, I found myself existing in a perfect Now, my past remotely distant, my future as enticing as a birthday present of unfathomable shape. I felt myself proudly alone but in no way lonely, ready for any experience, bringing with me an exotic baggage; almost as a 'young man from the provinces', a Stendhalian figure about whom, one day, there might be something to tell. Such egocentric euphoria, such references to a past century, to a romantic, almost Byronic conception of the travelling Englishman, were much aided by the fact of the *carrozza*, the sound of its wheels, the sharp, small explosions from the shoes of the horse on hard stones, and the unfamilar shapes and silhouettes, now barefaced, now half-erased by darkness, the lit shops and shifting crowds of a foreign town.

For the last few minutes of the journey I could feel that we had gone beyond the old city, that the buildings strolling past us were of later date, the street lighting different. As we crossed a wide piazza set on a slope our progress slowed to a walk while the poor, thin horse leaned into his collar for a sharply steepening hill. One more short, narrow street to be slowly climbed, and then came a small square, open to one side, out of which our road ran still more steeply upwards; to our left the tall, rectangular bulk of a house, a crowd of cat's-tail cypresses, a small baroque chapel beside a high, blank wall in the centre of which were imposing gates of wrought iron. The carriage stopped. On one of the gate-piers I saw, in white on a blue plaque, the number three.

Feeling suddenly nervous I got down. Between us the cabman and I tugged and slid the Revelations to the ground. The evening was still. Only a faint murmur came up from the city below. In the piazza there was no sound. The Casa Brewster loomed vast and impressive. Some of my euphoria left me. How should I get through those frowning gates? What should I do if no one answered the bell? Or if I failed to find a bell at all? The cabman was waiting expectantly, his horse attempting to browse on the cobbles. During the train journey I had succeeded in learning Italian numbers up to a thousand. What the man was then asking — and I had to get him to repeat it — sounded little enough for a twenty-minute journey. I paid him, once more adding a probably over-generous tip.

After the carriage had turned, the weak light of its lamps just touching the dark corners of the piazza, and had rolled off down the hill, I stood for some seconds peering at the mass of ironwork in front of me, searching for a bell-pull. When I found one I gave it a hard tug, felt the resistance of a long wire, and heard its rusty screech. No bell sounded that I could hear. Silence lay all around me. The high walls, the great, dark building, the long fingers of the cypresses black against the sky, gave an impression of waiting to know what I would do next. Then, from the gate itself, came a loud click. At that time I was unfamiliar with the practice, common in continental cities, of using an electrical impulse or, as in this case, a long wire to control the catches of faraway doors and gates. That click meant nothing to me. Again I gave the bell-pull a tug, the violence of which expressed the anxiety I was feeling; and again there came that loud, authoritative click. This time I was looking at the lock, and saw one leaf of the gates move slowly inwards. Light dawned. I gave the gate a push and, a minute later, was inside, grappling the Revelations, in a semi-darkness where I could just make out tall shrubs, a statue on a plinth with a wild, wavering baroque outline, a wall of dark trees and, some way off, light streaming from a wide-open door.

A woman's voice called something on a questioning note, ending, 'Il signorino americano?' 'Si!' I called back, 'Si, si!', hoping that it was really I and not some vague American who was expected. The household at the Casa Brewster, like the majority of the citizens of Florence, was, in those late days, more accustomed to American visitors than to the once ubiquitous English. I was to find myself classified 'americano' more often than 'inglese' throughout my stay.

A small dark woman, dressed in black, came forward from the arched doorway, beaming, to welcome me. A weak electric light, hanging high, showed behind her a broad passage, flagged with stone, which led through a corresponding arch to darkness and the shapes of trees, their trunks and the shrubs beneath them just showing. I shook my head, smiling, at her flood of Italian, unable to give her back more than my name and the fact that I was English, a point which she was never to take. Bustling ahead of me, and looking back constantly to smile encouragement, she led me into the loggia which separated the house from its garden on that side, and sharp left until we reached a tall glazed door. Through the glass I could see light from a chandelier and the suggestion of an enormous room. My heart leaped. Here I had been marvellously well advised: here my fancies for myself, for the setting which I thought I needed, were suddenly, wonderfully, made real.

Briskly, and with many expansive gestures, my guide made me free for my new domain. The *salone*, which we entered through the glass door, seemed vast, its floor a wide expanse of dark tiles, covered in places by small rugs. Down the centre, under the chandelier, ran a long refectory table bearing a silver vase of antique shape and a couple of majolica dishes. There was one window, opposite the door, set high in the wall and barred outside with iron. In the corner to the right of the window stood a tall, cylindrical cast-iron stove, alight and giving off a faint smell of coke. Opposite, to the window's left, an open doorway showed the start of a narrow flight of stairs. Those, it was at once revealed, led up a short distance to my bedroom, the red-tiled floor of which met the wall of the *salone* at half its height, so that its ceiling was lower, its feeling homelier and less august. A single window, shuttered at night, and also barred externally with iron, gave on to the loggia, the courtyard, and the dark green wall of ilex and stone-pine beyond.

I had been filled with contentment merely on seeing my apartment for the first time; the huge sitting-room with its delicate sixteenth-century vaulting in grey stone blocked in with white plaster; the bedroom, monastic almost in the simplicity of its furnishings, but showing my hosts' infallible taste in the glowing ancient embroidery of a counterpane; the bathroom where a deep iron bath on four feet had, at its tap end, a geyser, a six-foot-high copper cylinder, made to burn wood; the dark cell of a lavatory and the short communicating passage to both, lined from floor to ceiling with books.

Glancing to my right as I came into the loggia, I had seen an open door spilling yellow light on to a flight of steps and some statuary. That was the way from which my Italian lady had come, and so she must be a servant to Mrs Brewster, whose apartments were on an upper storey, the *piano nobile* or 'noble floor' of the house. Now my guide and welcomer was looking at me anxiously, and evidently asking a question. I caught the word *mangiato*, guessed correctly that I was being asked if I had eaten, and vigorously shook my head. I may even have patted my stomach, for I was desperately hungry. With a comprehending nod my benefactress disappeared into the darkest corner of the loggia. I heard a door close and the sound of voices.

With frowns and head-shaking I had forbidden Maria to lift the Revelations which were still making their unhandy presence felt outside the door. I heaved them inside, and was on my way with them to the bedroom, almost wafting them along, they seemed so much lighter now that I was at journey's end, when the door from the loggia opened again and Maria came in with a short, elderly grey-haired man whom she introduced as Giulio. There were smiles all round, and another friendly bout of near-communication. Giulio, whose lined brown face, drooping moustache, and striped flannel shirt fastened with a brass stud, would not have looked out of place in Oxfordshire, was clearly going to do something about my supper, for he set off with a reassuring wave down the passage to the bathroom which, I then discovered, had a door at its darkest end leading to the kitchen. I followed him, to find him blowing busily at a pile of glowing charcoal on a wide stone hearth. Seeing that all was going well, and with many more smiles, and a short speech from which I could detach the words '*la padrona*' and '*domani*', Maria left with a final '*Buona notte!*' as a kind of benediction. Knowing that *domani* meant 'tomorrow', I guessed that *la padrona*, Mrs Brewster, meant to receive me then.

That evening I had my first meal from Giulio's hands, a meal both simple and sustaining, article of a diet which I was to come to think the healthiest and most reliably appetizing of any that I had ever had. There was spaghetti, liberally snowed with fresh Parmesan cheese, in quantity sufficient for two hungry men; there were round, crisp rolls, and white butter, and a green salad, and another cheese which I had never tasted before, and small, sweet oranges for dessert, the whole accompanied by Chianti from an outsize straw-covered flask. Coffee came afterwards in a battered percolator, that black Brazilian coffee which inspires conversation and aids composition, a strong stimulant which, taken in quantity, makes the heart beat extra fast. Seated at one end of the long table, listening to no other sound than the flutter and clink of the stove — an imposing, ancient artefact, made in Essen — looking round me with gratitude and pure satisfaction, or up to the vaulted ceiling so high its groining was in dusk scarcely touched by the low-powered lights of the brass chandelier, I had a strong sense of having floated free. London and all that had happened there seemed infinitely far away. The pains and protests of the past weeks were present, certainly, at the back of my mind, but dimmed a little, their sharpness blunted. I have mentioned that when ill, I had been given injections of morphia which had had the effect, not of abolishing pain, but of removing it to a distance, so that it could be contemplated rather than felt. Florence, it seemed to me, might be going to produce a similar effect.

After supper I unpacked my Revelations and shoved them out of sight, not wishing to be reminded of the day when I should have to leave these so satisfactory surroundings and go home. Part of their great weight was accounted for by books, writing materials, one large framed photograph, and my Zeiss-Ikon camera with its accompaniments of lens-hood, filters and rolls of film. Those things I scattered about the vast sitting-room where they made only a moderate personal impression on its majestic atmosphere. My suits I had hung in a curtained recess of the bedroom; shirts, pullovers and such were stowed in a fine, curvaceous old chest of drawers. I was accustoming myself to great spaciousness, to the sound of my feet on tiles, to the weighty, enveloping quiet of the great house. I was alone but still in no way lonely. Somewhere under the same roof were Mrs Brewster and her servants and, for all I knew, any number of others like myself, each as perfectly self-contained, almost, as the monks of San Francesco da Paola must once have been in their cells. It was as well, perhaps, that I was not to learn until much later that monks were said to be buried under the floor of my bedroom, a fact which, if true, would account for its raised-up position in relation to the rest of the ground floor. Such news, at that moment, I might have found disturbing. Later, so much did I absorb the feeling of the place, I should have paid it little attention. In any event, they were good, quiet dead monks who never disturbed my sleep.

After bestowing my stuff I flopped on to the sofa and considered my situation. It was too early to go to bed, and I was certainly too excited to sleep. After those hours in boat and train I was physically tired. Parts of my body ached, but my head was turning like a kaleidoscope from one bright image to another. For a while I relived my journey. For a while I considered the reasons for it, and even gave thought to possible reactions from parents in Canada, or from friends and relations at home. I was well aware that my sudden dive to Florence would come in for criticism; that really I had no right to use the allowance I had from my father to please myself in quite so dramatic a fashion. My aim, therefore, must be to derive as much from a couple of months in Florence as could fairly be counted under the heading of 'education'. After all, I said to myself, all living, however unconventional, is educative; and, anyway, I seriously intended to write. And so, before giving the stove a last feed of coke, and extinguishing the lights in preparation for bed, I laid out on the darkly gleaming table a box of quarto paper, pens and pencils, and a loose-leaf book containing notes and sketches for stories yet to be written.

Many people would find it hard to recall any one period of

continual happiness in their lives, and some would gloomily deny ever having been continually happy at all. Looking back at my brief sojourn in Florence I can, without equivocation, reckon it one period of my life which, in every respect, was golden. Seldom before those days, or since, have I spent my time on so high and happy a level of exhilaration. More important, I have never fitted so comfortably into any scene, so that I passed my days untroubled by irritation, peacefully open to all that I saw and heard, delighted by every human contact, wholly untempted to any word or action that might be cross-grained, intemperate, or in any way cause for regret. From bewildered unhappiness I passed swiftly into a state of positive anticipation, something surprisingly sensible in me having decided to embrace whatever might come, while the irrational romantic hung on to an unformulated but persistent hope, which soon grew to a near certainty, that I should find, on my return to England, things changed for the better in a relationship my side of which I refused to let drop. Meanwhile — *carpe diem*! — I was going to make the most of my dash for freedom, whilst fully realizing that from one's self one can never be free; merely hoping that experience to come might help to steady that self, so scattered and so immature, into something a trifle easier to manage.

18

TIME OUT OF LIFE

Coming downstairs next morning I found Giulio raking out the stove, which soon made an encouraging roar. One end of the long table was laid for breakfast, which Giulio, with a broad smile and a murmur about *colazione*, went off to prepare. Of many surprises that day the first was the introduction by Giulio of two women, one middle-aged and one about eighteen years old. The elder, his wife, was introduced as Giulia, the younger, his daughter, as Giulietta. I was at once delighted and slightly appalled. Giulio's wages, whatever they might be, I could manage; but three people to look after me, charming though they were, might be more than I could afford. My bank in London had been instructed to send me ten pounds a month via the Banco di Roma. Paying a whole family to see to my needs might cripple me financially. We should have to see. Meanwhile, there they were: Giulio with his broad, wrinkly smile; Giulia graver, less forthcoming, flitting about the place, setting things to rights with occasional sharp exclamations, the Italian probably for 'Drat!'; Giulietta, who served my meals, a stately girl, tall, robust, high-coloured, with a dark down on her upper lip and, although a Florentine, the very type of girl who would once have posed as a gypsy or a dancer for visiting English painters by the Spanish Steps in Rome.

Giulio and his family, I discovered, lived not in the house but in one of a row of cottages at the lower end of what I soon learned to call the *podere*. This was the attractive, not wholly tamed expanse of ground, at several levels, on the city side of the monastery, and sloping away from it. The *podere* was a good place for walking in, when the weather allowed: for meditation, and for enjoyment, from a grove at its highest point, of the unique view over Florence where wave upon wave of russet-tiled roofs lapped the dome of the cathedral, the white tower of the Campanile and the upward-pointing finger of the Signoria. (A friend once, boarding a Florentine tram, and asking a particular direction from the conductor, was rewarded by a magnificent showman's gesture

235

and 'Yonder, signora! Where the marvellous Campanile of Giotto rises to the sky!' That was said in Italian, of course, in which it sounds particularly thrilling.)

The *podere* had spaces of rough grass, shrub-bordered paths, and many tall cypresses and broad umbrella pines. It was less a garden in the strictly architectural, Italian sense, than a farm turned pleasance and grown a little wild. A few yards below the terrace of the house was a two-storeyed cottage, known as the *villino*, and beyond was a smaller building to house carts and implements. At the far, or eastern, end, the land was cultivated and there was a grove of olive trees; and all this at the very edge of an important city. Behind the house the hill of Bellosguardo rose steeply, clothed in dark woodland, and showing a couple of Renaissance villas with canopied towers, and stone-buttressed formal gardens half-hidden among the trees. There was something about the view of Florence, with its cluster of significant buildings at the centre, and the green frame made by the trees of the *podere*, which held a faint reminder of the view of Oxford from the far end of Pond Close at Elsfield.

My next surprise, on that first morning, came not long after I had finished breakfast. I saw a shadow beyond the glass door, heard a sharp tap, and looked up from my guide-book to see a figure advancing into the room. This was a young man of about my own height, brown-haired, bright-eyed, with every smile and gesture proclaiming welcome to San Francesco and to Florence. We beamed at one another. I gave my name. He gave me his: Wolfgang Braunfels. He was, it appeared, a lodger like myself in that huge and hospitable house.

On many counts Wolfgang was going to earn my gratitude and respect. To begin with he was able to fill in for me some details lacking from my rather cloudy impression of San Francesco. He was the source of accurate information about Florence itself, and about those of its inhabitants whom I was likely to meet. Beyond all that, his gaiety, his lively curiosity about myself and my English background, his sympathy and his bubbling enthusiasm for life, seemed interestingly remote from my idea of the serious scholar that he certainly was. Wolfgang was a couple of years older than I, son of a distinguished German conductor, and, like several of his compatriots, had settled in Florence to study the history of art.

Once, many years later, my mother was to look at me rather quizzically and say: 'I believe that you really *like* foreigners! Other

236

people pretend to, but you actually *do*...' She had put a finger on a crucial trait in my make-up but, as so often with parents, had never made the connection between what must have been fairly evident, even in my schooldays, and what might have been a sensible way of putting it to work. That I had been trying to read French ever since I could make out three consecutive words; that French had been my one continuing success, both in school work and in examination; that I had decorated the old nursery, at a pleasantly melancholy stage of adolescence, with French proverbs in gold paint — 'Tout passe, tout casse, tout lasse...' and so on — must surely have shown a powerful inclination. My spoken French has always been serviceable rather than elegant, but by the age of eighteen I could read it fairly well, quite well enough to derive enormous pleasure from my reading. At Eton I had been much influenced by Cocteau, later on by Gide and Montherlant, later still by Proust.

My elder brother has often remarked that the most futile conjunction of words in English is 'If only...', but I feel obliged to use it just the same. *If only*, after Eton, I had been sent to a French university, I believe that the benefit to me, and to those who worried about me, would have been very great. What struck my family and some compatriots as wild, unsafe, eccentric in my temperament would, I am certain, either have passed unregarded in France, or would have been briskly put into shape by Gallic positiveness. A restraint, however light, of French logic and French practical sense, together with French tolerance of human oddity, I might easily have accepted, where any English equivalent would have made me shrug myself into fits. Above all, I should have been amongst foreigners and obliged to find my way in a foreign language, which was perhaps the sole form of discipline which my undisciplined nature would have unquestioningly obeyed.

I can imagine that such an idea never even came to discussion. Although my mother's family might have thought it reasonable, even traditional, my mother herself would not have been in favour. For all that she had brought me up on French folk-songs, and had murmured French poems to me at bedtime, and although she read French herself and spoke often of certain excellences in living which could only be found in France, yet she would never have agreed to letting me be out of sight for so long a time every year. The real obstruction, however, would inevitably have come from my Scottish grandmother, who would have thought an education in France an unacceptably definite stride down the primrose path to damnation. It would have been a waste of time to talk to her about the quality of French education, the high seriousness of French intellectual life. She would only have smelt licence and luxury and moral ruin; the awful Saturnalia of the Continental Sunday; the well-known frivolity and light-mindedness of the French; the real danger that I might enjoy the process altogether too much, finding wicked foreign connivance, at every turn, with all those aspects of my character of which she most disapproved.

It was always to be the sheer foreignness of foreigners that would appeal to me. Travelling in foreign countries I could feel free of the burden of other people's expectations, the weight of the past, the imponderability of the future. What I could not tolerate in my fellow-countrymen, I should find amusing, or negligible, or even appealing, in members of another race. Not having to bear any responsibility for them, even the tenuous responsibility of historical kinship, I could allow my foreigners all kinds of licence, and treat their prejudices and inherited attitudes with calm indifference of even, sometimes, with real respect.

With Wolfgang I was soon to find another attribute of foreignness, German this time, in an education of extraordinary scope and thoroughness, and its effect on a good mind combined with a questing spirit. It was not only his knowledge of painting and architecture and, naturally enough, music that was superior to my own, but the breadth of his interests, the extent of his reading — he read English in the original where I had had to make do with translations from German — which won my admiration. He was to endear himself to me in many ways, and not least by a genial forthrightness in criticism which, phrased as he phrased it, gave me continual pleasure. Having been often and severely criticized in my twenty-two years, I could easily have become over-sensitive, and might well have been so with a compatriot on first acquaintance; but Wolfgang's radiant good nature, together with his command of English which, though very good, nevertheless possessed its own particular idiom, made his criticism as palatable as his continual flow of questions was un-irritating.

One morning I was standing on the terrace, looking out over the *podere*, and whistling what I thought I could remember of a Bach toccata and fugue, a favourite among my seventy-eights at home, Wolfgang came up behind me. 'Ha!' he said. 'That is Bach that you whistle. Very poor, very wrong, but still Bach!'

Wolfgang was to make another critical contribution later in my stay; one which, had I possessed greater self-knowledge and less impractical romanticism, should have served as a warning for the future. One day he asked me if he might see something that I had written, and I gave him two poems, each addressed to the same person, which I had caused to be conveyed to an address in London, as a gauge of my continuing state of feeling. Wolfgang took the poems away with him and, when we were next alone together, handed them back. I could see that he was hardly overcome by my efforts and waited, feeling let down, for his opinion. What he had to say was, I now see, both accurate and just. He had liked the poems very much, and found them elegant and accomplished. 'Anything more?' I asked anxiously. No, just those things. He gave me to understand that I had achieved what the eighteenth century would have called 'good copies of verses', but that the poems were no more than sufficiently skilful, somewhat mannered, exercises in a particular genre. What I now know that he thought, although he did not say it in so many words, was that I was working on an emotion deliberately kept inflated by artifice: that the primal afflatus was gone, and that I was applying technique to celebrate something which had lost, or was in process of losing, its exclusive force in my life.

Since Wolfgang, by his usual method of questioning, which was persistent without, somehow, ever being impertinent, had got out of me the whole of my recent history, he was perfectly aware of what those poems should have contained. My flight to Florence amused him as a fairly ripe example of English romanticism, poetic, perhaps even aristocratic in mode. To so mature and well-instructed a person my comparative immaturity must have been evident, but he never for a moment made me feel callow, nor that my pains and anxieties might be less important, above all less lasting, than they appeared in my own eyes. Meanwhile he set about introducing me to Florence, and to people he knew there, and was at all times a source of useful information and enjoyable talk.

That morning of my first day at San Francesco we went together to visit Mrs Brewster, whose long range of rooms looked down on Florence from a commanding, but in no way diminishing, height. There was something about those rooms which reminded me of the Feildings' home, Beckley Park: the solid old Italian furniture, sparely placed and darkly gleaming, pictures or looking-glasses hung against sheets of Perugian damask, many books, a sense of the past as a living force inter-penetrating the present. Mrs Brewster was a painter, and there on the *piano nobile* she had her studio. She welcomed me kindly, if with a touch of vagueness. I was later to learn of the wide ramification of family and friends all over Europe and America which meant, at San Francesco, that someone was always turning up, announced or otherwise, accredited by a friend or relation in one of half a dozen countries.

We spoke for a while of Susan. It was indicated that I should be asked to visit again, for luncheon or dinner, on some unspecified occasion, and then Wolfgang and I took our leave. Our hostess turned back to her easel, needing as much of the pale, clear light as she could get from the winter's day. As we went down the stone stairs and out into the loggia, Wolfgang said: 'She lives for two things, her painting and her religion. She is Catholic and very devout. Oh, but that is not true! Mrs Brewster lives also for her children. Harry and Ralph are the sons. Ralph is in Greece, and Harry is not here at the moment; but you will meet him soon…And then there is Cloclo, her daughter. She too paints and is devout. One day she will come to this house. Everyone, the whole world, is in love with her, she is so beautiful and so good!'

I wonder how many miles I walked each day during those happy weeks. In the earliest days walking began each morning immediately after breakfast. I had been given a key to a small door in the wall beside the iron gates of San Francesco, a door through which I could go in and out without troubling the household. For all my good resolutions about writing, it was some time before a growing familiarity allowed me to leave the city of Florence alone for more than the space of a morning. There it lay below me, all that most mattered to me in it still contained in its medieval and Renaissance plan: a trunkful of jewels which demanded inspection at almost every hour of the day and night. The walk down, in any case, was exhilarating, whatever the weather, which latter was capricious. There were days when a harsh wind from the north threatened to slice me in half, when the German stove was powerless against the chill of the great *salone*, when frost lay in the furrows among the olive trees at the far end of the *podere*. It could also rain with fierce persistence. Robert Browning, who lived in and above the city at various times between 1846 and 1861, wrote:

> What I love best in all the world,
> Is a castle, precipice-encurled,
> In a gash of the wind grieved Apennine.

240

Sheer bravado, that was, I am inclined to think, since what came down to Florence from that same Apennine was enough, on some days, to make one wonder how Italy ever gained its reputation for warmth. Fortunately I had had the sense to bring with me a number of thick sweaters and some highly-coloured shirts, in a sort of tartan, which I had bought, the year before, for a few dollars at the Lumbermen's Store in Ottawa. They had been made by people who knew much about cold weather. Wearing one, and sometimes two of them I would tuck myself into a corner beside the stove, which Giulio and I had stoked nearly to red heat, and write, or read, or simply muse, until the fumes of the coke made my head ache. I would then put on still more clothes and rush out and climb briskly the long winding road which led up from the piazza to the village of Bellosguardo and, by one of a number of narrow, stone-walled lanes, into the rolling country beyond.

For the first days of my stay, however — and those could be days of sunshine and respite from the fierce wind, when the light was so clear that the city centre seemed a mere hop and step away, instead of the half-mile or so that it was — my daily route was downhill from the piazza, through narrow streets strung with the many-coloured washing of the Florentine poor, to the Porta Romana, and thence to the river. There it was necessary to pause, first to look across at the long white front of the Palazzo Corsini, with its wrought-iron window grilles and grey stone quoins, and then upstream to the wonderful survival, faintly reminiscent of London Bridge in old pictures, only in miniature, the regular roof-line and piled-up narrow houses of the Ponte Vecchio. Between that and the Ponte alla Carraia, beside which I would be standing, there flew from bank to bank the Ponte Santa Trinita, which Ammanati completed in 1569 to a design of Michelangelo, perhaps the most beautiful bridge in the world. From that point of view the river, at its eastern end, began at the Ponte Vecchio where it came rustling through three broad arches. Downstream to the west it curved away, old houses and churches dwindling into modernity, towards dark green feathers of woodland framing the Cascine on the farther bank.

Over the past forty years, since the last war in fact, Florence has become increasingly noisy and, at any season, more crowded than it was when I first saw it. In the 1950s came the Vespa, the motor-cycle so rightly named 'wasp'. Most young Italians, it seems, love noise, perhaps conceiving it as part of a *bella figura*;

they were obviously enchanted by this invention which could be made to sound like a whole nest of furious wasps at a turn of the throttle. Now there are also a hundred times more cars than there were in 1938, when it was still possible to step off the pavement without risking worse than collision with an ordinary bicycle, although one had to beware of the bull rush of a tram. There were many bicycles and, of course, people moving about very briskly, sometimes to be brought up all standing to greet acquaintances (much raising of black felt hats), or to gather into a group round someone who had news of some sort to impart. News and rumour, especially the latter, were the daily currency of Florentines of all classes, as I was soon to find out, to my great pleasure and, occasionally, slight embarrassment.

In the cafés and small bars, the hotels and restaurants, the little *trattorie* so numerous that any visitor can find one to return to again and again and make his own, in the smart teashops of the via Tornabuoni and the Piazza della Signoria, the more prosperous side of Florentine life was on display. I noted a high degree of elegance, especially among the younger men, who dressed and bore themselves with a discreet but definite panache and looked, sometimes, so hauntingly like the figures in paintings and frescos which I had just been seeing. Florentine women, then, were apt to lose early the marvellous bloom of their young years, particularly if having rather little to do combined with superb Tuscan cooking had led them to prefer comfort above all other things. As children, as adolescents, girls could be astonishingly beautiful, and even if not so were somehow blessed with a fine sense of the value, the preciousness, the desirability of being what they were. This could be told from every motion of their walk, the carriage of their heads, the proud and often disdainful glances from black or amber eyes. In those days one tended to think of all Italians, men and women alike, as dark, black-haired, with 'olive' skins and snapping black eyes; but often in the streets of Florence there were women of a striking fairness, blonde and blue-eyed, or tawny as lionesses, with golden eyes to match.

The population of Florence used once to be divided into the *popolo minuto*, the 'little people' and the *popolo grosso*, also known as the *Grandi*, the 'great ones'. The former were the artisans, small tradesmen and workers of the city; the latter the rich burgesses and the nobles. Those distinctions, which must have been so clear, and often and bloodily underlined in earlier centuries, were no longer, of course, so generally evident in my own. Nevertheless, if I left the playgrounds of the contemporary Grandi to walk the streets and explore the courts and alley-ways of the old city, or joined the crowds which streamed across the bridges or congregated in squares or marketplaces, I found a people which, whilst not enjoying wealth, yet certainly did not think of itself as 'little'. Enormous energy, devotion to a task, pride in work were all evident amongst the men, together with what is to be found almost everywhere in Italy, a fine quickness of understanding and an amiable readiness to give and receive pleasure. The young girls might be poor and obliged to work hard for a living but they, too, could show touching pride and satisfaction in being what they were. It was wonderful to watch a pretty girl, perhaps one of those lionesses which seemed to be a speciality of the place, walking up to and past a group of youths lounging at a street corner, passing them without a glance, armoured in splendid pride, and showing no sign beyond, perhaps, a slight frown, of noticing them, or of hearing the kissing sounds and loud exclamations of *bella, bella!*' which came her way.

Someone once remarked that Italian men are possessed of a sexuality which verges, sometimes, on the farcical. There was evidence of this all around; and there were also tales told by Englishwomen who, wishing to act as they did at home, ventured out into Italian cities on their own, and suffered harassment in one form or another, from sly pinches to outright propositions. I went often to those strange entertainments which were neither tea-parties in the English sense, nor gatherings for drinks, which took place at about five in the afternoon. One was offered sweet vermouth and sugar cakes, and one stood about and talked. Usually the ladies were seated, the elderly and the middle-aged presenting a picture more lively than that of the young ones, who sat demurely, eyes cast down, whilst the young men stood as close to them as possible, their faces drawn with frustration, and tried to get a glimpse of a pretty bosom down the open neck of a dress. The air, on the occasions when the young and handsome of both sexes were present, fairly hummed with a two-way traffic of desire. Remembering the innocent, if rather tiresomely hearty, free-and-easiness of an equivalent gathering at home, I wondered whether the rules here applying, especially among the old Catholic families, might not tend to make the game of passion more exciting for the young by making it so much more difficult.

I cannot now remember just how I first came to be introduced to Florentine social life. Certainly Wolfgang took me, at an early moment, into his own circle of German expatriates, all so busily pursuing studies of one kind and another, mostly to do with the history of art. Many of them were Jewish, and had already had the best of reasons for putting a good distance between themselves and their Führer. Others were self-exiled, from dislike of Nazism. Others again cared little for politics, but had been obliged to escape from a world of narrowing opportunities into the clearer light of Italy, to the particular solace which she has always provided for the scholarly or poetic spirits among their countrymen.

They were a lively and attractive lot, who welcomed me with warmth, treated me as one of their own — that is to say someone seriously intent on acts of creation or apprehension — and included me in all the amusements they made for themselves at the end of their intensive working day. Those delightful friends were enjoying a period — how brief was shortly to be demonstrated — of freedom to follow their cultural bent without interference from authority. Each was highly qualified for his chosen profession; all possessed doctorates of one sort or another. It would not be very long before Mussolini, under orders from his German master, would institute a form of persecution for those of Jewish blood; and the other Germans were soon to find their presence required by their government for purposes which had never made part of their view of life. For the time being, however, they were under no especial stress, and — since each was outstandingly intelligent — in spite of very clear ideas about what, if things went really wrong, they and those they loved would have to face, they managed to pursue their studies and take their pleasures with a mixture of high seriousness and high spirits which was extremely appealing.

The political climate of Italy, at that time, was a curious mixture of ebullience and foreboding. For the more thoughtful and the better informed there was little about Fascism, and less about an alliance with Nazism, which could give comfort or hope of better things. For a large number of Italians, however, the visions of glory, of a powerful and significant future constantly put forward by Il Duce and his party, had a considerable appeal. Seen from England, Italian politics appeared both detestable and dangerous. People imagined an Italy darkened by fear, ringing with the sound of jackboots, its people betraying at every turn their marvellous past, and presenting, through excessive ambition, a serious menace to that very civilization which we shared, and of which Italy had been an essential source.

On the spot, in Florence at any rate, things wore a different look. True enough, there was plenty of tension. Voices would drop suddenly in conversation, sentences stay unfinished. People looked over their shoulders a good deal, but the natural volatility of the Florentines, their gift for energetic living, their love of laughter, of commentary and gossip, and their delight in the human comedy as daily enacted, saw to it that days could continue to be passed in pure pleasure, so long as one did not glance too closely into the shadows.

Altogether there was not too much evidence of Fascist activities at that time, or not, at least, of an overt nature. Once in a while a discordant music sounded in the streets as children of the Fascist youth movement, the Balilla, came marching by, dressed in black shirts and shorts, with small black forage caps cockily planted on their heads, and an air at once cheerful and exalted. 'Giovinezza!' they sang, 'Giovinezza, Primavera di bellezza!' How true, I thought, how touching — and how deeply tragic; for here youth, beauty's springtime, was being dedicated, not to love, or productive work, or to any art at all other than that of war. Soon enough those lively children would learn how to kill, and far too soon, probably, put that learning into practice. In the meantime they would become imbued with a horrible kind of pride, be eager believers in the rubbish of racial superiority, and practise espionage and delation even among their own families. Those robust and healthy boys would have their natural thuggishness nurtured and encouraged so that, before very long, they would be ready and able to beat the life half out of some dissident with an iron bar thrust through a bull's pissle (no attributable bruises), or make another spill his guts on to the floor of a cell after enormous doses of castor-oil.

Here and there in the city I read, painted roughly on walls: 'Viva il Duce!' or, in a useful shorthand, 'W il Dux!' but these mural manifestations were no more common than others urging the populace to a rally promoted by a leading bicycle-maker. Such political evidence as I saw at that time did little more than nudge me into brief awareness of the time's volcanic possibilities, and only strengthened my determination to see, smell, taste, hear, examine in detail, and store up for a lifetime's use all that the city of Florence so prodigally had to offer.

My first introduction to Il Duce, or rather to his opinions, came when I was invited for drinks to the home of Baroness Franca Pecori-Giraldi. In those days there existed in Florence an

245

English-language newspaper, *The Florentine Weekly News*, of which Franca was part editor. That publication had quite a long history, going back to the second half of last century, to the great days of English and American travelling when, at any one time, there would have been sufficient English-speaking expatriates, whether residing in Florence or merely passing through, to make it economically worthwhile. The little paper was mainly a kind of social register, of comings and goings and the doings of Florentine society. That society was small enough for the advent of almost any newcomer, especially if he or she had some distinguished connection in the world beyond, to be thought worth a paragraph, perhaps even an extended interview.

Baroness Franca was short, brisk and definite. She was also rather deaf. On my arrival at her party, and after the necessary courtesies of introduction, she proceeded to pin me down. Why had I come to Florence? Well, apart from all the obvious reasons, to try to do some writing. 'You are a writer, then. Do you write psychological novels?'

'No indeed! Just short stories at present.'

The Baroness looked at me severely. She said: 'Il Duce does not approve of psychological novels.' I protested, eloquently. We were speaking English, but, unfortunately deafness had intervened. In the next issue of *The Florentine Weekly News* I read quite a long paragraph about myself, mentioning my father, and stating that I had come to Florence to write a psychological novel. For a moment I wondered whether I might be expelled from Florence, from Italy itself, as a contaminating influence on the pure air of Mussolini's state.

If Mussolini read *The Florentine Weekly News* he must have had other things on his mind at the time. I was not molested. It was easy to forgive Franca, who soon became a valued friend and an admirable guide to the ins-and-outs of Florentine life. She was also a rich source of gossip.

Florentine gossip a little resembles the gossip of Paris, in that it can expand a small nugget of fact to a breathtaking architecture of imagination and conjecture, without the smallest restraint of likelihood or any consideration of slander. Furthermore, the place — like certain sections of Parisian society — is a perfect sounding-board, or whispering gallery. At home, we used to play a game called Russian Scandal, at which the first player whispered something quite banal into the ear of the second, who passed it on to the third. After six or ten repetitions breathily muttered into successive ears the final result, told out loud, could sometimes be wildly funny, even rude, according to the imaginations that it had passed through. Something of the sort was apt to happen in Florence, and very probably still does, to the great pleasure and enrichment of all but the subjects of the scandal themselves.

It should surprise no one that I did rather less work at writing than I had originally intended, since Florence absorbed my attention so imperiously. That least contemptible of lusts, the lust of the eye, led me to feast after feast of happy contemplation: a rather muddled diet, but none the less enjoyable for that. From Santa Maria delle Carmine to Santa Croce, from Santa Maria Novella to the Duomo, to the Bargello, the Pitti Palace, the Uffizi, I gave my eyes the time of their life, and stored in my memory not, I fear, a complete and detailed and logical conspectus of Florentine history and achievement, but a glowing mass of impressions, all clear-lit and comprehensible at their respective centres, but blurring, merging at their edges into a haze of scarlet and gold and blue, like altar-pieces seen through incense-smoke.

Sometimes, to give my eyes a rest, I would sit in the Bobboli Gardens and stare into the green darkness of an ilex hedge, or close them and watch a procession of coloured images, from primitives stiffly composed but vibrating with a humble piety, to vast Assumptions swirling upwards, foreshadowing the Baroque; a noble lady nursing an ermine, the flowery draperies of Ghirlandaio, and rows of impressive males, dressed with a rich sobriety and presenting, with pride, with thought, with sensuality, and sometimes with cruelty, a *bellissima figura* to their age.

During my three months' stay in Florence I do not suppose that I saw a thousandth part of what was there to see. My German friends were probably a little shocked at my haphazard way of going about things, but they looked with indulgence on my waywardness, only occasionally suggesting a particular excursion, or providing a clue or pointer which I could never have found for myself. We met often in the evenings and sometimes, on a Saturday or Sunday, for luncheon in some small trattoria. Conversation proceeded in three languages, most of my new friends being proficient in English, and some in French as well. If a longish interchange went on in German, someone would always turn to me, courteously retailing the gist of it in English, and once more I was awed and made ashamed by the extent of this foreign culture.

It was not lost upon me that, had my performance at school and university been more diligent; had I not, for some cause integral to my nature but at that time obscure, positively rejected (as the body will reject a transplant?) a large part of the admirable instruction then offered to me, I might have met those wise and brilliant young people upon a more level intellectual footing. I could, however, also see that a worthy educational career, toeing a number of traditional lines, would have meant my being already, at twenty-two, a junior member of a merchant bank, or (heaven forbid!) a schoolmaster, or bowed beneath a load of study for the Foreign Service examination, trying for the one 'respectable' career I have ever regretted not seeking to follow. I should certainly not have been enjoying myself hugely in Florence, scarcely troubled by the thought of any head-shaking that might be going on elsewhere.

What I was, however, and perhaps what I seemed to promise, appeared to be enough for my foreign friends, who probably thought that I was doing what was right for my own nature and, anyway, presenting them with a subject for discreet curiosity and kindly amusement. They believed me a poet and, in their philosophy, that was a perfectly adequate passport to acceptance. Whether or not I was any good as a poet was of secondary importance: the impulse itself was enough.

One of my pleasures was to visit Nicolai Rubinstein, who lived in the village of Bellosguardo, high up on the hill above. This walk, on the days when Florence called me less strongly, or when the weather was especially fine and I wanted country rather than town, was one of my favourites. I set off up the sinuous hill road, past the high wall with its heavy door and plaque reading 'Villa Brichieri-Colombi', past the gardens of the Villa Franchetti, and the tower where Nathaniel Hawthorne spent some years, to the single street of Bellosguardo with its small dwellings and hump-backed ancient church. Here Nicolai had an apartment in an old house, comfortably furnished and full of books: full, also, of his welcome — warm, enthusiastic, even though I was probably interrupting important work.

Nicolai was a scholar engaged on some research, but not all the foreigners then living in Florence were studying Renaissance humanism, or Dante, or the history of art. There were professional people as well, exiled, voluntarily or otherwise, from their native lands. I remember with great clarity an evening spent in the house of a Pole called Jablonski who was, I think, an oculist. It was a 'literary' evening in the sense that all present spoke of, and sometimes even quoted, the poets of their particular countries.

Perhaps because no one at that party was by profession a literary man, except in the sense that most of them were at work on theses or expositions of one kind or another, the atmosphere was buoyant and quite untinged by the soured egotism and ill-concealed jealousy usual on literary occasions. I was invited to quote from English poets and even, rather nerve-rackingly, something of my own. At some point in the evening, for what cause I cannot remember, an argument developed, which, from the intensity of feeling expressed between two people, seemed likely to alter the temperature and cause discomfort. With my customary frivolity I must have interjected a comment which caused general laughter, thus lightening the atmosphere, because, a day or so later, Nicolai Rubinstein (who was to become so good a friend) presented me with a poem in German, dedicated to myself, recording my assistance in preserving the gaiety of that evening. Nicolai was not the only friend capable of producing verses, almost at a moment's notice, to record a happy occasion or convey an affectionate compliment, but this form of expression particularly suited the elegance of his mind and the warmth which he brought to friendship. His verses in German — so far as I could tell — and also in French, had a special quality of freshness, economy and immediacy. Beside them I began to think that my own recent productions seemed a trifle forced.

Another of Florence's exiled professionals, Dr Levi — a medical doctor this time — saved me, by his skill and promptitude, from an illness which might have ruined my Italian stay. During a week of really extreme cold, when I shivered in the salone, and could hardly warm myself in bed, I developed a bad sore throat, a throat so painful that I had a panicky feeling that I might be going to suffer, once again, what had attacked me in England two years before. Dr Levi, who came for several visits (and charged me in the end for saving, if not my life, at least my time of freedom, the equivalent of ten shillings), was more than a match for streptococci. He produced a drug, Prontosil Rosso, so new that it had scarcely been heard of in England. That was the very first of the sulphanilamide compounds which were shortly to be refined and marketed at home by May & Baker, and to play so valuable a part in medicine during the coming war. ('The wonder drug M&B', as Churchill called it.) Prontosil was compounded with a red aniline dye: hence its title, Rosso. One of its effects was alarming, or would have been had Dr Levi not given me fair warning: urinating, after taking it, produced a vivid blood-red stream, a preview of what I should see when, later, I had hepatitis in India.

I wonder what became of Dr Levi, small, slight and quick as a lizard, and like some lizards, brilliant. I pray that he escaped, somehow from the evils Mussolini was preparing for his race. They would not be long in coming: the drying-up of consultations, the falling-away of patients, the dismissal from teaching and clinical employment, the cancellation of work-permits, and, finally, the forced repatriation. It would be good to think that he escaped in time, and made his way somewhere, the United States perhaps, or Egypt, or even India, where his art would be appreciated and his racial origins disregarded. I have to wonder what became of so many people. Remembering those of German origin who did so much to make my stay in Florence a rich experience, and paying them this inadequate tribute, my tone must turn sometimes to the elegiac; for I do not know what happened to so many of them after September 1939. Of the later history of six I do know, and know too that all was well in the end. They were to become part of my life in London, where the qualities which had delighted me in Florence continued to show undimmed. But of the rest, and of their families, their connections not only in Germany but in Austria, Holland, Czechoslovakia, a world within a world of cultivated, gifted, creative people leavening the teutonic lump — of these I have had no further word.

In a way, the company I kept in Florence, although varied by pleasurable excursions into the Florentine *beau monde*, was not unlike that which I had enjoyed during my short stay at Oxford, albeit infinitely more mature and better instructed. Through the lives of those intent, hard-working young scholars ran a strong strain of romanticism. Poetic feeling was not confined to the written word. Side by side with scholarship and scholarly ambition it had a definite place in their lives. Some had been severed, by their need to go to Italy, from long-held affections, even projects of marriage, which must hang fire, kept alive only by letters, while they tried to make a future for themselves in Florence. Others were prosecuting serious love affairs on the spot, and suffering all the traditional emotional fluctuations of those. The women who came to their parties tended to be the wives of guests, or girls who, like themselves, were far from home and engaged in the same lines of study. It was scarcely possible, in those days, for young, unmarried Italian women of family to attend parties unchaperoned, unless invited by relations. As for the young ladies — American, English, French — who attended Mrs Lestrange's or other finishing schools, they mainly existed to be glimpsed in churches or galleries, and perhaps sleeplessly yearned for, but were so closely guarded as to be next to impossible to meet.

It seems, now, very difficult to believe that a young man could live in Italy on ten pounds a month, paying for rent and servants, smoking, eating and drinking, and — an important item — having films developed and printed, giving occasional dinner parties, and still having enough over to buy presents to take home. It seems so to me, and yet I know it to have been true.

The rent of my apartment came to about ten shillings a week, the wages of Giulio and his family to the same. Strong cigarettes of black Macedonian tobacco were priced in pennies, the comfortable great flasks of Tuscan wine in a few shillings. Coffee, now very expensive in Italy, was cheap enough to drink frequently, and a substantial meal in a small trattoria could be had for half a crown. When it came to having films developed and printed, I found this, too, perfectly possible — moreover the quality of the work was first class. The prints which I have kept are as good as the day they were made, fresh-looking still, neither faded nor yellowed by the passage of more than fifty years.

As the weeks went by my Italian progressed, but unscientifically, so that I could never do more than find my way about, ask for things in shops and cafés, and make the most elementary polite noises when invited out. Any of a number of serious linguists that I have known would have pored over grammatical constructions, pinned up lists of nouns and verbs to be learned while shaving, read every line of the *Corriere della Sera* every day, and engaged in serious conversation on every possible occasion. It was partly that I was spoiled by German and Italian friends, whose English was anything from good to excellent, and who wanted the chance to practise it on me. Mostly, I fear, the faults were laziness and the almost hectic gathering of sensations which engaged me, the same factors which were to prevent me from returning home with more evidence of serious artistic endeavour than a couple of short stories and a handful of poems.

With Giulio and his wife, I did succeed in establishing

251

satisfactory communication, since all that we needed to talk about concerned such simple matters as baths, laundry, food and various small supplies. Bathing was an adventure. At some point during the day I would tell Giulio that I would like a bath at seven o'clock — 'Bagno alle sette, Giulio!' — and he would answer with pursed lips and a vigorous nod. At round about half past six the great drama would begin with Giulio carrying piles of short logs into the bathroom. I soon learned that it was wisest to undress completely and be ready in my dressing-gown with anything up to half an hour to spare. That was the time for exploring the bookshelves which lined the passage between salon and bathroom, so as to be near at hand for Giulio's grand dénouement. They were a remarkable collection of books mostly in English, and mostly belonging to the time of Henry Brewster, Susan's grandfather. There were presentation copies from Henry James and 'Vernon Lee', many books of essays, works on travel, in all a library sufficient to last the most voracious reader for many months. From the bathroom came roaring sounds, the clank of the fire-door being opened and shut, the clop of logs being thrown in and then, with great suddenness, Giulio would appear at the bathroom door, beckoning urgently. I soon realized why he seemed to think it important that I should come at once. If all was going well, and the towering inferno of the geyser was doing its work, a thin trickle of scalding water would be coming from the tap. It was absolutely necessary to seize the moment, watch the hot water as it flowed, test it for heat and, the moment it showed signs of cooling, turn off the tap. For, once the geyser had provided as much hot water as Giulio's skill could elicit from it, and though the furnace might still be roaring like a dragon, and the tall copper cylinder be too hot to touch, there was evidently a point of no return past which the water would inevitably run cold. Sometimes I tried on my own to heat the bath-water, and only once succeeded — on other occasions I simply burned a great deal of wood without producing any usable result. Four years later, in Cyprus, I lived in an unheated hut at the bottom of a stony *wadi*, in a winter season so cold that I had to sleep in my clothes, with a flying-suit over all. Even in icy weather that practice was unhygienic. Once a week, at least, I simply had to have a hot bath and a complete change of clothes. This was achieved by telephoning to the nearby town, Nicosia, to the George Hotel, and ordering a bath for a specified time. It was important to arrive punctually for that event, since the hotel bath-water was heated by the identical twin of Giulio's copper tower. Lying there and enjoying a bath which was sinisterly close to a delousing operation, and gazing at a square of wintry Mediterranean blue through the window, I was happy, transported back in time and sentiment to San Francesco and my idiot's carefree existence there.

The British and Americans had for so long made pilgrimage to Florence, had so established themselves and even to some extent, their customs that one had a real sense of being easily accepted by the people. Florence had adapted over the years to its mixed bag of self-exiled noblemen, professors, literary ladies, pederasts and poets. There were the English chemist, an English tailor, several *pensions*, tearooms and hotels with English names and, thanks partly to my father, a British Institute for cultural exchanges of many kinds.

I saw few English people in Florence during my stay. There seemed to be little point in fleeing abroad to spend time with the sort of people I would have been happy to avoid at home: for Florence, then, was apt to serve as a refuge either for moneyed transients with artistic pretensions, or for people who had left their native land, not exactly to live abroad 'at His Majesty's pleasure', but probably because they had made some corner a shade too hot to hold them, rendering a stay in Italy as much a convenience as a pleasure. The former would only reproduce the endless circular round of gossip about personality interspersed with commentary on aspects of the arts currently in fashion, a stale ragoût which could be happily left to stew in London; the latter tended to be seedy, sponging, and self-justificatory rather than romantic and buccaneering. From recent visits to Florence I have the impression that things, in those respects, have not greatly changed. What has changed, and enormously, is the number of tourists, of all ages and most nationalities. A twenty-two-year-old Englishman would no longer be a novelty in Florentine society: there are too many of them about, not all of them presenting much of a *bella figura* on their country's behalf.

Echoes from an English past did, nevertheless, sometimes reach me in my happy corner of a foreign field. One April evening Mrs Brewster gave a reception in honour of a young Frenchman, Comte Reynal de Simony, who was either a relation or a friend of the family, I never knew which. He had arrived in the sunshine of a warm afternoon, in an open sports car, having driven straight from the south of France, bringing with him a pretty girl cousin. I remember thinking how attractive they were, that young couple,

253

and how great a confidence Reynal's family must have in him to allow them to travel unchaperoned. That, I have no doubt must sound quite extraordinary to anyone even half my age, but the fact remains that in the world of those young people, in those days, many would have thought such liberty little short of criminally insane. That such a thought should even have occurred to me, who believed myself generally beyond convention, shows how strong a hold such conventions could still exert.

Reynal and his cousin were staying in the house. The reception, which began at about six o'clock, started as a stand-up affair like a cocktail party, only the drinks were vermouth and Tuscan wine, and shaded on into a buffet supper, with much coming and going, and conversation in several languages until a late hour. For a short while Mrs Brewster's big salon was fairly sparsely populated. Reynal, his cousin and I stood by one of the windows watching the evening light where it seemed to detach from their surroundings and float upon a scarf of blue mist the dome and campanile of Florence. Reynal was regaling me with stories of an old lady, whose reputation for *galanteries*, even in her eighties, was a subject for awe and delight in her part of France. A sexual appetite of unusual force had early shown itself in this lady's life. At twelve she had seduced the gardener's boy at her family's château. By the time that she was fifteen, she had caused enough scandal to be a dreadful anxiety to her parents, who one day brought a priest of great age and acknowledged saintliness to reason with her. The interview ended abruptly, with the priest tottering from the room, declaring that he had never been so terribly tempted in all his life.

I was laughing at Reynal's story, and reflecting on how much pleasure the French derive from instances of an amorous temperament which makes no concession to advancing years, when a small crowd of people came through the door, among them two tall young Englishmen whom I knew. I knew them, but not well, not having seen much of them since Eton days, but there was some warmth in our meeting which even I, not having been overwhelmed by compatriots during the past weeks, was able to feel. One of the young men was Benedict Nicolson, elder son of Harold Nicolson and Vita Sackville-West. The other I shall not name. He came of a rich and, as Americans would say, 'socially prominent' family, and his version of the standard adolescent's revolt against his parents' ideas had been to embrace communism. Later on he was to die, bravely enough, in the coming war, fighting for the democracy which he professed to despise.

Those young men gravitated at once to my small party where others soon joined us. I then found myself alone with the two of them, giving and receiving news. It appeared that they had just come from Spain where they had been trying to get their services accepted — by the Government's side, of course, since very few of our acquaintance would have admitted to a sympathy for General Franco. Not knowing Spain, having no emotional link with country or people, and knowing little that was good of either side in the conflict, I had never felt the feeblest wish to help or hinder in that civil war. Others, I knew — and admirable, brave and brilliant men among them — had seen the long and weary business symbolically, romantically as a contest of political forces which they believed as clearly opposed as black and white. The civil war, for them, was a proving ground of politics, and also of their own manhood, their own earnest, urgent anxiety to do something positive, even at the risk of their lives, about the evils of their time. To many of my contemporaries, and particularly to myself after conversations with my German friends, the Spanish Civil War seemed a proving-ground, sure enough, but not so much for young Anglo-Saxon idealists as for the respective war-machines of Germany and the USSR. That war on a vaster scale was coming one day I had no doubt, but had equally no desire to hurry it on.

Ben Nicolson was already a serious student of painting, and I could not believe that anything but friendship had taken him on that Spanish adventure, Florence seemed so much more the proper place for him to be. In the late 1930s a variety of people went to Spain, either as observers for one cause or another, or out of a kind of anguish at witnessing (as they thought) wrong about to triumph over right. I remembered Michael Clark, à propos some British and American journalists who were making personal capital out of their Spanish visits, saying scornfully, 'They never get any farther than the Hotel Colón!' and pronouncing that name as the English word for the lower bowel.

For a space I had to listen to complaints about their difficulties from my two Englishmen, but chiefly from Ben's companion. It seemed that he had laid hands on all the influential political and social strings he knew of to help him to his objective. When he said: 'I pulled all my right-wing, aristocratic connections!' I opened my eyes wide. Not only did this seem entirely the wrong way of going about things — for what could such connections avail on the extreme political left? — but the phrase itself was not from any language that he and I had been brought up to use. It had the sour, flat ring of communist polemic, something from the *Daily Worker*, perhaps, or from some pamphlet dealt out to the faithful at a political rally. In those days I knew little about the activities of the Cominform, beyond the fact of an unswerving and dreary diligence. I wondered through what channels, whether at school or university, they had come to influence that young man.

With April came a spell of milder weather, after so bitter a February, so dramatically uncertain a March. Spring sunshine fell in long, slanting shafts between the cypresses of the *podere*, and lit the landscape around Florence through a faint, gold-powdered haze. One morning, going out on to the terrace in front of the house, I found three great terracotta pots containing lemon trees, their wax-white buds just starting into flower. '*Kennst du das Land...*' Well, I was beginning to, and there were the *zitronen* to prove it.

I began to find red and blue anemones, scarlet tulips, and small, sweet-scented narcissi in the furrows under the olives at the far end of the property. Walking in the city I felt a warmer breath coming round street corners and out of narrow alleys, smelling of woodsmoke and horse-dung and also, in some unplaceable way, of flowers. City sounds, the wrenching slither and clash of trams, the incessant barking of motor-horns, deep bell-notes from churches, voices of children playing on the pavements, rang clearly, sounded sharply in the dry bright air.

Although my explorations of the city continued, now that the weather was kinder I sometimes took myself off for a long walk on the Marignolle hills above and beyond San Francesco. There narrow, stone-walled lanes led out into a countryside of plough-land and vineyard with, here and there, set on knolls or the sides of hills, the country villas of landowners, some with square lanterns. to their roofs, some with umbrella-like structures raised on pillars above their towers. Spring, a *primavera* of Botticellian sumptuousness, was bursting all around me in young leaves and bright green wheat and, growing wild, the sort of flowers which would scarcely yet be seen in gardens at home. A light spring wind, still edged with a chill, came darting and pouncing from some quarter a trifle less rigorous than that of the 'wind-grieved Apennine'. I met few people in the lanes. There were dark figures bending among the vines or hoeing small, irregular fields, and occasionally I would meet a man with a face of dark wood, scored deep by wind and sunlight, driving a few sheep with the aid of a thin, slinking dog.

One morning I turned into a lane narrower than the others, walled high with rough stone on either side, which seemed to lead to a small villa which had caught my eye. There was something about that house which had so instant an appeal that I knew at once I must see it close to. Like many others it was square and white, its hipped roof crowned by a small lantern. Like them it stood on an eminence, and there was a screen of trees to one side. The lane which I was following was distinct from the rough tracks of earlier on by being paved with slabs of stone. After a while I came to a gate, a tall, slim affair of wrought iron between stone piers, bearing the coronet of a count. Directly opposite the gate stood a small baroque chapel. That effect was pleasing enough in itself, but the real wonder lay beyond the gate where a high flight of steps led up to the house. They were no ordinary steps but broad, shallow, three-quarter circles of dressed stone, widening out from the house like ripples from a dropped pebble. The effect was breathtaking. I pulled my camera from one pocket, selected a filter from among the plastic boxes which had been rattling about in another one, and prepared to trespass. Whether I should be risking guns, dogs, or merely picturesque abuse, I had to get closer to that house and, in a sense, claim it for my own.

The gates, which were secured with a rusty padlock and chain, had evidently not been opened for a long while. I found a piece of wall near by which I could climb, and so the first of several trespassings began. If all is fair in love and war, and if love at first sight makes closer acquaintance imperative, surely the same must apply to house property, giving at least a romantic if not a legal justification for the trespass. I climbed the great sweep of steps which curved away on either side of me, and stood on the terrace facing a view over fields and distant trees to the blue glitter, half rubbed-out by haze, of Florence and the Arno valley. There were no sounds but faint cries from distant fields, the faraway barking of a dog. The house stood silent, sufficient to itself, telling nothing. Its ground-floor windows, behind elegant iron grilles, were blind from closed shutters. No one came. I had the whole place absolutely to myself.

People talk of 'dream houses'. That villa has come to me since in dreams, but I could not have dreamed it before I saw it, simply because I could not have imagined any building so wholly original, so entirely satisfactory in its own architectural terms. Naturally, that evening, back in Florence, I asked several friends if they knew anything about it. On the whole they were not great explorers, being too engrossed in what they were doing in the town, and in any case, knowing much better the villas and gardens of Fiesole and Settignano on the other, more famous, side of the river. One man, however, did respond to my enthusiasm. He, too, had found the villa for himself, and had been haunted by it, as I was surely going to be. He too had made enquiries, and had been told that the building might, just possibly might, have been designed by Michelangelo.

I have never seen that villa again. I do not even know if it still stands — it might easily have been a casualty of the war. At the time I imagined many things about it. Perhaps, I thought, its proprietor, like so many Italian noblemen, preferred to live in the town, perhaps even in Rome, crossly upbraiding his steward and notary for not seeing to it that the property produced enough income to enable him to present a suitably *bella figura* to his world. Perhaps there had been a death, and the house and all its rooms were sealed whilst cousins and aunts wrangled, and lawyers grew fat, in Florence, Siena, or Pistoia.

I have never returned to see the house, preferring to keep it in my mind's eye as I saw it on those first bright, blowy mornings half a century ago. I should not at all care to know that it had become a ruin, or a motel, or a depot for fertilizer, or the possession of a property speculator from Dorking or Utrecht.

19

CLOSE OF PLAY

By this mound the crocus covers
Now the Spring is here
The city's sick and sallow lovers
Hide and seek with fear.

Who would be a city lover?
When the light has gone
And the hard-bought hour is over
Fear will claim its own.

Like a sustained sour chord beneath the trills and runs of a
seemingly lively piece of music, fear lurked under all activities, all
hopes and plans and aspirations in the year 1938, and was felt, like
the chord's remorseless vibration, in different ways by nearly
everyone. As I left Florence in early April of that year I was only
too well aware of the fear, the creeping anxiety which were
beginning to affect my friends. I could not help feeling that I was
abandoning them, the more so since they so touchingly seemed to
regard the country to which I was returning as unassailably sound,
impregnable, safe, by contrast with the growing menaces of their
own.

I came to London once more, and to the renewal of what, in the
winter, I had thought almost irretrievably lost. There was a
peaceful reunion, and soon it was possible to suppose that all was
as before. Those more experienced than I in affairs of the heart
might have doubted that. The frail, unhandy boat which is a love
affair only very rarely survives a wreck. Patched up, repainted,
pronounced seaworthy, the effects on it of shock and strain can be
thought quite repaired. Only later will they begin to show and
then, too often, the craft becomes unmanageable, is abandoned or
simply sinks. However that might be going to be, I returned to
my London courses full of energy and cheerfulness, hoisting the
small, coloured flag of my private life with solipsistic bravado

259

against the somewhat thunderous tinge of the sky.

Briskly, enthusiastically, I set about finding somewhere to live. I had grown fond of Campden Hill, and so determined to look for my lodging there. In all conscience I should be ashamed of having been less than kind about my Scottish grandmother who, dying in December of the previous year, had left me two hundred pounds which, in those days, was quite an important sum, the equivalent of a couple of thousand today. With that in hand I felt able to house myself rather more amply than in a single bedsitting-room. I began to haunt house agents and quarter the streets of W8 looking for something suitable. The choice was wide. Those streets offered a perspective, not only of Georgian brick or Victorian stucco, but of receding ranks of boards which read 'To Let' or 'For Sale'. The economic depression was still at its nadir, and house property was hard to move. In the end I found a small house to let in a very small square between Holland Street and Kensington High Street. The square was what would now be called a pedestrian precinct (or, in Venice a *campo*), since its approaches were — still are — too narrow for anything but a bicycle or a pair of feet. The little house stood in a row of three, with a shop on the corner, facing another identical short row. The minute square was paved with stone flags and had, on one side, a blank wall with trees beyond and, on the other, the gates and short avenue leading to St Mary Abbot's church. The whole, north and south approaches and open space together, was called Church Walk, and the house to let was Number 11. The houses were of the simplest construction, built, probably, in the reign of William IV, and run up inexpensively, I have been told, to house the outdoor staff of Kensington Palace. Six rooms altogether, with a bathroom and a tiny kitchen, looked a bit like overhousing for a single man and would certainly cost more than I wanted to pay. I parleyed with the proprietor, a woman who was a small-time speculator in the district, asking if she would let me have four rooms, kitchen and bathroom as a flat, she retaining the right to let the top floor to someone else. Perhaps unwisely she agreed, and I signed a contract to pay £85 a year for my portion of the house, with an undertaking to show the remaining rooms to possible clients when asked to do so. I say that this was unwise because the handful of people who came to 'view' the top floor over the next eighteen months lost heart at once on seeing that they would have to share a bathroom and somehow provide a kitchen of their own. So I had the whole house to myself, from the beginning, and at once set about the furnishing and decoration of my four rooms.

> What lasting joys the man attend
> Who has a polished female friend!

Thus, in about 1845, wrote Cornelius Whurr, and if he wrote anything else I do not think that it has survived him. I would not quarrel with either his sentiment or with its expression. It comes into my mind whenever I think of Susan.

Writing of my sister's schoolroom companions and my later flight to Florence, I mentioned Susan Feilding. By the year of which I am writing she had been married for some years to a regular soldier, Hugh Hibbert, and was the mother of two children. Her husband's regiment, at that time, was almost continually abroad, in India or Burma. Susan had dutifully visited both countries but felt, I suppose, that once, in each case was enough. Hers was evidently not an easy marriage at the best of times. Duty done, Susan preferred the life of a grass-widow and lived for most of the time in London.

When I first came to know her again, after years of school, on my side, and of marriage on hers, she was living on the ground floor of her family's house at the southern end of Queen's Gate. There began a friendship which was greatly rewarding, and which lasted through all upheavals of war and separation until her death a few years ago. On my return from Florence, that spring of 1938, I went to stay with Susan while first my house-hunting and then the making-ready of Number 11 Church Walk were going on.

Once Church Walk was ready there had to be considered what Philip Larkin has so memorably called 'the toad work'. Even I thought that I had spent enough time trying my hand at various inconclusive things, and that I must find myself a proper job. I had no wish to return to the film industry which, in any case, was suffering badly from the Depression. My excursions into journalism had not given me any relish for newspaper life; my own writing was still too slow and undirected to give much hope of a useful income and, strangely enough, I was beginning to feel the need of doing something directly concerned with the anxieties of the period. That need, of course, was related to, was in fact an expression of the personal anxieties which I had been feeling increasingly for some time.

The late 1930s were the era of 'news-letters'. A growing number of intelligent and instructed people, 'concerned' citizens as they would now be called, were becoming seriously dissatisfied with what they read in the newspapers. Disgustedly they

261

compared what they reasonably thought was happening or likely to happen in Europe with the anodyne messages handed down by editors and politicians. A hunger had developed for more exact, detailed, even 'inside' information, and certain alert and politically minded people were quick to try to appease it. News-letters, sometimes printed, sometimes mere cyclostyled sheets began to appear from every point of the political compass. They ranged in ethos from extreme left to extreme right and were, in almost every case, the brainchild of individuals rather than of groups. Among such of the country's young people as were politically aware, and had not sold themselves irrevocably to communism or its supposed opposite, irritation with the government and its apparent blindness and complacency led to much savage condemnation of the 'Old Guard' and 'guilty men', and a strong desire for information which might provide the basis of action for effective change. Business men, anxious for the future of their markets, the younger Members of Parliament, many civil servants were also likely takers of crisply authoritative news-letters, subscription to which seemed to give a kind of insider status, access to privileged information in a still largely ignorant world. If shrewd editors of popular papers restricted their coverage of foreign affairs it was because they knew that their readership had only the most limited interest in the goings-on of a pack of foreigners, and in any case, deeply needed reassurance about the possibility of war. Travel abroad, and hence knowledge of foreign peoples was, as I have already suggested, the province only of a few.

In the summer of 1938 my father came home on leave, to see many people, have many discussions and, most important, to put himself in the hands of a well-known specialist, at his clinic in North Wales, in an attempt to alleviate, if not to cure, his persistent duodenal trouble. His stay at the clinic, where I joined him as a visitor for a couple of weeks, came at a time of fiercely mounting tension as events moved towards what, although it settled nothing, came to be called the Munich Settlement.

During my father's leave which, incidentally, was the last time I should ever have his company, for he died in Canada eighteen months later when I was living in London, I met a man who spoke at length on foreign policy, and seemed to be admirably knowledgeable about it. When I heard that he too was issuing a news-letter, I went to see him. At once — and very likely I owed this also to admiration for my father — he agreed to take me on to his staff, and so I found myself as close to the political centre of things as, with no official position, it was possible to be.

So it came about, one winter day, that I found myself flying from Paris to Brussels and being, for the first and only time in my life, air-sick. The machine, belonging to the Belgian Sabena airline, was a Fokker trimotor, neither large nor fast nor, apparently capable of much altitude. All the way up northern France we flew below cloud, at no great height, and faithfully following, it seemed, the rolling contours of the land. The previous night I had spent little time in my bed at the Hotel Meurice, having passed the evening convivially, until a very late hour, with a good deal to drink. In consequence I had embarked for Brussels with a bad headache and a decidedly queasy stomach. The bucking and yawing, the sudden lift-like drops and ascents, were too much for the latter. Half-way through the trip I was obliged to reach for that depressing little brown paper bag. When the city of Brussels turned up grey and chilly and patched with dirty snow I was, although glad to be on solid ground, rather limp, and not very enthusiastic for my mission.

In so far as anything was 'serious' in those hectic, unstable, rumour-ridden days, my mission was serious. I had someone to see, some questions to ask, some letters to present, all as discreetly and as inconspicuously as possible. On many occasions in my life, however — perhaps rather unfairly many — comedy, and even farce, have turned up to destroy seriousness, whatever my good intentions. The comic spirit was certainly abroad on that cold, unpromising day. I had got the Meurice to telegraph to Brussels for a car to meet me at the airport and take me to a destination some miles beyond the city. It had not occurred to me to specify the kind of vehicle I should have thought suitable. If I had, it would certainly not have been a vast, gleaming black Packard limousine with white side-walled tyres and a liveried chauffeur. My arrival at the château of Steenockerzeel was going to be as inconspicuous as if I had come in a helicopter or a coach and four.

We drove out of the town until the crowds of small, neat houses had thinned out to market-gardens and fields, with lines of poplars sending their last yellow leaves spinning in the brisk winter wind. Then came a cluster of houses, gates, a short drive, and standstill on the cobbled forecourt of a small castle, a castle from a story-book, built of old brick and stone, with crow-stepped gables and turrets capped with cones of gleaming blue-grey slate. Silence, but for the sighing of the wind, enfolded us as the chauffeur switched off his engine. The Packard, in all its sumptuous modernity, seemed to take up a great deal of space, looking huge, incongruous and embarrassing. There was said to be a Nazi cell located in the village post office. I murmured to the chauffeur that I should be obliged if he would answer no questions, should anyone from the village approach him. His look was stern, confidential. 'Je ne dirai rien à personne!' he said. I turned away, crossed the bridge to the castle door, and stood looking around. The land on all sides was dead flat to the horizon; there was nothing anywhere to mitigate or divert the icy wind. The sky was flat as well, and near-seeming, leaden grey, shedding a kind of snowlight, promising more snow to join the white blankets on the fields. A wide moat surrounded the castle, its water ruffled to a dull gleam by the wind, and on it, in splendid indifference, rode a pair of swans.

I have written elsewhere of my 'idiocy', my absorption by my private concerns, my generally blinkered neglect of larger affairs. Nevertheless, from time to time, I have been led to a small part in matters which, one day, might be part of 'history'. As I looked, with some anxiety, at the castle's heavy door, I knew that what lay beyond it belonged to many centuries of the story of Europe, something once fabulously powerful now reduced, rejected but still, for its connotations, immensely impressive. My earlier malaise, a mixture of hangover, fatigue, irritation and doubt of my capacity to perform properly the duty laid on me, had evaporated. In its place came excitement, a strong wish to taste the atmosphere beyond that forbidding door. I was also shivering with the cold. Supposing that it must, even in that ancient place, be warmer indoors than outside, I looked for a bell.

A long iron rod with an openwork handle was fixed to the stonework at one side of the doorway. I pulled it gently downwards, only to hear the screech of rust and feel the resistance of disuse. There was no sound to be heard. I pulled harder, then harder still, and the bell-pull came away in my hand. Far inside the castle I heard a faint clash. Mortified, furious, ashamed, I was still trying to reinstate the bell-pull when the door opened a short distance and a face appeared. Its owner hauled the door a little further open, acknowledged my name and beckoned me inside. I pointed at the dangling bell-pull with apologetic smiles, but the short, elderly man in a dark blue suit seemed scarcely interested. It was as if any happening outside that stronghold was, for him, an irrelevance, wholly remote. I do not think that he noticed the Packard at all.

I knew his name, and that he was a courtier who had chosen to go into exile with those whom he had long been happy to serve. After we had exchanged small courtesies he beckoned me on, without further word, across a stone-floored hall where a grand staircase drove upwards into a kind of dusk. At the very top, motionless and looking straight down at me, stood a tall woman dressed in unrelieved black, one hand laid on the banister, her face a pale mask under a cloud of dark hair.

The young man who rose to greet me from a broad desk stacked with papers was, at twenty-seven, less than four years older than myself. Of his seventeen given names, beginning with Franz Josef Otto, he had chosen to use the third. As, unsmiling but courteous, he took my hand, I made my best court bow, as taught me by Colonel Mackenzie in Canada. I took in his appearance, his black suit and white linen, his alert eyes, his rather sombre seriousness. The Archduke Otto of Hapsburg, born in 1912, had had less than seven years as heir to the thrones of Austria and Hungary before, in April 1919, his father, the Emperor Karl, was deprived of his Imperial title and expelled from his country. I wondered what had brought the Archduke, twenty years later, to settle in that bleak Belgian countryside. The castle, from its antique and well-used air, its rubbed gilding on old dark wood, its threadbare velvets, might seem to have stood, cared for but unlived in, for very many years. Was it a grace-and-favour residence provided by a friendly monarch, or might it be, simply, one of many dwellings all over Europe collected by the Imperial family at one epoch or another of its past? Otto von Hapsburg's ancestors had once ruled over the provinces, such as Brabant (where I found myself) and Hainault, which make up the present-day Belgian kingdom. It was possible that the château of Steenockerzeel might have been something which the family still 'had by them', now come to strategic usefulness after centuries of near oblivion. Also, however sympathetic the Belgian royal famiy might be to their distinguished visitors, the geographical proximity of the German Reich, whose annexation of Austria had taken place less than a year before, would have made a too open partisanship diplomatically unwise.

For the time that it took my host to read the letters I had brought him I sat quietly considering my surroundings, shaping and defining in my head the impression that he made on me. That the room was warm I do remember, but remember little else about it

265

for the powerful interest provided by the still, intent figure across the desk, except that a flood of wintry light was coming in through tall windows of clear glass. At length the papers were laid aside and I was invited to put my questions.

My employer's chief concern was with the political information needed for the compilation each month of a memorandum to private subscribers. It was not difficult at that time, with all Europe in a state of upheaval, and everywhere a continuous movement of refugees or of people voluntarily displacing themselves for political reasons, to come up with items of information, often accurate enough, which had to be assessed, compared, collated before being distributed to interested parties. The trouble was that events, after Munich, were moving so fast that political situations changed pattern at every shock, like the coloured glass in a kaleidoscope, and so information could be outdated or even falsified almost at the moment of being gathered. However, I put my questions and, feeling that I should not take written notes, tried hard to store the lucid, considered answers in my, by then, somewhat clearer head.

It came to be my turn to be questioned, closely and in amazingly knowledgeable detail, about the political temper of my own country. I found myself wishing desperately that I had paid proper attention to the results of British by-elections, the state of the parties, the calibre of different politicians, the government's most recent views on foreign affairs. I fear that my interlocutor may have found some of my answers distressingly vague.

Otto von Hapsburg was exceedingly well-informed about the political condition of most European countries. On Germany and Austria his opinions were clear, unsentimental and by no means optimistic. I could imagine that his sources of information, many of them belonging to a complexity of ancient relationships which no new republic could hope to wish away in one generation, were as good as anybody's at that time. What he had to say I took in as best I could, determined to get it written down on the way back to Brussels.

When whatever time had been allotted to my visit in the Archduke's carefully planned working day was over I was courteously dismissed. Once again I followed the elderly courtier across the ringing stones of the hall. I gave a quick glance upwards to the head of the staircase but the ex-Empress Zita — was it really she? — was no longer to be seen.

As the Packard rolled back towards Brussels I made my notes.

The chauffeur, whose sense of occasion was clearly acute, sat stiff as a post at the wheel and drove as though we were leading a royal procession. At parting he received my tip with dignity, gave me a look of profound significance, then glided his impossible vehicle away.

Whilst eating a delicious dinner that evening at the Epaule de Mouton I had much on which to brood. I thought of the Austrian Empire stretching from Germany to the Adriatic and of the shocks and disasters which affected it even before the débâcle of the 1914 war. Contemporary Austria, for several years before the Anschluss of March 1938, had enjoyed great popularity amongst my countrymen — those of the travelling kind, that is. The Salzburg Festival had become a prime summer resort for the fashionable, whether musical or not, largely through the influence of the Austrian ambassador to London, Baron Franckenstein, whose charm was compelling and whose parties were famous. Smart women wore dirndl skirts and peasant blouses to frequent cafés where young Austrians in *lederhosen* slapped their knees and each other's faces in various kinds of country dance. Against the steely menace of a Germany grimly vowed to expansion and overtly militaristic, *gemütlichkeit* as expressed by the Austrians seemed especially appealing. Few, very few, guessed that, beneath so charming an exterior, uglier forces were at work; that many Austrians would soon join gleefully with their new masters in dreams of world conquest, in vicious intolerance and the practice of genocide. It would be many years before George Clare's *Last Waltz in Vienna* would help to set the record straight.

As the year 1939 began to gather momentum, each month outstripping the last in causes for anxiety, I went more and more often to France, sometimes on my own, sometimes acting as private secretary to my employer. With the increase of international trouble our organization had grown. Others, young men of my own age, had joined in the work of finding facts. My comings and goings were a source of surprised amusement to friends and relations. One day, when he found me wearing a new and voluminous winter overcoat bought off the peg in Oxford, my younger brother suggested that I must have had it made by the best tailor in Zagreb.

Among the new recruits to our organization was Michael Clark, introduced by myself and warmly welcomed for what he had to offer. Michael had bought himself a motor-bicycle, and on

that he proposed to travel across Europe and Asia Minor to
Palestine, sending back as he went some articles for a newspaper
and, privately to us, a report on his political findings in each
country through which he passed. A great friend from his
schooldays was yet another Michael, the son of Chaim Weizmann
the Zionist leader. Weizmann and my father were warm friends
and saw much of each other when the latter was Chairman of the
Parliamentary Pro-Palestine Committee. The final aim of Michael
Clark's long and difficult journey would be to join the Weizmanns
at their villa in Rehovoth, near Tel Aviv.

After a great send-off in London Michael was not heard of for a
couple of weeks. Eventually news came in a letter to me from the
Ritz-Dunapalota in Budapest. Michael, as I have said, was already
a connoisseur of great hotels; the Ritz in Budapest had always been
one that he particularly wanted to try. The letter, I should judge
from a downhill tendency in the lines, must have been written in
the course of a most enjoyable evening. It is in red ink on the
hotel's writing-paper, and signed 'Yours Michael (you know, Red
Michael!)'. It was the last I was ever to hear from him. Coming
into the office some weeks later I was taken aside by the senior
secretary and asked if I had heard the news — that Michael had
been killed in Palestine. The shock sent the whole world spinning
for some moments; then came my terrible grief. Soon we should
all become accustomed to random death, to the loss, taken
dry-eyed, of our contemporaries, but at that time such violent
ends for the young were unthought of, unallowed for. It would
have been bad enough to hear of a fatal crash on some far-off
mountain road — but this was murder.

The newspaper paragraph was bald. A young journalist had run
into an ambush while riding his motor-bicycle near Tel Aviv. By
inquiry of newspapers and the Colonial Office we found out a
little more, but not very much. The story, for me, lacks essential
detail. What was thought to have happened was that Dr
Weizmann, one evening, had gone to a meeting in Tel Aviv,
leaving Michael behind at Rehovoth. Someone whose duty it was
to watch over Weizmann's safety must have telephoned the news
that Arabs were preparing an ambush somewhere on the Tel Aviv
road, and that he must be warned to take another way home.
Michael allowed, I think, no second thought, simply jumped on
to his machine and headed for Tel Aviv. The Arabs in ambush,
either because they guessed his intention, or simply from the
tendency to unpremeditated violent action for which they are

noteworthy, opened fire as he came by. With thirty-six bullets in his body he must have died instantly. I took my sadness to my grandmother, who had known and appreciated Michael. A week or so before his death the office had received his first report, which was brilliant and highly original, and I had told her of this. Typically of a generation well-used to sudden death in the service of Empire, she thought to comfort me by reminding me of Michael's work. I could only say that the price was too heavy, that this was, for me, the first shot in a war.

A fine spring led on to as typically, traditionally lovely an English summer as anyone could remember. One day a letter came from Italy, from Nicolai Rubinstein. Leaving Florence in April of the previous year, I had warmly invited him to come to England, where he should be my guest for as long as he liked. His letter, guarded in tone, spoke of the disagreeable weather in Italy, and asked whether he might accept my invitation to come and visit me. Knowing that Mussolini, prodded by Hitler, had begun to make serious difficulties for Nicolai's people, I had no trouble in interpreting his message. I wrote at once, couching my invitation in the most definite terms. Not long afterwards, to my great relief, I learned that Nicolai was on his way.

His entry to England was achieved without difficulty. The two of us then set up house together very happily at Number 11 Church Walk, and it was not long before something of the Florentine atmosphere I had so enjoyed was re-created in that little house. Others, whose assessment of the immediate future was as shrewd and timely as Nicolai's, also found their way to England. I was able to repay hospitality received in Florence, for instance to Wolfgang von Leyden, in whose rooms at the top of a medieval tower in the Borgo San Jacopo I had often been entertained.

Nicolai was an historian, with a speciality in the history of Florence. Even at his then age of twenty-eight his scholarship must have been impressive, and seen to provide a needed contribution, for he was quickly made welcome by the English academic world. I gave him one or two such introductions as I thought might be useful; otherwise he went to work on his own. He is now Emeritus Professor of History at the University of London, a Fellow of the British Academy and of the Royal Historical Society. I honour Nicolai for many things, but most, perhaps, for his decision, at the very darkest moment of the war, to become a British citizen.

It was a great pleasure to see Nicolai applying a formidable intelligence, a lively, amused interest in people and in social life in all its aspects, to comprehending the new world in which he was now to make his life. His conversation, the originality of his observations, were a constant source of pleasure, and also he brought into my life a feeling of Europe, a touch of that 'foreignness' with which I had always felt at home.

That exquisite summer found most people in two minds. With one set of thoughts they pursued their avocations, made their plans, enjoyed their normal pleasures, perhaps appreciated as never before the splendid natural pageant put on for them in park and countryside, the new paint and fresh-filled window-boxes of London's residential quarters still quite intact. With another set of thoughts, cropping up unpredictably and too often amongst the first, there was the uneasy weighing of the news, the recurring leaden reminder that work and planning and pleasure, the ability to regulate and order life at will, were shortly going to be subject to pressures and necessities as unavoidable as they were undesired. Rumours, meanwhile, like dust-devils, rose up from nowhere and scurried about the town, whirling wildly and then subsiding, only to rise again in another place. Stories of Nazi Germany proliferated. We all heard of the English motorist who accidentally rammed a huge German tank, only to have it splinter all round him, being made of nothing but plywood. There were many such instances of desperate desire to play down, euphemize, discount the grim evidence increasingly coming our way.

Ever since Hitler's rise to power in 1933, first a trickle, then a stream, and finally a flood of refugees had been coming into Britain. Their arrival had stirred feelings of every degree from acute compassion to affronted annoyance. Many of them went half-mad with despair at the stolid inattention they met with when trying to inform, and, above all, to warn their new hosts. They *knew*; they were anxious to tell what they knew, but could not always find a hearing. Deep down, I believe that the British were preparing for a great ordeal in their own way. Something dreadful was probably coming, to face which they must brace themselves, but it did not help to be too alarmed beforehand.

Meanwhile the beautiful summer burned on. The traditional festivals took place — the Derby, Ascot, Henley, the Eton and Harrow match at Lord's. On the evening of the last, Lord and Lady Astor gave their traditional yearly ball at Number 4 St James's Square. Although, as I have said, I tended to spurn conventional invitations, the Astors' ball had been a regular fixture for me ever since leaving school. The setting was sumptuous; it was altogether a pretty spectacle, and I had there a chance to meet, for once in a while, acquaintances whom otherwise I rarely saw.

As I got myself up in tails and white tie, and hunted for the pair of white kid gloves which were then an essential part of the dancing man's uniform, I told myself that this ball would very likely be — what? — not quite the Ball before Waterloo, because war was still only, although ponderably, in the air, but the very last of its kind that I should ever attend. As I walked up the great staircase in a press of other young men, of sashed and bemedalled seniors, of matrons in tiaras, and eager girls in the pretty, so 'suitable' dresses of the period, I consciously took in every detail, determined to note and remember each aspect for recollection in the dark days which I believed sure to come.

I have written of this ball as a conventional occasion, but conventionality was largely foreign to my hostess, a fact which tended to make her parties more entertaining than most. The tiresome business of the 'generation gap' had not yet declared itself and so, that evening, the great house was filled with people of all ages, some old and very grand, the majority young, a few very young indeed. Amongst the last was a selection of the large Kennedy family, children of the American ambassador. Kathleen, the eldest child, was surrounded by admirers; her younger siblings wove in and out of dancers and conversers, unawed, uninhibited, a bright shuttle of anarchic high spirits unaccommodating to stateliness. Wandering at some point into one of the suite of smaller saloons surrounding the ballroom I stopped in my tracks, feeling myself an intruder. There, showered with light from a crystal chandelier, were the Duke of Kent and Princess Marina, he wearing the Garter sash and she (to my eye by a long way the most beautiful woman present) one of Hartnell's romantic creations, full-skirted, almost a crinoline. They were engaged in happy conversation, quite absorbed in one another.

Harsh fates in store cast, that evening, no shadow before them. Kathleen Kennedy and George, Duke of Kent would both be killed in aircraft accidents. Some of the young men there would not see many more birthdays; some leading politicians present would soon endure obloquy, relegation, a sour end to their careers. I turned away into a smaller room, perhaps a study, in which a bar had been set up.

271

Lady Astor was a fervent teetotaller, to a point where it was a wonder that liquor should be served at her parties at all. I was just taking a glass from a footman when a concealed door in the wall burst open and Philip Toynbee appeared, clutching a bottle of champagne. He had evidently been anxious about supplies and, with customary forthrightness, had gone foraging for himself. At prep-school Philip and I had been great enemies in spite, or perhaps because of, an irritating sort of attraction which we felt for one another. In later years he would claim that I bullied him. The truth was that we both had gangs of adherents and, depending upon whichever gang was temporarily in the ascendant, each of us 'bullied' the other. Philip had come to terms with his distinguished heredity in ways impossible to me. His father, Arnold Toynbee, historian and polymath, must have been as they say, 'a hard act to follow'. Philip, reacting against the almost excessive high-mindedness of his forebears, carried their social anxieties to a conclusion which, perhaps, their logic could not countenance, and became a communist. Somehow, nevertheless, he did manage to enjoy the best of several worlds, which explains his presence, tail coat and all, at the Astors that evening. In her book *Hons and Rebels* Jessica Mitford tells a wonderful story of Philip staying in a miner's home and concealing the evening clothes and other 'class' paraphernalia which he would need at his next port of call, Castle Howard. As a grandson of Lady Mary Howard, who had married Professor Gilbert Murray, he had, of course, as much hereditary right to be there, as the right he had acquired for himself to be the guest of a miner.

There is one more dance to remember before this chronicle comes to an end, my brother Alastair's Commemoration Ball at Christ Church, Oxford. For that we had a small house-party at Elsfield, returning to sleep in a perfect summer dawn, and breakfasting late, chiefly on platefuls of raspberries, under an elm tree on the terrace. It still seemed just possible to make plans, that July of 1938, and plans were discussed rather sleepily that morning. Alastair intended to go to the University of Virginia, as soon as he had his degree. The girls of the party seemed to have full and busy lives before them. I alone was in limbo, quite unable to believe in anything but futility where plans were concerned.

White haze hung in the distance, the grass was still wet with dew. It was going to be a hot day.

TAILPIECE

Once again, after more than thirty years, I have visited the demesne of Elsfield Manor, participating in a broadcast for the BBC on John Buchan, his work and his Oxfordshire home.

Our party of three started off at the gate into Pond Close, between Jack Allam's cottage and the gardener's 'gothick' house. We made our way to the point where once the elm trees framed a famous view of Oxford. The going was not easy. Forcing a path through waist-high grass and hogweed five feet tall, climbing through fallen boughs and over prostrate logs, we arrived — I panting almost too heavily to be intelligible on the air — at the far corner of Pond Close. The elms, of course, had gone with the elm disease which has so altered the look of the land, and nothing remained to shield the eye from sight of Headington's sprawl and the vast, pale bulk of the new hospital there. The towers and spires of the University were still in place, but now encircled, competed with, to memory's eye diminished.

The green-painted door in the wall, which had once opened on to the pleasures of kitchen-garden and hothouse, was nowhere to be seen, or not immediately at any rate. When I found it lying flat in a tangle of nettles I nearly let out a yelp into the microphone. The walls of the walled garden still stood, as they had stood for two hundred years, but the hothouse had gone and the rest was incipient jungle.

Nature, in these islands, is never slow to reclaim her own, and to fill with some serviceable material any vacuum created by neglect or disease. Going through to the main garden I could see the Crow Wood much thinned out where the elms had died but filling with brush and saplings the space between the remaining trees. I also saw that the roof of the Doric temple where Doctor Johnson used to sit was falling into decay. Beyond the wood, in front of the house, the lawns had become a kind of savannah, waving in the wind.

In an earlier chapter I wrote of James Adams, the head gardener, and his gallant effort to prove the worth of his garden by providing superb fruit and vegetables 'even as weeds and grass took hold all round their places of growth'. Weeds and grass had had their victory: what was now to be seen was wilderness triumphant. Standing below the library windows to make — with commendable restraint, I believe — my part of the commentary, I felt strangely heartened when a cock pheasant took furious flight from the long grass at my feet.

Such observations as I have made are a commonplace of our time. The Elsfield property once required three gardeners to keep it in shape, together with hands for cutting down trees, carting wood, scything in paddock and meadow. A proprietor would nowadays have to be carelessly rich or utterly, unselfishly devoted to maintaining his surroundings, to produce such an effect again. Let the birds and animals have it, I thought, as we went on into the stable yard: they are only repossessing what was once their own.

Observing the stable yard I was interested to see that things had been done which we had considered doing in the 1950s and had been obliged to abandon. In the high range on the road side two stables and a loft had been converted into a dwelling and, lower down, the 'Edwardian' barn seemed to have become a house; and so there must still be life and movement in the place although, apart from the pheasant, we had seen none that morning.

There is really nothing here for tears. The Elsfield I knew is clear-lit, bright-edged in my memory. Its significance for others will be different; different but not diminished, since they will be looking for, and I hope finding, food for recollection of another kind. 'This disordered century', for those who have lived a large part of it, has quite got out of hand. I can only echo the Wife of Bath:

> ...whan that it remembreth me
> Upon my yowthe, and on my jolitee,
> It tickleth me about myn herte root.
> Unto this day it dooth myn herte boote
> That I have had my world as in my tyme.

July 1990

INDEX